REBEL IN THE RANKS

To Denis,

with all best wishes —

Brad S. Gregory

REBEL
IN THE
RANKS

Martin Luther, the Reformation,
and the Conflicts That
Continue to Shape Our World

BRAD S. GREGORY

HarperOne
An Imprint of HarperCollins*Publishers*

REBEL IN THE RANKS. Copyright © 2017 by Brad S. Gregory. All rights reserved. Printed in the United States of America. No part of this book may be used or reproduced in any manner whatsoever without written permission except in the case of brief quotations embodied in critical articles and reviews. For information, address HarperCollins Publishers, 195 Broadway, New York, NY 10007.

HarperCollins books may be purchased for educational, business, or sales promotional use. For information, please email the Special Markets Department at SPsales@harpercollins.com.

First HarperOne hardcover published in 2017

FIRST EDITION

Designed by Ad Librum

Library of Congress Cataloging-in-Publication Data has been applied for.

ISBN 978–0–06–247117–8

17 18 19 20 21   LSC   10 9 8 7 6 5 4 3 2 1

To my parents

CONTENTS

WHY THE REFORMATION MATTERS

T HIS IS A BOOK about the Reformation and why it still matters. Regardless of our own religious views, the Reformation remains important because we can't understand secular and religious ideas and institutions today without it. What happened five centuries ago affects us today. If we want to know why the early twenty-first century is the way it is—and how it got this way—we need to understand the Reformation and its impact. The Reformation ended the Middle Ages and made the modern world—but not in any simple or straightforward way.

Much of the Reformation's influence remains indirect and unintended. This is a major theme of this book. Protestant reformers five centuries ago were not heralds of modern individual freedom and autonomy. Neither did they envision modern democratic states or advocate for consumer capitalism. They did not support modern religious toleration or champion the modern separation of church and state. And yet we cannot understand any of these ideas, institutions, or practices—or many others—without a proper reckoning of the Reformation and its enormous effects.

Martin Luther would be horrified by most of the long-term outcomes of the Reformation, as would John Calvin, the other most influential Protestant reformer of the sixteenth century. Yet though horrified, they might not be surprised by how things have gone because they viewed human nature as utterly sinful apart from God's grace. They and their colleagues were trying to reform what they regarded as terrible problems in the Church and, in the process, to make people and society more authentically Christian. In some areas of Europe, especially in the later sixteenth and seventeenth centuries, they perhaps would have thought they had succeeded. But they would be appalled if they could see how their actions led indirectly to a profound diminishing of Christianity's public influence in Western societies. The religious disagreements and conflicts that followed the Reformation set the stage for religion's eventual separation from the rest of life. That too will be a major theme of this book. It's part of why the Reformation remains important, regardless of our opinions about the past or the present.

A Hard Life

Seeing how this happened, and why the Reformation still matters today, means seeing how the Europe of five hundred years ago gradually and unintentionally was transformed into the modern world. One of the hardest things at the outset is to get a sense of what life then was like. Then as now, wealth was distributed with radical inequality, but we can hardly imagine how little wealth there actually was. Human life was more demanding, more difficult, and less comfortable. People lived closer to nature and to its daily, seasonal, and annual cycles.

　　Whether in Scandinavia, central Europe, or near the Mediterranean, the large majority of men and women lived in small villages. They were illiterate and worked by farming the land. The impressive surviving medieval churches, Renaissance city halls, and homes of wealthy merchants should not mislead us: especially in central and northern Europe, most buildings were made of wood and were vulnerable to fires, which occurred regularly. The materials, texture, and furnishings of buildings bore the marks of human crafting, devoid of modern industrial surfaces and finishes. People had little mastery of the natural world. Uncertain weather left them vulnerable to poor harvests. Epidemic diseases, above all the dreaded bubonic plague, constantly threatened. In part because medical care was largely ineffective, the average life expectancy was much shorter than today: 32 to 34 years at birth in England around 1500, with few adults living beyond their fifties.[1]

Traveling was difficult and frequently dangerous, and overland trade with heavy or bulky commodities meant expensive and cumbersome transport—which is why grain, timber, wool, and cloth nearly always went by water, whether in ships that hugged the coastlines from the Baltic to the Mediterranean or in barges that navigated the many rivers—the Rhine, Loire, Danube, Elbe, Po, and more—vital to Europe's trade. Even the fastest communications were slow: around 1500, letters dispatched by courier from Brussels to Venice, for example, took ten days to arrive at their destinations.[2]

Despite Europe's overwhelmingly rural character, cities were disproportionately important as centers of trade, artisanal manufacturing, education, and culture. Still, Cologne, the largest city in the vast expanse of central Europe, had a population of only around 40,000, while London's 60,000 residents were largely concentrated within a square mile. In fact, aside from London, before the Reformation England boasted only two towns with as many as 10,000 inhabitants.[3]

In cities and villages alike, when the sun went down it got *dark*. There was no electricity, there were no gas street lamps. Paris, the largest city in all of Europe, with maybe 200,000 people, was lit at night with torches, as was every other city. And dark meant dangerous, which is why city dwellers guarded their urban walls night and day. In a world without professional police forces or standing armies, keeping out suspicious travelers and would-be intruders was a priority.

Religion as More-than-Religion

Besides these radical differences in the material conditions of life, religion held an utterly different place in society than it does in Western countries today. In our time religion is considered an individual choice, and that choice includes the option not to be religious at all. Religion today is a distinct area of life—separate from your career, professional relationships, recreational activities, consumer behavior, and so on. None of this was true in the early sixteenth century: religion was neither a matter of choice nor separate from the rest of life. Except for the Jews, who made up a tiny percentage of Europe's population around 1500, everyone became a Christian through being baptized with water; baptism was a prerequisite for the possibility of eternal salvation after death. Almost always baptism took place just days after birth. That way, if a baby died—as one in four did from disease or malnutrition before their first birthday— she would be saved by God. Baptism was a rite of initiation into the local parish church and into the community in which you lived. Like the other sacraments, it also conferred God's grace—his spiritual presence and power in and through the material world he had created. Except in emergencies when there was immediate danger of an infant's death, baptism was administered by the local priest. He had joined the clergy through a special ritual of ordination, and his vow of celibacy and duty to administer the sacraments set him apart from laypeople, who made up the large majority of Christians.

A parish was coextensive with the local community; a small

village would often be a single parish, while a city might include many parishes, each of them an urban neighborhood. Europe included tens of thousands of parishes reaching from Scandinavia to the Iberian and Italian peninsulas. Rural and urban parishes alike belonged to the Catholic Church, which had its administrative and symbolic center in Rome and was headed by the pope. Parishes were geographically organized into dioceses, the Church's administrative units, each headed by a bishop responsible for overseeing all the parishes and priests in his diocese. For most Christians, however, the pope and even bishops remained remote figures. Local experience of the Church meant participation in a web of social relationships of family, kin, and neighbors linked by customs, rituals, and worship led by a priest.

Though for most Christians Rome lay far away, religion played a central role in everyday life—from the primary relationships between family and kin to the practice of politics and commerce. Social relationships and gender expectations were inseparable from Christian norms. And both public and private morality were conceived in Christian terms. Rather than standing apart from government or courts of justice, religion informed both politics and law. At the same time, Christianity was not aloof from the buying and selling of goods and pursuit of profit; Christian ethical teachings sought to shape economic transactions and restrain greed. Education, from the teaching of ABCs in humble small-town primary schools through instruction in one of Europe's sixty or so universities, was imbued with Christian ideas. In short, religion included a lot more of life than religion includes today. Known as Latin Christendom, this social, political, intellectual, and cultural totality was the medieval predecessor of today's European nation-states.

This does not imply that everyone, or even very many people, behaved like saints. Far from it. That was one problem the Reformation sought to address, though it wasn't the main concern of its leaders. Long before Martin Luther, conscientious Christians had been voicing their criticisms of sinful behavior. For literally centuries before the Protestant Reformation, medieval men and women who *were* devout lamented the gap between Christian ideals and lived realities—from St. Bernard of Clairvaux in the twelfth century to St. Catherine of Genoa in the early sixteenth, with dozens more in between. Sinful shortcomings in the Church and the lives of its members, including its clerical leaders, affected every part of society precisely *because* religion was intertwined with every part of life. Luther was hardly the first to notice sins, point out problems, or condemn abuses of power, whether among local priests or in the conspicuous consumption of Renaissance popes. But as we'll see, for Luther, all these were just symptoms, not the heart of the matter.

An Inherited Christian Worldview

The medieval Church leaders who infused politics and economics with religion, regulated law and education, and shaped family life and culture shared a worldview and vision of history upon which hung the eternal fate of millions of Christian souls. This collective vision was based on the Bible. Starting with the Old Testament, the inherited story of the Christian worldview in the early sixteenth century went something like this: In the beginning, as a supreme act of love, God created Adam and Eve in his image as the first human beings, the crowning achievement of his creation of everything *ex nihilo* ("out of nothing"). God set them in the paradise of the Garden of Eden. But Adam and Eve disobeyed God, thinking they knew better what was good for them. Pain, suffering, and death entered the world through their act of rebellion. All human beings who came after them were subject to this original sin not because of anything they'd done personally but by virtue of shared human nature.

Yet in his mercy and love, God called Abraham and through him a people, the Israelites, to make a covenant with him. God delivered his holy law to Moses so that the Israelites could lead just and righteous lives. Repeatedly they sinned and strayed from the covenant, but repeatedly God chastised them and called them back through his prophets. Through Israelite prophets such as Isaiah, God foretold of a messiah, a savior, who would lead the beleaguered nation of Israel to triumph over its enemies in a future age of peace.

According to Christians, this prophecy was fulfilled in the first century in the person of Jesus of Nazareth, the *Christ,* or "anointed." The New Testament told his story and that of his earliest followers. Christ was an unexpected kind of savior, not the sort who would lead Israel to political success. According to Christians, he wasn't merely a great ethical leader or prophet; he was the very incarnation of God—a real man in all respects but also actually God himself. The same God who created the universe and championed the Israelites had reached deeply into human history—gotten his hands dirty, so to speak—and taken on the fullness of human temptation, weakness, humiliation, and suffering in this lowly carpenter's son. A shocking notion, to be sure, and an unlikely storyline for a savior—and according to Christians, it was what set Christ apart from everyone else who had ever lived or would live.

It was Jesus Christ's self-sacrificing death by crucifixion in perfect obedience to God's will that undid Adam and Eve's *dis*obedience and made eternal salvation with God possible. Shortly after his execution, God raised the crucified Jesus from the dead in the resurrection, a triumph over death that ratified the incarnation. Subsequently, this stunning event was celebrated annually as Easter, the most important Christian feast day. Before joining his "Father" (as Jesus called God) in heaven after his resurrection, Jesus told his followers to preach the good news—the gospel—to all nations, baptizing them in the name of the Father, the Son, and the Holy Spirit. The movement of Christ's

followers that ensued was the Church, described by the Jewish convert Paul (whose writings were included in the New Testament) as the
mystical body of Christ. The Church was made up of all Christians,
past and present—that is, all those who believed in Christ as their
savior and were united to him by their common faith.

The Church derived its authority from Christ as God-become-
human. It was God's instrument on earth for eternal salvation until
Christ would come again and make a world-ending Last Judgment,
an event foretold in the New Testament. Fidelity to the Church's
teachings was necessary for eternal salvation. That's why heresy, the
deliberate dissent from church doctrine, was so dangerous.

How you lived dictated how God would judge you for eternity.
That's why Christian teachings were meant to inform every aspect of
life. Nothing was irrelevant to religion because nothing lay outside
God's creation. Religion was meant to influence how Christians worshipped and prayed, of course, but also how they ruled and worked,
bought and sold, taught and learned, related to their families and
understood their lives. Because religion was so interconnected with
everything else, changes in religion automatically affected every area
of life. Changes in Christianity and disagreements about it had consequences that reached far beyond religion as we usually think of it.
And the Reformation brought changes in Latin Christianity unlike
anything else in the Middle Ages in its geographical scope, its staying
power, and its transformative influence.

From Then to Now: A First Glance

The Reformation had the long-term impact of gradually and
unintentionally transforming Europe from a world permeated
by Christianity to one in which religion would be separate from
public life, becoming instead a matter of individual preference.

This separation from public life is what I mean by *secularization*. Multiple areas of life in Western societies ended up getting secularized because the Reformation inadvertently made Christianity into an intractable problem.

This was a different *kind* of problem from that decried for centuries by medieval holy men and women—the problem of Christians not living up to the Church's teachings. Protestant reformers differed from medieval reformers by asserting that many of the Church's teachings were themselves false. The problem wasn't just bad behavior; it was also erroneous doctrine. Defenders of the Roman Church, however, disagreed and condemned Protestants as heretics—*they* were the ones teaching the novel, false doctrines. A crucial, unintended result of the Reformation was that it introduced sustained, widespread disagreement about Christian teachings.

Martin Luther not only condemned abuses in the Church and attacked the papacy but also rejected many beliefs and practices that had been integral to Latin Christianity for centuries. If everyone (or almost everyone) had agreed with him, the Reformation might have transformed the Church and society as a whole. But defenders of the papacy and inherited Christian teachings rejected Luther's rejections as well as those of John Calvin and other Protestant reformers. Roman Catholicism not only persisted; its leaders also undertook major reforms of their own, reasserting traditional teachings, defining others for the first time, and encouraging religious practices and institutions that Protestants condemned. This unprecedented division of Latin Christianity brought about unanticipated and unintended consequences.

Because Protestants and Catholics disagreed with one another, and because religion at the time was embedded in politics, economics, society, and culture, we cannot understand the significance of the Reformation by concentrating on Protestantism alone. It is the Reformation *era*—the period from around 1520 to 1650—with its disagreements and conflicts *between* Protestants and Catholics that remains essential to understanding the Reformation's lasting impact today. Together, in relationship to each other, Protestants and Catholics created major new problems that couldn't be ignored.

What emerged was essentially a redefinition of religion in relationship to the rest of life. New ideas came to stand in for religion; they inspired novel practices and reconfigured institutions. Taken together, these new ideas, practices, and institutions became the foundations for the modern world. They led eventually to the modern secularization of Western life—an unintended outcome of a sixteenth-century religious revolution.

Protestant reformers agreed with their medieval predecessors that Christianity should inform politics and society, and they sought to make it happen in their own ways. Protestant rulers agreed with their Catholic contemporaries that human life ought to be ordered in ways sanctioned by God. Conscientious Catholic and Protestant rulers in the Reformation era agreed that true religion should be defended and promoted. Because they *dis*agreed, though, about what true Christianity was *and* at the same time regarded it as so important, they fought a series of military conflicts in Western Europe from the 1520s through the 1640s. These are commonly known as the Wars of Religion. Considering religion's influence on all areas of life, it would be more accurate to call them the wars of *more*-than-religion.

These more-than-religious wars were destructive, expensive, and inconclusive. By the middle of the seventeenth century they had drained and exhausted Europeans. The disruptive conflicts of the Thirty Years' War (1618–1648) and English Revolution (1640–1660) wreaked widespread devastation, and weary Europeans started looking for alternatives. Understandably, more rounds of large-scale violence involving religion weren't appealing. Starting in the seventeenth century, some Europeans began to reconceive religion as separate from politics, which led to the political protection of individual freedom of religion as the first important modern human right, beginning across the Atlantic with the United States in the late eighteenth century.

But the religion protected in the post-Reformation world would not be religion in the medieval or Reformation sense. Because religion had become such a problem, it had to be redefined and its scope restricted. People would be free to believe whatever they wanted and to worship however they wished. At the same time, explicit religious beliefs or practices could no longer inform the wider society. Even in European countries with state-supported churches, politically protected space was eventually carved out for dissenters. Europeans and North Americans gained individual freedom of belief in exchange for the shared social, political, and cultural influence of religion. Neither Luther nor any other major Protestant reformers sought this goal; it was prompted instead by the conflicts between Protestants and Catholics that followed in the wake of the Reformation.

The Protestant reformers also did not intend another consequence of the Reformation that remains deeply influential today: people's ability to answer questions of meaning and morality in an open-ended variety of ways both religious and secular. Individuals today can believe whatever they want about morality or purpose and lead their lives accordingly. This is a big part of what we usually mean by *freedom*. Early Protestant leaders had a very different vision: they wanted to recover what God said in the Bible as the basis for reforming the Church and informing all of human life.

But from the very start of the Reformation in the 1520s, Protestant reformers disagreed about what the Bible meant and how it should be applied. Ironically, their disagreements stemmed directly from Luther's insistence on scripture as the bottom-line authority for Christian faith and life. And these disagreements were never resolved; there existed no mechanism or process for resolving them. Instead, modern democratic states would centuries later move toward protecting secular answers to the deepest questions about human life through the same political measures that guaranteed religious freedom.

The history of Protestantism in the Reformation era and since is much more than just the history of Lutheranism. It's much more than the history of Martin Luther's ideas and their reception. It's the history of all the rival and frequently divisive interpretations of the Bible and of all the Protestant churches, traditions, and groups associated with them. In the Reformation era, Protestant and Catholic authorities largely succeeded in suppressing other Protestant groups, such as the Swiss Anabaptists, Hutterites, Mennonites, Schwenckfelders, Socinians, Familists, and more. This kept their numbers small and their impact minimal. Only Lutheranism and Calvinism (more accurately known as Reformed Protestantism) influenced large numbers of people in a sustained fashion. Not coincidentally, Lutheranism and Calvinism were the only two Protestant groups that, like Roman Catholicism elsewhere in Europe, were politically protected and promoted by civic magistrates or territorial rulers. Once religion had been redefined as an individual choice that could and should be politically protected, other forms of Protestantism could and did become more common and influential. Nowhere has this been more evident since the eighteenth century than in the United States.

Many people today answer questions that have traditionally been central to religion—about how to live, what to care about, how to treat others, and so forth—in secular ways. Their responses are in crucial respects the indirect outcome of the Reformation as well. These modern nonreligious alternatives became possible because certain disagreements inherited from the Reformation era remained unresolved. In various forms, those standoffs have remained part of the Western past for the last five hundred years. As noted already, starting in the seventeenth century, some people began to reimagine the relationship between religion and politics in order to navigate problems stemming from unsought Christian pluralism. Where theologians remained deadlocked, new attempts arose to justify politics, ground morality, and imagine society in terms that were independent of religion.

Religious disputes inspired secularism. Disagreements about God's Word and God's will remained intractable. To find persuasive answers to questions about politics, law, morality, and society, disagreements about God would have to be set aside. The political and moral thought of the Enlightenment and the secular philosophies of the modern era were born out of the divisive conflicts among Christians in the Reformation era. Most people, however, are not aware of how they have been influenced by ideas that arose in response to the Reformation. They are also not aware that modern institutions arose as they did in order to address concrete problems inherited from the Reformation era. Today, the politically protected individual right to believe whatever you want so long as you obey the state's laws is an unintended consequence of the unresolved religious disagreements of the Reformation.

Where We Are Going in This Book

This is the bottom line: anyone who wants to understand how and why we have the Western ideas and institutions we have today must understand the Reformation and all that followed in its wake.

The story of the Reformation rightly begins with Martin Luther. Chapter 1 focuses on this intense man and the extraordinary years from 1517 through 1521. During these four years an unlikely series of events catapulted him from an unknown Augustinian friar and university professor to the most famous author in Europe, a man who dared to defy both pope and emperor.

As soon as Luther published his ideas, he became a public figure, and the Reformation swelled into a movement he couldn't control. Chapter 2 moves from man to movement, the volatile early Reformation in Germany and Switzerland from 1521 through the mid-1530s.

If the Reformation had remained within these borders, it wouldn't have had nearly the impact it did. But, as the Reformation spread to other countries, rulers opted for or against it, which resulted in the construction of new Christian traditions as well as contentious and sometimes violent Christian pluralism. Men and women everywhere had to decide how to respond to rulers' measures in the midst of rival religious claims. Chapter 3 moves beyond the early Reformation as a German movement to the Reformation era throughout Europe, covering the period from 1520 to around 1650.

Chapter 4 takes the widest perspective of all in analyzing how the modern Western world since the seventeenth century was formed through a series of interrelated responses to problems inherited from the Reformation. During this period, religion was redefined to accommodate doctrinal disagreements and to insulate public life from religious influence. The processes of secularization that followed continue to operate in the early twenty-first century—which does not mean that the citizens of Western liberal democracies are all coming to believe or value the same things, as political developments in both Europe and North America demonstrated in 2016 with disturbing clarity.

The book starts small and expands outward—from one Augustinian friar to a German movement, a European era, and Western modernity. We will start where the Reformation itself started: with the restless anxiety of that Augustinian friar five hundred years ago.

CHAPTER 1

A RELUCTANT REBEL

T HE Reformation, an unlikely series of events that transformed Latin Christianity and with it Western civilization, begins with an equally unlikely figure: Martin Luther, a pious and spiritually anxious Augustinian friar solemnly devoted to God. In 1517 on the eve of the Reformation, hardly anyone knows Luther except for his confreres and townspeople in the obscure German town of Wittenberg. Mostly, Luther keeps his anxieties to himself. He lives with thirty-some fellow Augustinians in a friary in a forgettably small town set in the oddly shaped territory of Electoral Saxony, which is part of the large stretch of central Europe known as the Holy Roman Empire. The empire is a collection of hundreds of cities and territories that includes the Germanic peoples, and it belongs to Latin Christendom, which encompasses Europe from Iceland to Poland and Lithuania and from Scandinavia to Spain and Sicily.

A Busy and Burdened Friar

By midsummer 1517, though Luther occasionally expresses a few hints of frustration and anger, he shares nothing that suggests rebellion, let alone a revolution. He's too burdened with responsibilities to imagine the *Ninety-Five Theses,* which he will write only a few months later.

The "lazy monk," a familiar caricature of the early sixteenth century, does not apply to Luther. Not at all. Neither does he look secluded, like the popular image of those whose religious vows of poverty, chastity, and obedience supposedly separate them off from society in lives devoted to prayer. The name of Luther's religious order, the Augustinian Hermits, is misleading in this way: they aren't hermits—loners seeking God in solitude. Neither are they monks, leading common lives of cloistered contemplation, like the Benedictines, who by the early sixteenth century have been around for almost a thousand years, or the Cistercians or Carthusians, newer contemplative orders with their origins in the monastic revival of the twelfth century. The Augustinians are friars, members of the mendicant ("begging") orders, like the larger and more influential Dominicans and Franciscans. Their religious vocations entail actively engaging with lay Christians in the wider world, known in Latin as the *saeculum* (the origin of our word *secular*).

In October 1516, Luther writes to his longtime friend Johannes Lang. Lang has recently been named the prior of the Augustinian friary in Erfurt, a bustling city more than a hundred miles to the southwest of Wittenberg, where years before Luther attended university and first entered the order. Unburdening himself to a friend he's known for years, Luther writes, "I nearly need two copyists or secretaries," adding later—in yet one more letter he's scratching out with ink-dipped quill pen on paper in his small, regular handwriting—"all day long I do almost nothing else than write letters." But despite his lengthy protestations to Lang, Luther does a lot more than letter writing as Wittenberg's autumn days grow shorter. Other more pressing duties and demands leave him feeling overwhelmed:

I am a preacher at the monastery, I am a reader during mealtimes, I am asked daily to preach in the city church, I have to supervise studies, I am a vicar (and that means I am eleven times prior), I am caretaker of the fish pond at Leitzkau, I represent the people of Herzberg at the court in Torgau, I lecture on Paul, and I am assembling a commentary on the Psalms. As I have already mentioned, the greater part of my time is filled with letter writing. I hardly have any uninterrupted time to say the hourly prayers and celebrate Mass. Besides all this there are my own struggles with the flesh, the world, and the devil. See what a lazy man I am![1]

So much for the life of contemplative seclusion he imagined when he chose his vocation more than ten years earlier! At that time he sought a highly regulated life of prayer, worship, self-scrutiny, and self-discipline. For more than another year after Luther writes this letter, only a few people—some German Augustinians, some townspeople and students in Wittenberg, and a handful of others in Electoral Saxony—know who Luther is and recognize his dedication and talent. Which is why at age thirty-three he is asked to do so much. And this hardworking friar and obedient servant of the Church does it well, not wearing his spiritual anxieties on the coarse woolen sleeve of his friar's cowl.

Augustinian Duties

Luther is first and foremost an Augustinian friar and Catholic priest. In fact, he took vows in a deliberately rigorous religious order, the reformed or Observant Augustinians. He could have chosen one that was less strict, but he didn't. In the course of the fifteenth century, hundreds of male and female communities from different religious orders deliberately undertook reform as their members sought to "observe" the original way of life, or *rule,* of their founders.

Luther laments to Lang that all those demands on him *as* a capable and conscientious Augustinian are burdening his core obligations to say mass, the ritual reenactment of Christ's suffering and crucifixion and the central act of Christian worship. Throughout Christendom, thousands of priests offer countless thousands of masses a day. Luther's duties are also impeding him from properly fulfilling the seven prescribed times for prayer that structure his daily life and the lives of thousands of others in religious orders. He dreads becoming a frazzled friar who just goes through the motions. Dedication to God, Luther believes, is meant to be deliberate, reflective, serious, and heartfelt.

Before his passion and death, at the Last Supper recounted in the Gospels, Jesus commanded his apostles to "Do this in remembrance of me" (Luke 22:19); hence the clergy re-present his sacrifice in masses throughout Christendom. Following Psalm 119:164, which says "seven times a day I will praise you [God] for your righteous judgments," those who pursue lives of holiness dedicated to God gather for monastic prayer seven times each day.

Augustinians eat most of their meals in silence while one of the friars reads aloud something spiritually edifying, which is what Luther means by his mealtime reading duty. It fits within the regular routine of his days and is not too burdensome. Preaching for his fellow friars takes more time and preparation, but it's also close to the heart of his vocation. It's an extension of his deep engagement with God's Word in scripture, which has been part of his life for several years.

Administrative tasks are another matter. They're not inherent to his vocation. But in Luther's time as in ours, someone has to do them if an organization is to sustain itself. Luther's role as vicar ("representative") over the eleven Observant Augustinian friaries in his province, the geographical administrative unit into which religious orders are parceled, doesn't actually mean he's in charge of each one as its prior. His passionate temperament makes him prone to dramatic exaggerations. He's not even the prior of the Wittenberg community, let alone ten others, and he's well aware that his friend Lang oversees the house in Erfurt.

But Luther is the provincial vicar under the provincial superior, Johann von Staupitz, and as such he has to address all sorts of practical matters, spending long hours on many days writing letters. He tells Lang that fellow friars have been relieved of or appointed to new duties in Munich, Culmbach, Neustadt, and Dordrecht; the plague "attacks quite cruelly and suddenly" and is killing people in Wittenberg, sometimes two or three in a day, including a nearby artisan's son buried just that day; two Augustinians have just come from Cologne among four newly arrived in Wittenberg, where in Luther's own friary forty-one men are now living "on our more than meager supplies."[2] Managing Augustinian practical affairs is encroaching on his Augustinian religious life.

A few years before, Augustinian affairs took Luther all the way to Rome, the center of the Catholic Church, more than eight hundred miles south over the Alps. In the winter of 1510–1511 Luther and a confrere were sent there and back on foot. It will turn out to be the only time Luther ever travels outside his native Germany. Rome is one of Latin Christendom's major pilgrimage destinations and has been for centuries. Like countless other men and women, Luther made the most of the opportunity. While there, he visited multiple churches, received special blessings, and said many masses. He was dismayed to see, in the city of early Christian martyrs, others whose dedication and devotion was less serious than his own.

Like his trip to Rome, Luther's administrative duties as vicar follow from his Augustinian commitments, even though these duties involve no overt prayer or worship. For centuries some religious orders, including the Augustinians, have been accumulating lands through bequests from pious laypeople. Someone has to look after all this property.

So we find Luther keeping tabs on a fishpond owned by the Wittenberg Augustinians nearly eighty miles to the west near Magdeburg. He also negotiates in a court case in Torgau, thirty miles to the southeast, about the use of a parish church nearby in the village of Herzberg.[3] This energetic, committed Observant Augustinian, like thousands of other members of mendicant orders, is living out a successful career in the Church as 1516 turns into 1517.

Getting to a New University
in a Small Town

At least to all appearances. Luther continues to keep his spiritual anxiety to himself even while he says prayers and masses; reads at meals and preaches in his friary; conveys news, receives brothers, and writes endless letters as provincial vicar; and plays Augustinian fishpond manager and local legal negotiator. Not to mention his teaching duties. He's busy as a professor of theology at the University of Wittenberg, where he tells Lang he's supervising the studies of other Augustinians, lecturing on some of St. Paul's writings from the New Testament, and preparing for publication the lecture notes he'd delivered on the Psalms.

Established in 1502, Wittenberg's university and Augustinian community are newcomers to the town. By contrast, the Franciscan friary has been there for two and a half centuries. Prince Frederick "the Wise," nicknamed for his decades of prudent rule over the territory of Electoral Saxony, made Wittenberg his main residence in the late fifteenth century. He spent years and considerable funds rebuilding his castle and its accompanying church in impressive

Renaissance fashion on the west end of town. But Frederick lacked a university, since his cousin George, in the parceling out of Saxony in 1485, received the larger town of Leipzig with its established university.

Frederick wanted a university of his own, as princes commonly did. Besides lending prestige, universities train the lawyers, physicians, theologians, and men of affairs useful for helping princes consolidate control in their territories. And so, needing more professors than the Franciscans could provide, he called on an old Augustinian friend, Johann von Staupitz, to establish the Augustinians in Wittenberg and help staff the faculty of his new university by providing two professors, one each in moral philosophy and theology. Luther's immediate superior in the order, Staupitz, is in charge of Germany's eleven Observant Augustinian friaries. At the time Luther writes to Lang, Staupitz remains, as he's been for years, an important confidant and spiritual adviser for Luther, one of the few who knows about his interior struggles.[4]

Luther's duties include overseeing the university studies for Wittenberg's Augustinian novices ("newcomers"). There were twelve in late 1516, about a third of the members of the community.[5] The novitiate was a tryout stage of religious life so men and women considering it would know what they were getting into before taking final vows. Those who went forward did so because they made a personal, voluntary choice. It's exactly the choice Luther himself made years before, after his novitiate in Erfurt, a commercial hub and culturally sophisticated urban center of nearly 20,000 souls with its prestigious university founded in the late 1300s. Luther made his way through Erfurt's faculty of arts (the equivalent of undergraduate education) and started on the study of law in June 1505, in accord with the wishes of his father, Hans Luder.

Hans wanted the best for Martin, his second son with his wife, Margarete Lindemann. He'd done well for himself as a small-scale businessman in the copper smelting industry of Mansfeld, another small town where Luther had spent most of his boyhood and attended primary school.[6] Ambitious for Martin, Hans sought for him a path through education that would lead to a financially successful career as a lawyer.

But only a few weeks after he began to study law, Luther got caught in a violent thunderstorm while walking back to Erfurt. Terrified by a bolt of lightning and roaring thunder that threw him to the ground, he reacted in characteristic medieval fashion: he made a vow to a saint, in this case St. Anne, the mother of the Virgin Mary. Luther promised St. Anne that if she preserved him in the thunderstorm, he would enter religious life. Within a month Luther, true to his word, knocked on the door of the Augustinian friary in Erfurt, defying his father's ambitions and startling his friends.

A year later, after completing his novitiate, Luther made his voluntary final vows, solemnly giving himself to God. He dedicated himself to a lifelong process of sanctification through prayer, worship, and ascetic self-denial in seeking to follow Christ's command to "be perfect as your heavenly Father is perfect" (Matthew 5:48). In 1507 Luther was ordained a priest and celebrated his first mass.

Luther showed himself eager for religious life. He was spiritually intense, intellectually gifted, and interested in scripture. Staupitz asked him to pursue advanced studies in theology to serve the Augustinian order and the Church. Luther did so, studying theology in the way necessary for anyone who aspired to become a theologian: through the curriculum, concepts, logical rigor, and argument-based method of scholasticism, which rested heavily on the thinking of the ancient Greek philosopher Aristotle, whose works had been translated into Latin from Greek and Arabic in the twelfth and thirteenth centuries. The scholastic curriculum emphasized logic and natural philosophy, the precursor to modern science in that it sought to explain phenomena in the natural world. Aristotelian concepts and its method of disputation, which employed precise argument and counterargument, were also used in theology, long the most important academic discipline because of its role in articulating and safeguarding Christian teaching.

Luther earned the customary degrees along the way to his doctorate in 1512 while simultaneously lecturing on Aristotle's ethics in Wittenberg during his first stay in the city in 1508 and 1509. Two years later, when Staupitz's own duties required him to travel too much to sustain his teaching, Luther was transferred to replace him in Wittenberg.

God's Word, Humanist Scholarship, and Christian Reform

By the time he sits down to write to Lang in late October 1516, Luther is about to lecture on St. Paul's letter to the Galatians; he's just completed a series of lectures on Paul's letter to the Romans. For the past two years as a professor, he's been immersed in the Psalms. These Old Testament prayers Luther knows virtually by heart, because like many other members of religious orders he chants all 150 psalms every two weeks, cycling through them again and again as part of religious life, internalizing their hopes and fears, their exaltations and exasperations. By 1513, the year Luther starts his lectures, seven years of communally chanting the Psalms have woven these prayers into the fabric of his daily life. He's also an heir to the centuries-old monastic tradition of *lectio divina* ("sacred reading"), the careful, patient, meditative pondering of scripture. He is practiced in seeking its relevance for his own life and, inseparably for Luther, for the stewardship of his soul. Reading the Bible in this way differs from scholastic theology, which uses scriptural verses in technical, logical arguments, though the two forms of biblical engagement have coexisted in Christendom for three centuries.

In addition to the scholastic theology in which he was trained and the meditative reading he practices every day, Luther uses yet another method for approaching the Bible in his lectures: Renaissance humanism. Like many other scholars of scripture in recent decades, including some other scholastic theologians, Luther sees the value in the humanist exhortation *"ad fontes!"* ("back to the sources!"). The Bible was originally written in Hebrew and Greek, not Latin or a sixteenth-century vernacular language. Because any text is better— richer and more nuanced—in its original language than in translation, Luther began studying Hebrew and Greek. But from 1513 to 1515, in his lectures on the Psalms, he still uses the traditional Latin translation of the Bible, called the Vulgate, the translation made by St. Jerome in the late fourth century that has been used throughout Christendom for more than a thousand years.[7]

In 1516, while Luther is lecturing on St. Paul's letter to the Romans, Desiderius Erasmus (ca. 1467–1536), Europe's leading humanist scholar, publishes the *Novum Instrumentum* ("The New Instrument"), his unprecedented edition of the New Testament with the Greek text and his own Latin translation running for over five hundred pages in parallel columns. Immediately, Luther starts using Erasmus's edition for his lectures. A master of impeccable classical Latin and superb Greek, Erasmus is a widely published author and the editor of many ancient texts by pagan writers and the church fathers. But in 1516 none of his publications is bigger than his *Novum Instrumentum,* which includes more than four hundred additional pages of annotations and commentary to explain textual difficulties and to justify his countless diversions from the Latin Vulgate.[8]

Erasmus's translation is something of a bombshell. The Latin Vulgate, after all, was embedded in the Church's worship, preaching, moral instruction, and scholastic theology. If some of its translations were misleading or mistaken, did that cast doubt on the Church's teachings? Not necessarily, but it did raise new questions about their relationship to scripture and the relationship between scholastic theology and humanist biblical scholarship.

Erasmus is critical of scholastic theology for what he regards as its abstractions and technical language, which he considers remote from the practice of the virtues at the center of Christian life. He's also critical of scholastic theologians who stubbornly deny the importance of linguistic study and textual criticism. He thinks classical languages and rhetoric are better equipped than Aristotelian philosophy to provide the intellectual foundation for the renewal of Christendom—a renewal for which so many conscientious Christians have been calling for so long.

In Erasmus's view, the main problems plaguing Christendom are superstition and ignorance, and largely to blame for them are the clergy's negligence and (often) ignorance. Schooling is the solution: through effective instruction in the Christian virtues by educated clergy and teachers, laypeople will know what to do and how to live. Humanist scholars are the key players in this enterprise: they know ancient languages, they read and compare manuscripts, and they prepare editions for publication in both the original languages and translations. They are the teachers of the teachers who will reform Christendom through education.

Because most Christians in the early sixteenth century are illiterate and have little or no formal education, this initiative cannot be realized overnight. Such a transformation across Christendom will take time. Despite Christendom's entrenched problems, patience is necessary. The Latin Church is an enormous, complicated institution made up of smaller institutions that have been layered over one another for more than a thousand years. Its problems can't be fixed all at once. But Erasmus and his colleagues hope that if the education-based reforms of the Christian humanists take hold, a better-educated clergy and laity in a less sinful Church will gradually emerge, which will lead to a more genuinely Christian society.

In 1516 Luther recognizes Erasmus's immense achievement as a biblical scholar in making the Greek text available while simultaneously pointing out problems with the Vulgate. He also likes Erasmus's criticism of scholastic theology, despite his own training in it. Luther has come to believe that Aristotle's philosophical categories hinder rather than help a person's understanding of God's Word in scripture. But Luther parts ways with Erasmus's confidence in languages and rhetoric to provide the needed substitute. His own experience has increasingly led him to believe that human beings can't be the agents of their own moral improvement. Try as hard as you want for as long as you want, you can't better yourself through your own exertion.

Here Luther's biblical scholarship intersects with his personal struggles over his own sense of sinful inadequacy. In late 1516, the best antidote to Aristotle he has found is St. Augustine (354–430), the namesake theologian of his religious order and Latin Christendom's most influential theologian by far throughout the Middle Ages. In particular, Luther loves specific passages in Augustine's writings that speak to his own experience of human weakness and impotence in the face of God's commands.

Exactly a week before he writes to Lang about his burdensome workload, Luther writes to George Spalatin, Frederick of Saxony's secretary, requesting that he send a letter to Erasmus on his behalf. He asks Spalatin to convey his esteem but also to tell Erasmus that he really ought to prefer St. Augustine to St. Jerome, Erasmus's hero among the Latin church fathers.[9] Several weeks later, in early December, Spalatin does write to Erasmus, inserting chunks straight from Luther's letter. He doesn't mention Luther's name, referring only to "an Augustinian priest, as well known for his holiness in life as for his distinction in theology,"[10] leaving the essentially unknown Luther anonymous.

Even into late 1517, the contrast between Erasmus and Luther as published authors could hardly be greater—the superstar humanist against a virtual nonentity. Luther's commentary on the Psalms remains unpublished despite the hopes he expressed to Lang in his letter. He manages only a brief German treatise on the seven penitential psalms, a traditional genre, which is published in the spring of 1517. Besides that, Luther writes the preface for a partial edition of a late medieval German mystical treatise that appears in December 1516.[11] Both are the work of Wittenberg's only printer, Johann Rhau-Grunenberg, whose shop sits near the Augustinian friary at the east end of town. Rhau-Grunenberg is basically a bottom-shelf service printer for official university announcements and textbooks.[12]

By contrast, as Europe's leading humanist scholar, Erasmus has been published since 1514 by northern Europe's cutting-edge printer of humanist texts, Johann Froben of Basel. In previous years he was the prize author of Italy's trendsetting humanist printer, Aldus Manutius of Venice. Besides Erasmus's pathbreaking edition of the New Testament, by the end of 1516 Froben publishes within two years an expanded edition of his *Adages,* two reprints of his best-selling *Praise of Folly,* his edition of Seneca's *Lucubrationes,* multiple monumental volumes of his carefully prepared edition of St. Jerome's correspondence, and *The Education of a Christian Prince,* a practical handbook of political theory, for the Habsburg teenager Charles of Spain.[13]

Wittenberg's Thriving Christian Piety

As an author, Luther is invisible by comparison. But he is known locally in a different capacity. The last responsibility he mentions in his letter to Lang is preaching in the local parish church of

St. Mary's, which he's been doing on a regular basis since 1514. Importantly, it brings Luther into sustained contact with ordinary lay Christians outside the university setting and provides a testing ground for Luther's effective communication in German. Although the mass was always celebrated in Latin, homilies (sermons preached on the specified biblical readings for each particular mass) throughout Christendom are offered in the vernacular in parishes like St. Mary's.

The church itself is an imposing, twin-towered Gothic structure adjacent to the market and city hall, more or less in the middle of Wittenberg's long east-to-west layout. A large parish church that had been expanded in the fifteenth century, St. Mary's with its impressive towers symbolizes the thriving practice of Christian faith in Wittenberg. Right next to St. Mary's is the Corpus Christi chapel, a much smaller structure built in the 1360s to accommodate the growing demand for masses. The Franciscan and Augustinian friaries have their own churches as well, of course.

There is yet another church, despite the fact that Wittenberg is a small, unremarkable town of no more than 2,500 people. Frederick the Wise recently built his castle church at the west end of town, and it's a jewel, displaying commissioned religious paintings by leading German artists such as Albrecht Dürer, and Lucas Cranach, whom Frederick lured to Wittenberg in 1505 to be his court artist. This structure is also known as the Collegiate Church of All Saints, incorporating a church institution called a chapter, established in the fourteenth century, and supporting dozens of priests called canons. Most impressively and distinctively, All Saints includes a special gallery that houses a large collection of saints' relics—over nineteen thousand—which makes the church a regional pilgrimage destination. Frederick, Luther's pious prince, has been building the collection over many years. In 1517, over nine thousand masses are said in the castle church alone, and over forty thousand candles are burned. That doesn't count St. Mary's, the Corpus Christi chapel, or the Franciscan and Augustinian churches.[14]

Wittenberg is like other communities in this respect: wherever you look, you can see expressions of Christian piety—in processions and pilgrimages, in the endowment of masses and prayers to the saints, in willing support for the rebuilding and upkeep of parish churches, and in voluntary contributions to religious orders. Ordinary people show their devotion through participating enthusiastically in the organizations of Christian fellowship called confraternities, through engaging in biblically based works of mercy, such as feeding the hungry and caring for the sick, and through purchasing and using printed prayer books. Since the 1450s, when Johannes Gutenberg invented the printing press, well over a thousand *editions* of these books have been published, many of them inexpensive, which means that probably over a million copies of them are in circulation by 1517.[15] And those who can read also read the printed Bible in vernacular languages (except in England, where the Bible in English has been generally illegal for a century because of its association with a heretical movement, the Lollards).[16] Twenty-two editions of the complete vernacular Bible have been published in German or Netherlandish by 1518, plus over 130 editions of the New Testament readings for the annual cycle of Sunday masses.[17]

Throughout Europe, as Luther lectures on St. Paul, preaches in St. Mary's, supervises Augustinian novices, and looks after a fishpond, Christians are participating with gusto in their religion in many different ways. And beyond a few basic expectations, most of those ways are up to them; how they want to practice the faith is largely their own choice so long as they don't stray from approved practices. The menu of options is rich and long. This doesn't look like a religious culture that's about to be turned upside down, any more than the busy, devout Augustinian friar Martin Luther looks like he's a rebel in the ranks, ready to start a revolution.

Sins, Reform, and the
Importance of Confession

Yet at the same time long-standing, pervasive dissatisfactions and problems are churning in Christendom. Not every Christian practices the faith with enthusiasm—far from it—and probably few people practice the virtues central to Christian life consistently or uniformly. The basic problem has long remained the same. Indeed, for centuries, many holy men and women have seen it clearly: despite all these devotional practices, there is a disconnect between what the Church teaches and the way many Christians live.

Alongside enthusiastic expressions of Christian faith in the early sixteenth century, sins are everywhere, from the top of the Church's hierarchy on down through the laity. Popes, the cardinals who advise them in Rome, and the bishops, who are frequently absent from the dioceses they are supposed to oversee, often live ostentatiously wealthy, worldly lives contrary to the biblical virtues of poverty and humility.

In Europe as a whole, very few Christians ever see the pope or a cardinal, while the bishops are hardly common figures in most people's daily lives. Certainly not in Wittenberg. But parish clergy and the members of religious orders are. Some parish priests keep concubines despite their vows of celibacy, and most of them, especially in rural areas, lack strong theological or pastoral training. A more common source of criticism is the clergy's greediness, manifest in tithes, rents, and fees for services. Members of the laity also resent them for taking advantage of their clerical privileges, such as exemptions from most taxes and the right to be tried for criminal accusations only in church courts. Laypeople often complain about the members of religious orders for the same reasons.

Anticlericalism of this sort is common in the 1510s as it has been for a very long time. And most members of the laity are hardly beyond reproach—whether merchants who seek profits at the expense of the common good, families whose members stoke violent feuds for years on end, or peasant villagers who superstitiously think the Church is a source of holy magic they can exploit to their own advantage.

Despite abundant evidence that Christians are religiously engaged, an elusive goal remains the same as it has been for generations: the reform of the Church by exhorting all clergy and laity to live better Christian lives in imitation of Christ. All this is old hat. St. Bernard of Clairvaux said it in the twelfth century, St. Catherine of Siena in the fourteenth, and countless others besides. In his fifteenth-century bestseller, *The Imitation of Christ,* Thomas of Kempen exhorted Christians to "earnestly desire to advance in virtue, love discipline, dwell in repentance, show prompt obedience, exercise self-denial, and patiently bear all trials for the love of Christ."[18] By the early sixteenth century, Christian humanists, led by Erasmus above all in northern Europe, are starting to put their own twist on this long-standing impulse by emphasizing reform through erudition and education.

Latin Christendom in 1517 is a paradoxical picture of pervasive piety and widespread human sinfulness—no great secret among those who care about the faith and the Church and therefore want things to improve.

Another of those who wishes to see reform is the Christian humanist Giles of Viterbo, the head of the Augustinian order. He preached the opening address of the Fifth Lateran Council, convened in Rome by Pope Julius II in 1512 just a year before the pope died. Giles has no illusions about the Church's shortcomings. But like other reformers, he thinks the key to fixing them lies with conscientious, educated clergy, who should carry out their duties and practice the Church's teachings by enacting the Christian virtues of selflessness, forgiveness, humility, and love of enemies. As Giles puts it, "Human beings must be changed by religion and not religion by human beings."[19]

Five years later, in March 1517, the Fifth Lateran Council concludes without fanfare. It gives no indication that any major institutional changes are needed or that any substantial doctrinal changes are called for. The problem lies not in the Church's teachings but in getting more people to live consistently by them.

For the many shortcomings of rich and poor, powerful and humble, learned and ignorant alike, the Church offers the sacrament of penance. It is the means, according to the Church, through which God forgives sins. Unlike the onetime sacrament of baptism, the initiation rite through which you became a Christian within days after birth, the sacrament of penance takes place once every year for most Christians. The most important medieval Church council (the Fourth Lateran) prescribed it as such in 1215, although practices of penance went back centuries earlier, based on the words of the resurrected Christ to his apostles, as written in John's Gospel: "If you forgive the sins of any, they are forgiven them" (John 20:23).

Just before Easter each year, Christian clergy and laity alike are required to confess their sins to a priest, in this role called a confessor. He absolves you of your sins provided you're sorry for them and carry out a penance, which provides "satisfaction" for your sins—something positive you do to satisfy God for having offended him. The more serious the sin, the greater the penance.

This annual confession of sins is a prerequisite for receiving the Eucharist—the consecrated bread that through God's power and by means of the priest's words miraculously becomes the body and blood of Christ during the mass. As we've seen, this too was biblically based on Jesus's words to his apostles: "This is my body," he said in reference to the bread at the Last Supper, and then, "Do this in remembrance of me" (Luke 22:19). Individual Christians can have a mass said for their specific prayer requests, and—as with anything else good and desirable—the more the better. All told throughout Christendom, the laity pay for countless thousands of masses to be said every day of the year.

Priests such as Luther consecrate both bread and wine at mass, but usually only they consume them, and only they receive the consecrated wine. (In Bohemia in the fifteenth century, laypeople demanded they receive "the cup," which became a symbol of the dissenting Hussite movement.) Most Christians receive the Eucharist only once a year, at Easter. However, in the decades before 1517, devout laypeople are confessing more frequently in order to receive the Eucharist more often.

Luther's Struggles Beneath the Surface

Devout, dedicated, and perceptive, Luther criticizes many of the problems that similarly bother others who care about the faith and the Church. But these are not the problems he has in mind when he tells Lang about the last thing that keeps him so busy: "my own struggles with the flesh, the world, and the devil." For Luther, this conventional monastic phrase veils something deeper than the usual dissatisfactions with sinful Christians who fail to live up to the Church's teachings. The phrase is as real to Luther as his own flesh and blood; it goes far beyond failing to follow Christ by inadequately practicing the virtues as taught by Christian humanists or scholastic theologians.

Luther is tormented nearly to the point of despair not despite but *because of* his life as an Augustinian and the exacting way in which he endeavors to live up to its demands.

Few others know this. Those who do include a few fellow Augustinians, such as Staupitz and Wenceslas Link, who also came to Wittenberg from Erfurt when Luther moved in 1511. Luther confides in Staupitz. He confesses his sins to him in the sacrament of penance and seeks Staupitz's advice about his spiritual struggles. Luther's basic problem is rooted in his own experience: despite the Church's assurances that God forgives his sins in the sacrament of penance, Luther doesn't *feel* forgiven. He doesn't feel as though things have been set right between him and God. And that is what he craves most in life, much more than an advance in his order, international fame, or even being recognized as an effective preacher.

The sacrament that seems to work for most everyone else doesn't work for him. He doesn't experience God's mercy despite how widely it's extolled as a counterbalance to God's justice in sermons and sculptures, paintings and prayers alike. For Luther the scrupulous Augustinian friar, there is only the God of judgment. And for Luther the relentlessly introspective pursuer of holiness, that's not a good thing.

In Luther's experience, God's judgment on him can only be a condemnation—the condemnation of a never-good-enough, constant sinner. His experience leads him to a shocking conclusion: the central commandment of Christian life is not simply difficult but *impossible* to fulfill. According to scripture, Christ said, "You shall love the Lord your God with all your heart, with all your soul, with all your mind, and with all your strength" (Mark 12:30). Who can live up to that? Anything less than being "perfect as your heavenly Father is perfect" renders you subject to divine condemnation. When you die, God will consign you to hell forever.

The more Luther seeks to obey, the more aware he becomes of his failures; the more he struggles, the harder the struggle becomes. He's a man caught in spiritual quicksand.

Luther's interior torments are the religious roots of the Reformation. Luther is no rebel seeking to undermine the Church. Neither does he aspire to start a church of his own; the very notion would have made no sense to him. In fact, Luther's own anxiety, intense as it is, by itself would not have produced the Reformation. Plenty of other devout men and women in the Middle Ages struggled with their own sinfulness. If Luther had kept his spiritual wrestling to himself, he probably would have remained mostly unknown. But he doesn't. The Reformation begins because Luther *acts* on his anxiety.

Between the summer of 1517 and the spring of 1521, the roots of the Reformation sprout and grow in unlikely fits and starts in Luther's spiritual struggles. His distinctive religious experiences are indispensable. But so too are the actions he takes as a concerned pastor and innovative theologian; so too are his temperament and his conviction that nothing less than eternal salvation is at stake.

Luther begins to speak out, and beginning in early 1518, others start to criticize him. Back-and-forth interactions gain momentum, and through them Luther sharpens his ideas and speaks ever more boldly. He writes his thoughts in letters; he preaches his ideas in sermons; he publishes his words in print. Fame begins to arrive as if out of nowhere, and Luther embraces it as he reacts to the resistance he faces. In less than four years he has become a reluctant rebel within his own Church.

The Wider Stage: The Holy Roman Empire

While the drama of this unexpected turn of events begins in Luther's anxiety, in his anger and actions in Wittenberg, it unfolds quickly in the vast expanse of central Europe known as the Holy Roman Empire. There is no Germany as we understand it (and will not be until the nineteenth century), though "the German lands" and "the German nation" are terms used in a cultural sense. Beer-drinking, hearty Germans have a sense of themselves as different from wine-drinking, effete Italians south of the Alps. To the west, France,

England, and Castile-Aragon (the heart of what will become Spain)
are all hereditary monarchies with budding bureaucracies that serve
their sovereigns' ambitions.

By contrast, the Holy Roman Empire is an elective monarchy
whose ruler oversees a crazy-quilt patchwork of several hundred territories and cities. These principalities and towns cover modern-day
Germany, Austria, the Czech Republic, Belgium, the Netherlands,
and parts of eastern France and northern Italy. Seven electors—
three archbishops from the Church and four nonecclesiastical rulers
of territories, including Frederick of Saxony—are the political officials who vote to elect a new emperor whenever the previous one
dies or steps down.

Or so it's supposed to go. The Holy Roman Emperor in 1517
is Maximilian I. He's fifty-eight years old, a member of the powerful Habsburg family, which rules Austria. For decades he pur-
sued aggressive military campaigns and acquired titles; then in 1508
he proclaimed himself emperor. Like other Holy Roman emperors
before him, Maximilian does not directly govern each of the empire's
many territories and cities. Because each city and territory jealously
guards its own traditional privileges, Maximilian does not—and
cannot—rule over them directly. Unlike his royal contemporaries,
such as Henry VIII of England or Francis I of France who inherited
their royal rank, Maximilian as an elected emperor cannot simply
coerce his subjects.[20]

Therefore the emperor must govern through negotiation, and
this he does especially when representatives of the empire's cities
and principalities gather in periodic assemblies called diets. Usually
these diets are held in one of the empire's leading cities, such as
Nuremberg, Augsburg, Worms, or Cologne. The boundaries of
imperial dioceses and principalities do not coincide, and this mis-
match plus the patchwork nature of the empire and the need for the
emperor to act collaboratively means that reforming the Church in

the Holy Roman Empire is especially difficult. Reforms are needed; this is as evident as the devotional practices of Christians are obvious. But who will lead the reforms, and how will they be carried out?[21]

Reforms for the empire are not coming from Pope Leo X in Rome. When the Fifth Lateran Council concluded in the spring of 1517, it advanced no major initiatives and instead asserted the Church's traditional position—that the problem lay not with Church teachings but with people failing to follow those teachings. At that moment there are few signs of religious dissent; by 1517 the Bohemian Hussite movement, inspired by the Czech preacher John Hus in the early 1400s, has long been contained.

Neither are bishops in the Holy Roman Empire likely to spearhead reforms. Most of them grew up in aristocratic families, and they pursue wealth in the same way as secular nobles. They are not about to foster reforms that might curtail their pleasure-loving lifestyles, even though they and other members of the clergy are being roundly criticized for their greed by many people throughout the empire.

Reforms might arise with the religious orders. As we've seen, the Observant movement influenced Benedictines, Franciscans, Augustinians, and other orders in the fifteenth century in many areas of Europe, including in the Holy Roman Empire. Because religious orders at the time were not bound to the structure of Latin Christendom's dioceses and parishes, they could act without bishops' initiative or approval. Yet their success was only partial. The Observant movement even created new problems because not all the individual monasteries in any order accepted the changes. Bickering and bitterness resulted *within* religious orders because the reforms provoked resentment and resistance among some of the monasteries. Conflict among the German Augustinians rooted in this issue, in fact, prompted Luther's one and only journey to Rome in 1510.

The hoped-for religious reforms in the empire, when they happen, are usually local and lay, led by either territorial princes or city councils. That's less odd than it seems once we remember that religion is not separate from the exercise of power and that Christian values are supposed to inform secular life. The empire's leading cities, including Nuremberg, Augsburg, Cologne, Strasbourg, Frankfurt, and Erfurt, are all politically independent, answering only to the emperor for their civic affairs, including matters of religion. These cities are also important centers of commerce, artisanal crafts, education, and culture—nodes in a network of communication and travel that connects the cities of northern France, England, and the Low Countries to the Italian peninsula. Their influence puts them in a position to shape the religious life of their communities in crucial ways. Over the previous couple of centuries, many of these cities have wrested control of church institutions away from bishops, precisely *because* many urban leaders were conscientious Christians who cared about the Church.[22] If the bishops wouldn't oversee reforms, secular authorities would.

Conscientious political authorities want to sponsor religious houses that are filled with devout friars and monks rather than cynically lax ones, and for just this reason Frederick of Saxony recruited the Observant Augustinians to help set up and run the University of Wittenberg. Other city officials regularly hire outstanding preachers from the religious orders to support religious life in their territories, most notably during the seasons of Advent, the four weeks before Christmas, and Lent, the six and a half weeks leading up to Easter. These preachers exhort Christians in the familiar message of "walking the walk": Remember that you will be judged by God after death, so obey Christ's commands! Practice the virtues, avoid sins, love God and neighbor, tend to others in need! It's not an esoteric message. But it's hard to live out, as Luther feels with such a piercing, painful acuity.

Going Public with *Ninety-Five Theses*

The first hint of what is to come occurs near the end of Luther's obscurity. In September 1517 the dutiful Johann Rhau-Grunenberg publishes a one-page broadsheet by Luther with a boring title: *A Disputation against Scholastic Theology.* In his broadsheet, Luther ironically lists concise propositions to be argued over—a central practice of scholasticism—in order to criticize scholasticism itself, sort of like a poet writing a poem to criticize poetry. He condemns theologians' reliance on Aristotelian categories. "No one can become a theologian," Luther argues, "unless he becomes one without Aristotle." Indeed, "the whole Aristotle is to theology as darkness is to light."[23] This fits with Luther's emphasis on the study of scripture and love for certain passages in the writings of St. Augustine. His argument is also consistent with the ongoing curricular reforms at the University of Wittenberg, which are bringing in humanism and edging out scholasticism.

Esteem for Augustine is hardly novel; his impact on medieval Christian theology can hardly be overstated. Ideas that Augustine wrote late in his life have inspired Luther's extreme (but not unprecedented) views in the *Disputation* about the sinkhole of human sinfulness and the human inability to do good. These views grow directly out of Luther's own spiritual struggles: "man by nature has neither correct precept nor good will," and the will is "innately and inevitably evil and corrupt."[24] Regardless of how hard you try, Luther's own experience has convinced him that you can't improve yourself on your own.

Luther's remarks and tone are provocative, considering how scholastic theology has shaped universities since the thirteenth century, but they aren't unheard of. They aren't even rebellious: humanists, including Erasmus in his *Praise of Folly* (1511), sometimes mock scholastic theologians in print for their arcane jargon and seeming detachment from real life. And just a few months earlier, in April, Andreas Bodenstein von Karlstadt, Luther's senior colleague at the University of Wittenberg, published his own theses against scholastic theology.

"In these statements," Luther concludes in his *Disputation,* "we wanted to say and believe we have said nothing that is not in agreement with the Catholic Church and the teachers of the Church."[25] Luther remains loyal.

Like Karlstadt's published theses, Luther's *Disputation against Scholastic Theology* fails to find a popular audience. As an author Luther remains invisible.

There is little reason to think anything will be different a few weeks later when Luther writes another series of propositions objecting to misunderstandings about indulgences. Indulgences were related to the satisfaction portion of the sacrament of penance; they were fees paid to the Church to reduce the penalties for your sins, and they constituted an important means of fund-raising for the Church. Once you confessed your sins to a priest and were sorrowful for them, you could buy an indulgence, which would eliminate some or all of the actions you would have been required to take to make satisfaction for them.

The specific terms of indulgences varied, depending on how the pope framed them. Indulgences filled two purposes at once: you helped raise money for some charitable cause in the Church while lessening the burden of doing actions to make up for your sins. What's not to like? The actions you *would* have undertaken were worth something, certainly, so they could be assigned a monetary value. If you paid what they were worth, you'd substitute an indulgence for the action and make a charitable contribution to the Church besides.

Indulgences had started centuries earlier as exceptional papal grants.[26] Over time popes democratized them, making indulgences accessible to lay Christians at large. They were extremely popular among the laity in the late fifteenth and early sixteenth centuries, including in the Holy Roman Empire. Beginning in 1476, Pope Sixtus IV permitted indulgences to be applied to souls in purgatory, the after-death state where souls are purified in order to prepare for God's eternal gift of heaven. This expansion of indulgences strengthened the solidarity between living and deceased Christians. It could help Christians counter selfishness: you could diminish the afflictions of your family members and friends and help hasten their way to heaven.

In 1515 Pope Leo X proclaimed an indulgence to raise money to help build St. Peter's Basilica in distant Rome, a project begun about a decade earlier. Now, in 1517, he makes the indulgence available in the Archdiocese of Mainz in the Holy Roman Empire, where he has arranged to share its proceeds with Albrecht, the new archbishop. The Archbishop of Mainz is one of the empire's seven electors, charged with choosing a new emperor. The young Albrecht is already the Archbishop of Magdeburg; this additional appointment makes him the most powerful churchman in Germany. This holding of multiple church offices by the clergy ("pluralism") violates the church's own (canon) law, yet it is common. Holding several offices at the same time means more income, though it also increases complaints about clerical greed.

To make an exception to canon law, a papal dispensation is required, which Pope Leo grants in exchange for an enormous payment from Albrecht. The archbishop borrows the money from the Fuggers, a wealthy banking family of Augsburg, then needs to pay it back. His profits from the indulgence will help. Albrecht's theological advisers prepare a Latin pamphlet promoting the indulgence. Albrecht then hires an experienced Dominican priest, Johann Tetzel, to journey from town to town in his dioceses, beginning in early 1517, to promote the indulgence through enthusiastic preaching.

Frederick of Saxony, concerned that the indulgence campaign will drain money from his lands and compete with the contributions he might receive from pilgrims visiting his relic collection in Wittenberg, bars the indulgence campaign from his territory. Though Wittenberg is outside the Archdioceses of Mainz or Magdeburg, it lies close by in the Diocese of Brandenburg. Wittenbergers, unable to purchase the indulgence at home, simply travel to nearby towns just outside Electoral Saxony to buy what they want.

The problem with indulgences isn't their existence, it's their abuse. Partly this is overexposure: by 1510 some areas of Germany seem to suffer from a sort of indulgence weariness, with Christians less willing to buy them than in previous decades.[27] Moreover, the laity can easily misunderstand indulgences: ordinary men and women are tempted to think that indulgences exempt them from having to be sorrowful for their sins or having to confess them properly—as if God's forgiveness itself were for sale.

For Luther, indulgences threaten to make things too easy—the very opposite of what Christian repentance should entail, Luther thinks, as he meditates on the crucifixion of Christ and agonizes about his own sinfulness and God's forgiveness. As far back as his Psalms lectures in 1514, Luther had started thinking about how indulgences jeopardize the struggle and striving that are integral to following Christ.[28] Indulging in indulgences can make you lazier about performing the virtuous actions for others that are commonly imposed as penances. For weak Christians indulgences are acceptable, he thinks, but clergy promoting them should do so only with consummate care.

In Luther's view, Tetzel is acting recklessly. Like the authors of the indulgence pamphlet Albrecht had commissioned, Tetzel is rashly cutting corners, sacrificing pastoral care in order to maximize profits. By implying that Christian life requires anything less than serious, sustained, strenuous striving, Tetzel—Luther thinks—is misleading the laity and thus damaging their religious lives, even endangering their eternal salvation.

Luther knows nothing about the arrangement between Pope Leo and Archbishop Albrecht or about Albrecht's financial arrangement with the Fuggers. But he reads the pamphlet Albrecht's advisers had prepared and sees the indulgence certificates that Wittenbergers are bringing back from nearby towns. As a conscientious pastor, he's alarmed, having already preached about the perils of indulgences earlier in the year. This is all happening on Albrecht's watch and with his official approval. On October 31, All Hallows' Eve, Luther sits down to write a letter to Albrecht. In it, Luther says that though he hasn't personally heard the preachers promoting this indulgence, he's heard what ordinary folk are taking away from their message, and he isn't pleased: "I do bewail the people's completely false understanding, gleaned from these fellows, which they spread everywhere among the common folk." Apparently, some laypeople believe that the mere purchase of this indulgence guarantees their salvation or that souls go straight from purgatory to heaven when they buy it. The implications, he tells Albrecht, are grave: "O great God! In this way, excellent Father, souls committed to your care are being directed to death." As a result, Luther writes, he "could no longer keep silent about these things," and very much in line with the emphasis on concrete Christian action in late medieval piety, he says that "works of godliness and love are infinitely better than indulgences."[29]

Concerned for Albrecht's reputation, Luther urges him to withdraw the indulgence pamphlet and correct the preachers lest someone refute them and disgrace the churchman. Luther concludes with an invitation for Albrecht to examine a series of propositions that Luther includes in the letter. These propositions are, of course, his *Ninety-Five Theses,* terse Latin statements that presuppose a firm understanding of theology and canon law.[30]

We know that Luther wrote to Albrecht and sent him the *Ninety-Five Theses*. We don't know for sure, and probably never will, whether Luther actually posted the broadsheet with his theses on the door of Frederick's castle church in Wittenberg. It doesn't really matter. If he did post the theses publicly, he certainly didn't conceive of it as a grand gesture of defiance against medieval Catholicism, a clarion call for a religious revolution and the high road to the modern world. Depicting it this way, as in modern celebratory paintings, is pure mythmaking.

The practice of posting theses for academic debate—and other notices—on church doors was commonplace. If Luther did tack up the *Ninety-Five Theses* on the door of Frederick's castle church, it had all the thrill of a professor posting an announcement on the faculty bulletin board. Luther's timing, though, was no accident. October 31 fell one day before the Feast of All Saints, when hundreds of pilgrims would pass through the door of the Church of All Saints to view Frederick's relic collection. However, if the large broadsheet did appear on the church door, very few pilgrims could have read it, printed as it was in two columns of densely packed Latin.

What matters about the *Ninety-Five Theses* is the fact that they were printed—four times in Latin: first (probably) in Wittenberg, then soon after in Nuremberg, Leipzig, and Basel, the important Swiss center of printing where Froben had been publishing so many works by Erasmus. Multiple editions appeared in different cities over a wide geographical area, increasing exposure and publicity. Luther helped by sending copies to friends in Nuremberg and Erfurt, both cities with important circles of Christian humanists. The theses were also translated into and apparently printed in German, though not at Luther's initiative.[31] He hadn't yet crossed the bridge into the language of the people when it came to complex matters of theology and politically sensitive issues of religious practice. That would soon change, along with so much else.

The publication of the *Ninety-Five Theses* turned Luther into a public figure. His *Disputation against Scholastic Theology* a few weeks earlier had not brought him fame, for it concerned matters in which only theologians were likely to be interested. But the *Ninety-Five Theses* addressed a popular practice related to one of the Church's seven sacraments. More importantly, that practice concerned issues of money and greed and the allocation of church funds in a culture that had long been critical of clerical avarice.

At first sight, the *Ninety-Five Theses* sound less than revolutionary. They assume rather than reject papal authority. They also presuppose that indulgences are legitimate, purgatory is real, and intercessory prayer works. Luther takes aim at none of that; his main target is the careless dispensation of indulgences by reckless preachers—none of them identified by name—who imply that indulgences entail more than the remission of church-imposed penalties and can do more than confirm God's forgiveness. Indulgences, Luther says, should be "preached with caution, so that the people do not mistakenly think that they are to be preferred to other good works of love." Giving to a poor person or lending to the needy—typical late medieval acts of piety—are better than buying indulgences, "because love grows through works of love and a person is made better."[32] Becoming better by practicing the virtue of Christian love was a cornerstone Christian idea.

The *Ninety-Five Theses* also contain some sharp edges, and like other critics of the Church's problems, Luther means some of them to be cutting. The genre of the disputation and his privileges as a professor of theology mean that he can float ideas in print without having to own them. They are not his *assertions* but rather "merely" propositions for debate, the bread and butter of scholastic theology.

Because popes grant indulgences, Luther's theses repeatedly mention the pope. Among the propositions Luther offers for consideration are many assertions about what the pope (supposedly) desires, understands, intends, and has the authority to do—and not do. Implicitly, Luther is talking about the scope and character of papal authority. Ten theses in a row begin with the assertive phrase, "Christians are to be taught ..." By *Christians* Luther means the laity—seemingly implying that they aren't already being taught correctly.[33] Eight consecutive statements near the end are couched as "truly sharp questions of the laity," in the voice of laypeople posing questions to the pope. These statements target papal avarice, tapping in to the long-standing frustration with clerical greed in general. "Why does the Pope," Luther's "laity" ask, "whose wealth today is greater than the richest Crassus, not simply construct the Basilica of St. Peter with his own money rather than with the money of the poor faithful?"[34]

In late November, Albrecht receives Luther's letter with a copy of the theses, written in Latin, and passes them on to the theological faculty at the University of Mainz. His theologians sound a tone of caution but do not immediately condemn them. However, because Luther is addressing issues of much more than provincial concern, they advise Albrecht to send Luther's *Ninety-Five Theses* to Rome, which he does. Albrecht won't hear back from Rome until the following summer. By then Luther's days as a virtually unknown Augustinian and university professor will be well behind him.

Unexpected Fame

In the first months of 1518, as Luther's theses continue to circulate publicly, several university theologians in the Holy Roman Empire recognize their danger and respond with harsh criticisms. Even if his theses only offer propositions for debate, Luther's critics correctly argue that Luther is speaking recklessly and, what's more troubling, *publicly* about complicated theological matters that can easily be misunderstood by the faithful. To make matters worse, he is presuming to speak for the pope and to restrict the pope's authority over Catholic doctrine and practice. Among Luther's earliest opponents are a personally offended Tetzel and Konrad Koch (known as Wimpina), his fellow Dominican, as well as Johannes Eck, a widely published scholastic theologian influenced by humanism at the University of Ingolstadt in Bavaria.[35]

Through the medium of print, thorny questions intended for debate among authorized experts have been made available for public comment for the first time. But only a tiny percentage of the population can read Latin. Writing about touchy theological issues in German would be something else entirely, which is why it's so alarming when Luther decides to respond to his critics publicly in the vernacular.

Luther's *Sermon on Indulgences and Grace* appears in late March 1518. Like the *Ninety-Five Theses*, it is brief, but unlike the theses it is written in German in a much more accessible style. Rather than single propositions, Luther writes in short, punchy paragraphs with the specific intention of reaching a wider audience, a *public* audience. Like never before, Luther writes with passion and power, a new energetic style that will continue in the following months to grow stronger during exchanges with his opponents.

Luther carefully refrains from referring to the pope as he had throughout the *Ninety-Five Theses*. But harking back to his *Disputation against Scholastic Theology*, he combines criticisms of theologians with a stronger attack on indulgences. Luther still accepts indulgences "for the sake of lazy and imperfect Christians," even though it would be "a thousand times better" if Christians instead preferred to practice good works and endure God's punishments.[36] Because Luther accepts the canon law that permits indulgences and the papal authority that sanctions them, he can't repudiate indulgences outright. But his message to Christian laity, whom he addresses directly in the sermon, can hardly be clearer: "My will, desire, plea, and counsel are that no one buy an indulgence. Let the lazy and sleepy Christians buy indulgences. You run from them."[37]

Luther also attacks scholastic theologians' views of penance, contrasting what "new teachers" of scholasticism (from three centuries earlier!) have "made up" and "invented" with a theology rooted "in Holy Scripture or in the ancient holy Christian teachers," the early church fathers.[38] Drawing on his engagement with scripture and favoring passages important to him from St. Augustine's works, Luther begins to drive a wedge between the Bible and the church fathers, on the one hand, and scholastic theologians, on the other. He will soon radicalize the distinction that Erasmus and other humanists previously formulated. Luther proclaims his own points "sufficiently grounded in scripture," arguing that the combined wisdom of scholastic theologians "do not have enough with their opinions to put together a single sermon."[39] All this even though scholastic theologians have been preaching regularly on scripture for more than three hundred years.

Moreover, Luther seems to reject the very notion of the sacrament of penance: "It is a tremendous error when people imagine that they can make satisfaction for their sins, which God instead always forgives gratis out of immeasurable grace while desiring nothing for this grace except that one live well from then on."[40] This goes far beyond raising questions about the sacrament; it suggests, if not claims outright, a radical reinterpretation of sin and of God's forgiveness. Underpinning the sermon are years of Luther's own struggles with sin and God's demand for perfection, plus Luther's restless search for a way out from under God's righteous condemnation. For Luther, these issues are far from academic. They go to the heart of what it means to be a Christian. Luther is coming to believe that nothing less is at stake than the Christian's entire relationship with God and the truth that makes eternal salvation possible. As such, ordinary Christians need to read, learn about, and discuss these issues and, most of all, live a Christian life according to them. Which is why Luther publishes the sermon in German.

Much more than the *Ninety-Five Theses,* the *Sermon on Indulgences and Grace* makes Luther famous. He has touched a nerve. Altogether a dozen printings of the work appear in Wittenberg, Leipzig, Augsburg, Nuremberg, and by the end of 1518 Basel, over four hundred miles away, with new editions appearing regularly thereafter. An untapped audience is eager to discuss matters of religion in a devout culture wanting reform in the Church.[41] Luther exploits the opportunity with gusto. Besides continuing to lecture and preach, for the rest of his life he will write and publish at a furious pace in both German and Latin, aiming at both general and scholarly audiences.

For the first time, Christian humanists recognize the author of the *Ninety-Five Theses* as a kindred spirit, a fellow reformer critical of clerical abuses and lay laxity. Through this community's "Republic of Letters," they help to distribute Luther's text far beyond Germany. Writing from the university city of Louvain in modern-day Belgium, Erasmus sends a copy to his friend Thomas More in London.[42]

Luther's influence also grows through direct contact with colleagues beyond Wittenberg. Most important is the long trip he makes to Heidelberg in April for a meeting of the Observant Augustinians from the German province. With theological critics attacking the *Ninety-Five Theses* and attention already coming from Rome, Staupitz asks Luther to prepare propositions and explanations to convey his ideas to fellow friars within the order. Luther performs well at the Heidelberg Disputation, impressing many attendees and widening his influence. Like sympathetic Christian humanists, Observant Augustinians begin to spread word about him beyond Germany.

Also present at the Heidelberg Disputation are influential non-Augustinians, including the Dominican friar Martin Bucer. Already influenced by Erasmus, Bucer is moved by Luther's showing. In contrast to Tetzel and Wimpina, Bucer makes clear that not all members of the Dominican order are hostile to Luther. Johannes Brenz, Bucer's teacher of Greek at Heidelberg, is equally impressed by Luther.[43] Both Brenz and Bucer will become important Protestant reformers in subsequent years.

Heidelberg sits nearly three hundred miles southwest of Wittenberg, a different university setting in a different region. The propositions Luther discusses, which affect Bucer, Brenz, and many Augustinians, don't mention indulgences at all. But they do concern issues related to human sinfulness, God's forgiveness, and Christian life that lie *behind* Luther's criticisms of indulgences. Speaking to an audience of other learned experts, Luther presents his ideas at Heidelberg much more extensively than in the bald statements of the *Ninety-Five Theses* or the short paragraphs in the *Sermon on Indulgences and Grace.*

More than any of his writings to this point, Luther's ideas in April 1518 reveal the distinctive core of his emerging theology. God's demands in scripture—his "law"—are *intended* to make sinful human beings aware of their complete inability to assist in their own salvation. By nakedly confronting the futility of all self-exertion, desperate sinners are driven to acknowledge their need for God's saving power—his "grace" and "gospel." "It is certain that one must utterly despair of oneself in order to be made fit to receive the grace of Christ," Luther says at Heidelberg. Luther's years of arduous effort in Augustinian religious life are again the backdrop: "The law humbles, grace exalts."[44]

Luther is coming to see the *point* of all his striving and straining in a different light. Exertions in the Christian life are not about making satisfaction for sins or gradually improving by doing good works to avoid damnation. They are *intended* to be spiritual quick-sand that sinks you, making you find in yourself "nothing but sin, foolishness, death, and hell."[45] Only if you feel how dreadfully sinful you are will you realize how desperately you need to be saved and that only God can save you.

At the Heidelberg Disputation Luther expands on themes he began to develop years earlier. To this point, only his students and perhaps a few fellow Augustinians have glimpsed them in an initial, tentative, inchoate form in his lectures on the Psalms. Pushback from critics of his *Ninety-Five Theses* and newfound notoriety help Luther to clarify and catalyze his ideas. Though Heidelberg remains a restricted academic venue, real-world events far removed from that setting will lead Luther to express his developing theology more explicitly—and more forcefully.

Making Political Waves

Activity in Rome impinges on events in Heidelberg. The first papal impulse is to handle Luther quietly within his religious order. At the prompting of Pope Leo X in February, Gabriel della Volta, the new head of the Augustinians, writes to Staupitz as Luther's immediate superior, exhorting him to make sure Luther isn't teaching "novelties." Staupitz responds by offering Luther a forum to expound his views at the Heidelberg Disputation.[46] Luther's successful performance doubles as his first refusal to back down. Why should he stop criticizing abuses and caring about the laity, especially when crucial insights are becoming clearer? Plenty of others have coupled pastoral concern with criticism of the Church they loved.

Luther has no intention of acquiescing and submitting, not considering what he believes is at stake. There's not a chance in hell. If he's mistaken, Luther wants an explanation of how and why he's wrong. He doesn't want to be told just to shut up.

Following the Heidelberg Disputation, in May Luther returns to Wittenberg. With abuses of ecclesiastical authority on his mind, he angrily preaches a sermon against the misuse of excommunication, the formal exclusion of Christians from the Church. This sermon isn't published right away, but accounts of what Luther supposedly said circulate and find their way to Maximilian, the Holy Roman Emperor. In August, Pope Leo X receives a letter from the emperor denouncing Luther as a heretic. In empire and church alike, Luther is starting to make waves at the highest political levels.

By the summer of 1518, Luther is no longer unknown; however improbably, he's becoming famous. Luther is delighted to secure for the University of Wittenberg a brilliant teacher of Greek named Philip Melanchthon, just twenty-one years old, who strengthens the university's commitment to a humanist curriculum and in subsequent years will become one of Luther's most important allies. But on August 7 Luther receives a summons to Rome to be questioned on suspicion of heresy. Accompanying the citation is a condemnation of the *Ninety-Five Theses* by Silvestro Mazzolini, better known as Prierias, a Dominican theologian who is also the Master of the Sacred Palace, the pope's official theologian at the papal curia (court) in Rome.

Prierias's brief refutation of Luther has a telling title: *Dialogue against Martin Luther's Presumptuous Conclusions on the Power of the Pope.*[47] What Luther initially proposed as debatable theological propositions, Prierias interprets as overt assertions. And whereas Luther concentrated on misunderstandings and abuses related to indulgences, Prierias takes Luther to be challenging papal authority.

Luther's German opponents have also called Luther out for his implicit criticisms of papal authority, but this rebuke comes straight from Leo X's official theologian. Luther can't dismiss it as the prattling of some provincial theology professor. And what Prierias says is clear, sharp, and uncompromising: "He who says in regard to indulgences that the Roman Church cannot do what it has actually done is a heretic."[48]

Luther is stunned and shaken. But he quickly recovers and gets angry, as he will do so often in the coming years (and throughout the rest of his life). Prierias's strong statement about Church authority flies in the face of Luther's personal experience and developing theology. Like some other scholastic theologians, Prierias explicitly sees the authority of scripture as dependent on the pope as the Vicar of Christ. Outraged, Luther writes a response no less dismissive and insulting to Prierias, which he publishes in late August. He accuses him of offering nothing but opinions from St. Thomas Aquinas, "without scripture, without the church fathers, without the canonists, and finally even without reason itself. And so it is my right, that is my Christian freedom, to reject and refuse both you and your *Dialogue*."[49] Yet except for his continuing disdain for scholastic theology, Luther's response remains traditional in its reliance on canon law, the church fathers, reason, and scripture.[50]

Nevertheless, Luther is now newly vulnerable, and his case has become irrevocably political. It has caught Maximilian's attention—and not in a good way. It risks the reputation of the University of Wittenberg and what its faculty is trying to accomplish with its humanist curriculum. And it reaches far beyond Wittenberg and Electoral Saxony to Rome, the spiritual, symbolic, and administrative center of Christendom. Pope Leo gives Luther sixty days, two short months, to appear in Rome. But Frederick of Saxony, as Luther's elector, refrains from ordering Luther to go. With some German distrust of Italians likely at work, Frederick shields his professor out of concern that Luther is unlikely to receive a fair hearing in Rome.

This is the first instance of the political protection Luther receives between 1517 and 1521, which will continue throughout the Reformation—for Luther and other reformers fortunate enough to receive it. Political suppression, its opposite, will become and remain critically important as well. From this moment forward, decisions and actions of political leaders—princes, city councils, sovereign kings, and the emperor—will crucially influence the success or failure of the Reformation. Without Frederick's political protection, Luther's sudden rise would have come to an immediate end, and with it the Reformation.

Instead, Frederick intervenes. Because Leo X is trying to finance a new crusade against the Ottoman Turks, he needs the financial support of German cities and princes, including Frederick, who uses this as leverage in his negotiations with Rome. Frederick directs his secretary and adviser, George Spalatin, whom Luther asked to write to Erasmus back in 1516, to keep in touch with Luther, and Spalatin in turn becomes Luther's key go-between with Frederick. In the meantime, the empire's political representatives convene a diet in Augsburg to discuss Leo's campaign against the Ottoman Turks as well as other pressing issues, including who will succeed the aging Maximilian as emperor.

A Sheltered Meeting in Augsburg

Leo X sends to Augsburg Tommaso de Vio, a leading Dominican theologian and experienced administrator, better known as Cajetan. Recently named a cardinal, Cajetan is a major player. For a decade he has served as head of the Dominican order in Rome. He's a reform-minded, distinguished interpreter of St. Thomas Aquinas, the most important medieval Dominican theologian. Like Luther, Cajetan has misgivings about the theology of indulgences: independently of Luther, in late 1517 he wrote his own treatise on the problems with indulgences; it went beyond a simple list of theses for scholastic debate.[51] And yet his primary task in Augsburg is to persuade the diet to agree to Leo's tax.

In late August 1518 Frederick meets Cajetan, who agrees to speak with Luther after the conclusion of the diet. Instead of making Luther travel to Rome as the summons ordered, Cajetan grants a meeting on German soil. It's a compromise, a sign of good faith, but the meeting is still not without danger for Luther, who is facing a threat of excommunication and possible execution if he's found guilty of heresy and refuses to recant.

In late September Luther makes his second long trip of the year, traveling another three hundred miles from Wittenberg to Augsburg. He arrives a few weeks later, in early October, after the diet has ended. By this point, Cajetan has carefully read Luther's *Sermon on Penance* and his lengthy *Explanations of the Ninety-Five Theses,* which Luther dedicated to Pope Leo. Cajetan is taking the encounter with Luther seriously. He is not a Dominican theologian poised for more polemics, like Tetzel or Wimpina, but rather a sophisticated, experienced professional. His study convinces him that Luther is indeed expressing views contrary to those of the Church. Cajetan has his instructions from the pope: get Luther to recant and desist from his errors, and make him promise to avoid any future problems with his preaching or publishing. If Luther complies, all will be forgiven and forgotten.

If he doesn't comply, Cajetan is free to excommunicate him and, under the full authority of the papacy, forcibly bring Luther to Rome. In preparation for his meeting with Luther, Cajetan composes several brief theological treatises based on his nuanced reading of Luther's writings.

For three days, from October 12 through October 14, Luther and Cajetan meet behind closed doors in the Fugger mansion in Augsburg. From the outset, their contrary expectations and convictions become obvious: Cajetan wants a docile apology for Luther's errors while Luther wants Cajetan to point out any errors in his preaching or publications. Honoring Luther's request, Cajetan notes that Luther criticized a papal bull (an official papal statement) about indulgences issued in 1343 by Pope Clement VI. Luther defends his criticism, arguing that the bull's claims lacked a legitimate biblical basis and distorted scripture. Cajetan also objects to Luther's idea that a Christian who receives the Eucharist after confession has to be *certain* of faith and God's forgiveness. Otherwise, in Luther's view, you doubt the very essence of God's promises in the Bible.

This latter point is crucial, reflecting Luther's own experience and his years of striving, straining, and yearning to *feel* forgiven and loved by God. It's fundamental to his emerging theology as the gift of God's gracious "gospel," which follows the pride-destroying hammer of his "law." In a statement prepared for Cajetan and given to him on the final day of their discussions, Luther develops what he has written on the nature of faith in his *Explanations*. It will become central from now on: "I stated that no one can be justified except by faith."[52] Nothing you do, whatever your effort or exertion, whatever the satisfaction for your sins in the sacrament of penance, makes you worthy to receive the Eucharist. Only your trust in God's promise of forgiveness can do that—and that trust itself is God's gift. "Through no works will you be prepared for the sacrament, but through faith alone, for only faith in the word of Christ justifies, makes a person alive, worthy, and well prepared. Without faith all other things are acts of presumption and desperation."[53] Luther testifies straight out of his own spiritual struggles.

Cajetan is unmoved and unpersuaded, though he promises to send what Luther has written to Rome. In his estimation, Luther's ideas about faith are weird, and his views on the forgiveness of sins are subversive. To accept them, Cajetan writes in one of the preparatory treatises for their meeting, would be to add a new requirement for salvation for Christians who've *already* properly confessed and done satisfaction for their sins—a requirement dependent on their felt experience—and thereby "to construct a new Church."[54] Cajetan has his orders from the pope and is trying to succeed in his mission—to get Luther to renounce his ideas. At the same time, with his theological acuity he sees more clearly than Luther how radical those ideas are and what they seem to imply.

For Luther, Cajetan's demand is outrageous. Here's an official papal representative and one of the Church's most distinguished theologians dismissing his deepest convictions about God's Word, its power, and its singular place in Christian experience! *His* Christian experience, with its tormented, tortured history stretching back through more than a decade of his life as an Observant Augustinian, with all those psalms chanted, masses said, sermons preached, lectures delivered, confessions heard, fasts completed, and hours spent wrestling with the meaning and magnitude of God's Word. There's no way he will give in; he feels he can't. Luther invokes his conscience: "I do not want to be compelled to affirm something contrary to my conscience, for I believe without the slightest doubt that this is the meaning of Scripture."[55]

Luther is certain he understands scripture correctly, which informs his conscience and makes it unmovable. Like Prierias, Cajetan asserts that papal authority ranks above the authority of church councils and scripture. Luther denies this, saying scripture's authority trumps papal authority: "For the pope is not above but under the word of God."[56] Luther traveled to Augsburg in good faith, ready to be corrected for any errors he might have unintentionally expressed. He was willing to submit to papal authority, provided he was shown to be in error. But he wasn't prepared for—nor could he believe—Cajetan's demand that he submit to papal authority without being convinced he'd said anything to contradict scripture. His discussions with Cajetan become a watershed in his ideas about the papacy: at Augsburg, Luther starts to see a rift opening up. On one side are his religious experiences and understanding of God's Word; on the other are claims about popes as the authoritative interpreters of scripture. Luther had traveled to Augsburg confident these issues were complementary. For centuries they had coexisted within the Church's traditional consensus and had been rejected only by medieval critics who were condemned as heretics. After meeting with Cajetan, though, Luther's confidence is shaken. Increasingly, he is forced to choose between a papal interpretation of scripture and his own reading of it.[57] As Luther stated to Cajetan, when one's conscience is on the line, there is never really a choice.

Following his tense meeting with Cajetan, Luther is secretly smuggled out of Augsburg on horseback because of a genuine fear that Cajetan will extradite him to Rome. Upon his return to Wittenberg, Luther remains vulnerable, but he's also emboldened, perhaps as never before, and he continues to preach and publish under the protection of Frederick, who rejects Cajetan's request to expel Luther from Electoral Saxony. Protecting his star professor, Frederick argues that most Germans find nothing objectionable in Luther's ideas. What's more, in his estimation Luther has neither received a fair hearing nor been formally condemned for heresy. In response, Leo X issues a bull reasserting papal authority over indulgences. Though Luther doesn't see it until January, he preemptively calls for a church council to take up the very issues he and others have been discussing for more than a year.[58]

Luther's invocation of a council against a pope echoes conciliarism, the idea that the authority of church councils trumps the authority of the papacy within the Church. Leo is not conceding the point that some papal claims conflict with the Bible, so Luther hopes a council will support his view. A century earlier, the Council of Constance (1414–1418) marked the high tide of conciliarism during a major institutional crisis within the Church. Constance declared the superior authority of councils in ending the Western Schism (1378–1415), in which rival popes excommunicated one another and split Latin Christendom for nearly forty years. Conciliarism imploded in practice after Pope Pius II officially condemned it in 1460 following the restoration of the papacy in Rome, although as a theory conciliarism still enjoyed some theological defenders in the early sixteenth century.

In calling for a council, then, Luther likely is trying to find some sympathizers. But, as Luther surely knows, the real obstacle to his plan in late 1518 is that only the pope has the authority to convene a council.

A Public Showdown in Leipzig

Following the Augsburg proceedings, Luther becomes increasingly bold in his thinking. In November, he publishes his reflections on the encounter with Cajetan. The difference between papal and scriptural authority is becoming clearer to him: "For divine truth is master over even the Pope, and I do not await the judgment of a man when I have learned the judgment of God."[59] "The judgment of God" refers simply to what scripture says, and in Luther's view popes are distorting it in multiple ways. He criticizes the traditional view that the pope's authority derives from the resurrected Christ, handed to St. Peter as the leader of the apostles and from him to the popes as his successors. The key biblical passage is Matthew 16:18–19, which will be argued over endlessly in the Reformation era: "And I tell you, you are Peter, and on this rock I will build my church, and the gates of hell will not prevail against it. I will give you the keys to the kingdom of heaven, and whatever you bind on earth will be bound in heaven, and whatever you loose on earth will be loosed in heaven." Luther attacks those who "brazenly state in public that the Pope cannot err and is above scripture. If these monstrous claims were admitted, scripture would perish, and nothing would remain in the Church but the word of humans."[60] Now Luther openly stands by scripture, which has brought him his hard-won experience of divine grace working in the hearts of sinners crushed by God's unfulfillable law.

By December Luther is more convinced than ever that papal authority and scriptural authority compete with rather than complement each other, and there's no question in his mind which one reflects divine authority. In a letter written late in the month, Luther privately starts thinking the unthinkable about the high-ranking churchmen in Rome: "Just like the Antichrist, now they're sitting in the temple of God, showing off as if they were God, having taken up power only for their own advantage, going about their fleecing and esteeming robbery (especially the pope), resting contentedly, serving no one, and instead pressuring everyone by force to be their slaves."[61] In the new year, once Luther sees Leo's papal bull confirming indulgences, he becomes convinced not just that past popes have erred but that the present pope is erring.[62]

Nevertheless, rather than excommunicating Luther, Leo still wants him to recant; he seeks reconciliation and obedience. He dispatches Karl von Miltitz, a young German priest employed at the papal court, to meet with Frederick of Saxony. Leo X wants Frederick's support in opposing Maximilian's grandson, Charles, as the Habsburg successor to the imperial throne. Three years earlier Erasmus dedicated his *Education of a Christian Prince* to Charles, but the pope now fears the further consolidation of Habsburg power. After Miltitz arrives in Germany, he negotiates with Frederick and Luther, intending to close the rift that threatens to open wider. For two days in early January 1519, Miltitz and Luther meet face-to-face in Altenburg, about thirty miles south of Leipzig. Luther is persuaded to draft a letter of apology to the pope in exchange for the silence of Luther's opponents. But he refuses to recant and never sends the letter.[63] Miltitz also tries to arrange for Luther's case to be heard before a German bishop rather than in Rome, which looks like it might yield a compromise solution to the conflict.

In the meantime, just days after Luther and Miltitz talk, the death of Emperor Maximilian transforms international politics overnight. It's a boon to Luther because it strengthens Frederick of Saxony's hand. A new emperor has to be chosen, and Frederick is not only one of the seven electors who will cast a vote, he's also the favorite of some parties to succeed Maximilian as emperor. His supporters include Leo X because of the pope's anti-Habsburg opposition to Charles, which plays to Luther's favor.

Frederick has no interest in becoming emperor, but as usual he keeps his cards close to his chest. Leo's preferred non-Habsburg alternative, King Francis I of France, will not be elected, in part because he doesn't have enough money to pay off the electors. But the pope's need for Frederick's political support puts the Luther affair on the back burner in Rome for several crucial months, which allows Luther, shielded by Frederick and this turn of events in the first half of 1519, to continue to write at a furious pace. He publishes a sermon in German about the popular late-medieval practice of meditating on Christ's passion, which is reprinted many times. He revises his Latin lectures on Paul's letter to the Galatians. He also studies more intensively the history of the papacy and canon law in preparation for a public debate that will mark a further stage in his challenge to the papacy and his ability to articulate his alternative vision of Christian faith and life.

Polemics in print precede the debate, continuing a pattern that started with responses to the *Ninety-Five Theses*. The main participants are Luther, his sympathetic Wittenberg colleague Karlstadt, and their opponent, Johannes Eck (1486–1543), from Ingolstadt in southern Germany. For a year already, since the spring of 1518, all three have been writing and publishing feisty theses and counter-theses. Eck argues for the divine basis of papal authority over all Christian churches, posing the issue of papal obedience more point-edly than ever. Luther counters, denying papal supremacy over the non-Latin churches, insisting again that popes and canon law are not above scripture. Long before the meeting of the three men, their publications have established clear battle lines. All parties agree that the disputation itself will be judged by the theological faculties of the Universities of Erfurt and Paris, the latter still the most pres-tigious in Christendom, as it has been since the thirteenth century.

In late June 1519, the antagonists finally square off in Leipzig under the patronage of Duke George of Saxony, Frederick's cousin and the ruler of Ducal Saxony, whose territory has been separate from Electoral Saxony since 1485. The local bishop objects to holding the debate at all, but Duke George ignores him, another instance of a political authority who supports Church reform and acts accordingly. The atmosphere in Leipzig is tense: some two hun-dred people, including many rowdy students, accompany Luther and Karlstadt south from Wittenberg for the event. The University of Leipzig has no room large enough for the crowd of observers, so Duke George hosts the event in the splendid courtroom of the city's Pleissenburg palace. Two lecterns face each other, Eck's decorated with a banner of St. George, the Wittenbergers' lectern with a ban-ner of St. Martin.

Everyone knows Eck's real target is Luther, not Karlstadt. Eck is a precocious scholastic theologian *and* humanist who earned his doctorate in theology at age twenty-four. He's published many learned treatises and demonstrated his skills in debate, establish-ing an international track record with appearances in Vienna and Bologna. The first week of the disputation between him and Karlstadt is a warm-up act for the main event. Eck and Luther start debating on July 4 and go at it for ten days straight with just one day off. Their most important exchange comes early in the proceedings, picking up on their published disagreement about papal authority. Right away Eck links Luther to a long line of heretics who denied the divine right of popes, including John Hus, the reformer from Bohemia burned at the stake in 1415. Luther takes the bait, saying that on some points for which Hus was condemned by the Council of Constance, his views were "most Christian and evangelical." Eck sees his opening: not only is Luther saying that popes can be and have been wrong, but also that *church councils* can be and have been wrong.[64] The whole point of conciliarism was to recognize councils, not popes, as Christendom's final authorities and arbiters of Christian truth. If both can be mistaken, where does that leave Luther? What remains?

Scripture alone. God's Word in the Bible. The repository of God's revelation, it contains everything necessary for eternal salvation. All other authorities—popes, councils, canon law, church fathers, theologians—are subordinate to it. If they depart from it, they cease to *be* authorities to the extent of their departures. "No faithful Christian," Luther says to Eck at Leipzig, "can be forced beyond the sacred scripture, which is nothing less than divine law."[65] For Luther the Leipzig Disputation is a watershed, a point of both arrival and departure. Almost despite himself, Luther sharpens the emphasis on scripture that has been central to him for years, the source of succor in his spiritual struggles dating back to long before he became a public figure in late 1517. With hostile intent, Eck draws Luther's position out of him.

After the Leipzig Disputation, Luther's cornerstone becomes more firmly settled. "By scripture alone"—or in Latin, *sola scriptura*—becomes his rock. On this basis he will criticize whatever in Church teaching and practice contradicts God's Word. On this basis he will reconstruct authentic Christian teaching and practice for the sake of laypeople, who have been sadly misled through no fault of their own. And on this basis he will become the unwitting progenitor of a revolution in Western Christianity—a revolution that will affect just about everything because of how religion is interconnected with the rest of life.

No one can see it in the summer of 1519, but the Leipzig Disputation will turn out to be critically important for the Protestant Reformation as a whole. Eck goads Luther to take his ideas to their logical extreme. The result is a rejection of the idea that scripture has to be interpreted *within* the Church's tradition, *in accordance* with papal or conciliar authority. Not so, Luther says: the Word of God is *its own* authority, distinct and independent from every merely human tradition, individual, institution, and idea.

As if any more drama is needed, another major turn in European politics coincides with the Leipzig Disputation. On the day after Eck and Karlstadt begin debating, the young Habsburg prince Charles, all of nineteen years old, is unanimously elected as the new Holy Roman Emperor. Massive bribes to the electors, channeled through the Fuggers of Augsburg, facilitate their choice. Born and raised in Flanders, in the northern part of modern-day Belgium, Charles has never set foot in Germany. Neither does he speak German. But he brings the Habsburg lands in central Europe together with Spain and its expanding overseas empire, becoming Europe's most powerful ruler. Frederick of Saxony now has to deal with Charles to protect his famous and infamous Wittenberg professor.

Luckily for Luther, his prince remains his protector in the following months. Shortly after the Leipzig Disputation, Eck writes to Frederick, as Cajetan had the year before, and urges him to take action against Luther. The disputants ignore their agreement not to publish on the proceedings at Leipzig while awaiting the verdicts of the Erfurt and Paris theologians. Dozens of dueling publications appear declaring that Luther trounced Eck or that Eck crushed

Luther, championing Luther or excoriating him, attacking the papacy or defending Rome.

The Erfurt theologians dally, never issuing an official response, and the Paris theologians delay for well over a year. In the meantime, two other important university theology faculties issue their own judgments. On August 30, Cologne condemns propositions from Luther's writings; on November 7, Louvain follows suit. The Church's institutional opposition to Luther is growing, with entire theological faculties from some of Europe's leading universities now condemning his claims.

Luther is undismayed: What else can be expected from self-interested scholastics ignorant of scripture and in thrall to the pope? And why should he be concerned? By now he feels that the wildly improbable course of events during the previous two years can be explained only as the expression of God's will, working through him as an instrument. He doesn't slow down: besides his teaching and preaching, he continues writing and publishing with extraordinary vigor. He writes on the sacraments of penance, baptism, and the Eucharist, reconfiguring each according to his new theology and criticizing the deficiencies he sees in received sacramental teachings and practices. Altogether, in the course of 1518 and 1519, Luther writes an astonishing forty-five different works, divided fairly evenly between Latin and German. Over 80 editions of his writings appear in 1518; in the following year that number more than doubles, to 170.[66]

In the wake of the Leipzig Disputation, the network of humanist correspondents from England to Italy hums with news about Luther and his challenge to papal authority. Word of him also continues to spread internationally among fellow Augustinians. At the same time, Luther's appeal reaches beyond learned Latinate circles to the laity at large, tapping into long-standing anticlerical sentiments and calls for the reform of the Church. His pastoral concern, which has motivated him since before the *Ninety-Five Theses,* continues.

Increasingly he couples his criticisms of scholastic theologians with confident appeals to laypeople to judge the disputed matters for themselves. More than once he simply reprints his opponents' attacks, adding a preface and his own caustic notes, sure that his readers will find his opponents' arguments wanting.

Something new occurs when *lay authors* start writing and publishing their own theological pamphlets in favor of Luther. Lazarus Spengler, the city council clerk of Nuremberg, writes a treatise supporting Luther in late 1519. This is unprecedented. A layman writing in the vernacular on matters of doctrine opposing the papacy is unlike anything since the invention of the printing press in Europe nearly seventy years earlier.

A Clarifying Anger

In the wake of the Leipzig Disputation, clergy with connections to the papacy start to oppose Luther more vigorously. Viewing Luther as dangerous and wicked, Eck urges the pope to resume the process of Luther's excommunication. At the same time, though, Miltitz renews negotiations with Luther. The two men meet again on October 9, this time in Liebenwerda, southeast of Wittenberg. Even into December hopes persist that Luther might be heard before the Archbishop of Trier.

In January 1520, months after the imperial election and the Leipzig Disputation, Luther's case is reopened in Rome, even as he continues to reach out to bishops for support. Two papal commissions are appointed in February to examine the situation and determine how to proceed. That same month, the university theologians of both Cologne and Louvain solemnly underscore and reiterate their condemnations of Luther. In the meantime, Eck makes his way from Germany to the papal court, arriving in March. He emphasizes what a serious threat Luther is, a danger—because of his growing popularity in Germany—that complacent cardinals and courtiers in Rome are underestimating.

Back in Wittenberg, Luther continues working like a man possessed—which his followers and detractors alike start to believe is true. In February, Luther reads two works that enrage him. The first is an exposé by the fifteenth-century Italian humanist Lorenzo Valla. Valla critically examined the Donation of Constantine, which purported to be Emperor Constantine's fourth-century grant to the papacy of political authority over secular rulers. Valla showed that the Latin in which the Donation was written couldn't belong to the fourth century, arguing instead that the Donation was actually a monastic forgery from the Middle Ages. Luther is incensed: here is further confirmation that popes have usurped control over the Church for their own selfish ends.

The second work, which concerns the nature of the Church, was written over a century earlier by John Hus, the condemned heretic whom Luther admitted at Leipzig was "most Christian and evangelical." Inspired by Hus's treatise, Luther develops and deepens his ideas into a distinction between a true, invisible Church of Christians united in genuine faith according to biblical teaching and a corrupt, visible Church of false Christians in which authority is exercised unworthily and power wielded tyrannically.[67] This meshes perfectly with how Luther sees Christendom in 1520. Shockingly, it was Hus who had been right, not the Council of Constance that condemned him. After reading Hus's treatise, Luther sides unabashedly with the Bohemian reformer: Luther and those who agree with him, he writes, "all are Hussites and did not know it."[68]

This expanded admiration for Hus's ideas and Valla's unmasking of the Donation of Constantine lend a sharper edge to Luther's already critical view of the papacy. Luther's reading, writing, and reflection lead him to a new clarity, at once terrifying and exhilarating: he comes to see his own defense of the gospel as the front line in an apocalyptic battle against the powers of Satan. An earlier suspicion now becomes his conviction: the Antichrist has taken over the papacy. He's now seething, and events will soon strengthen his conviction that the situation is much more serious than he had imagined before.

In the spring of 1520, Luther and Rome continue moving more decisively away from each other.[69] Eck publishes yet another treatise on St. Peter and the papacy. By May he's drafting the bull that threatens Luther with excommunication, based on the propositions condemned in Cologne and Louvain. In both Latin and German, other theologians join in publishing opposition to Luther, including a Franciscan from Leipzig, Augustine Alfeld. Prierias too, the official papal theologian who authored the critique of the *Ninety-Five Theses* two years earlier, publishes another treatise against him. In late May and early June, a committee of cardinals and theologians meets four times in Rome to prepare the final version of the papal bull. Luther responds with vitriol in *The Papacy at Rome,* his first vernacular treatise against the papacy. He also continues writing and publishing pastoral treatises, works that aim to instruct and encourage ordinary men and women in Christian life. The most substantial of these from the spring of 1520 is his *Treatise on Good Works,* which he begins in March and publishes in early June, right when the committee in Rome is finalizing its bull against him.

Luther's *Treatise on Good Works* instructs laypeople in his new theology and criticizes Christian practices incompatible with it. His new theology is at odds with medieval Christianity. Luther bemoans how "ignorant and blind instructors" among the clergy have led laypeople away from the right understanding and practice of good works. He denounces "Roman whores and buffoons" who seek their own self-aggrandizement. "There is no longer any spiritual authority in Christendom," he asserts, saying that "popes, bishops, and priests" are "the princes and leaders of the devil's army."[70] Luther criticizes as unbiblical and self-serving many common religious practices, including the endowing of masses, participating in pilgrimages, praying to saints, and of course buying indulgences as "not good works at all but a complete waste."[71] Genuine good works can flow *only* from faith in Christ, faith being the foundational and unmerited good work bestowed by God, which must be the basis and moving force of all good works. All actions done in faith, no matter how seemingly mundane, *are* good works; all actions done without faith, however seemingly pious, are presumptuous hypocrisies.

In some way or other, Luther says, authentic good works fulfill one of the Ten Commandments, which are biblical and commanded by God. Properly understood, such actions are infinitely available and more than enough to keep you engaged in a lifetime of ceaseless activity, for God "is served by everything, whatever it may be, that is done, spoken, or conceived in faith." But without faith, and the feeling of certainty that comes with it, all your "good" works are actually worse than worthless: "If there is no faith or good conscience toward God, your works are decapitated, and your life and goodness amount to nothing at all."[72] If you're not certain, it means you don't really trust God—that is, you don't really have faith. And without faith as your foundation, you're not really a Christian at all. Reinforced by resistance and deepened through debate, Luther's years of frustrating experience in the friary are finally bearing fruit in his new theology.

On June 15, 1520, the papal bull *Exsurge Domine* appears. It calls on Christ, St. Peter and St. Paul, and "the whole communion of saints" to "rise up" and oppose Luther, for "a wild boar from the woods has undertaken to destroy this vineyard [that is, the Church], a wild beast seeks to devour it." It condemns forty-one propositions, all but one of which were taken directly from Luther's writings, as "deadly poison," and orders "each and every Christian believer of either sex, under no circumstances to read, speak, preach, praise, consider, publish or defend such writings, sermons, or broadsides or anything contained in them."[73] Luther himself is prohibited from preaching. His writings are to be burned throughout Europe, and he's given sixty days formally to recant his errors or face excommunication as a condemned heretic.

The bull will not be delivered in Wittenberg until October 10, nearly four months later, which is when the sixty-day clock will start ticking. But already in June, when *Exsurge Domine* is being finalized and published and before Luther ever sees it, his attacks on the papacy reach a new intensity. He reprints Prierias's latest treatise with his own biting marginal comments, adding an introduction and conclusion. In the latter, Luther exhorts political authorities to violence against the pope and cardinals: "If we punish thieves with the gallows, robbers with the sword, and heretics with fire, why do we not turn with force of arms against these teachers of iniquity, these cardinals, these popes, and this whole collection of filth of the Roman Sodom which unceasingly lays waste the Church? Why do we not wash our hands in their blood, so that we and all who are ours can be free from a general conflagration that will be extremely dangerous for everyone?"[74]

Luther no longer thinks of reform or reconciliation. Rome's endemic corruption, according to Luther, is actually much worse than anyone had thought: the official Church is not just deficient but diametrically opposed to the gospel! Satan himself has conquered the papacy and installed the Antichrist on the papal throne, presaging the apocalypse foretold in the New Testament's Book of Revelation. If there is to be any hope of salvaging Christendom before God's Last Judgment, emergency measures are required. A drastic intervention is needed, and it's going to have to come from *outside* and *in opposition to* the Roman Church. But how? By mid-June, just when *Exsurge Domine* appears, Luther is working on a treatise that will be more revolutionary and more influential than anything he's written so far.

Liberation and Denunciation

To the Christian Nobility of the German Nation appears in August, a scathing manifesto in German by a man now convinced of his role in a cosmic battle between God and Satan. The first edition of four thousand copies sells out in less than two weeks—an indication of the crescendo of enthusiasm for Luther's writings. He continues to pour forth publications. Together with *To the Christian Nobility*, two of these works—*The Babylonian Captivity of the Church* and *The Freedom of a Christian*—sharply reject papal authority and powerfully articulate Luther's alternative vision for Christian faith, life, and the Church. Together with political events, they mark the late months of 1520 as another escalation in the increasingly stark clash between Luther and his growing number of supporters, on the one hand, and the papacy, its loyalists, and those committed to the established Church, on the other.

Because Leo X, the cardinals, and the papal court are not willing to reform themselves or the Church, Luther turns in *To the Christian Nobility* to the newly elected Charles V and the German nobles. He urges political leaders to do what the Roman hierarchy and its loyalists refuse to do. In one sense, Luther urges them to walk the path that reform-minded political authorities were treading when they tackled the Church's problems in their own territories. But in another way, Luther blazes a dramatically new trail. Previously, political leaders took for granted that they would promote Christian practices according to the Church's teachings. Luther turns this upside down, repeatedly insisting that for the sake

of Christian truth they must act against those teachings—because
in his view many of those teachings are the root of the problem.

In order to justify this audacious imperative, Luther has to
persuade political authorities of its legitimacy "in these evil latter
days."[75] Going for the jugular, he attacks the papacy's claims about
clerical authority over the laity, the interpretation of scripture, and
church councils. Once these three "walls," as Luther calls them,
are destroyed, the way is clear for secular authorities to oppose the
papacy. In an emergency overshadowed by the expectation of God's
Last Judgment, secular authorities are delegated by God to maintain public order even regarding the Church.

Because "we are all consecrated priests through baptism,"
Luther argues, Christendom consists of a priesthood of all believers.
The claim is utterly radical—in effect, an act of insurrection against
a foundational pillar of Western Christianity, the idea that clergy
enjoy a special character. "There is no true, basic difference between
laymen and priests, princes and bishops, or (as they say) between
spiritual and secular, except that of office and work, not that of status." Abolishing the special character of the clergy will enable the
Church to be reformed by secular authorities taking action against
the pope, "who has neither faith nor intelligence," and whose claim
to monopolize the interpretation of scripture is "an outrageous fan-
cied fable." Because all Christians are priests, all have the duty and
"the power to test and judge what is right or wrong in matters of
faith" based on the proper interpretation of scripture. This startling
implication flows from Luther's emphasis on the Bible as the sole
authority for Christian faith and life. In Luther's bold words, "It
is the duty of every Christian to espouse the cause of the faith, to
understand and defend it, and to denounce every error."[76]

Skillfully Luther exploits long-standing desires for church reform,
widespread resentment of clerical greed and privilege, and German
sentiment against Rome, where "the devil himself is in charge." In

Luther's view, the avaricious papacy and the "swarm of parasites" at the papal court, colonized by Satan, seek ever greater worldly self-aggrandizement at the expense of the gospel: "Now that Italy is sucked dry, the Romanists are coming into Germany." Indeed, the exploitation is already afoot: "How is it that we Germans must put up with such robbery and extortion of our goods at the hands of the pope?" Playing on political authorities' sense of duty, Luther places the matter squarely in their hands: "O noble princes and lords, how long will you leave your lands and your people naked and exposed to such ravenous wolves?"[77]

German complaints about the Church's problems have been common currency for generations, but never has anyone appealed so brazenly to political leaders against papal authority and the Church's teachings. "The Christian nobility should set itself against the pope as against a common enemy and destroyer of Christendom for the salvation of the poor souls who perish because of this tyranny," Luther explicitly states, while repeatedly erupting in anger against the papacy—"O that God from heaven would soon destroy your throne and sink it into the abyss of hell!"[78]

In *To the Christian Nobility* Luther exhorts German political leaders to take up twenty-seven measures to reform the Church. Many of these imperatives concern ending the procedures through which money is extracted from the Church in Germany by the "nest of devils at Rome." Other directives, however, advocate for rejecting practices and teachings central to medieval Christianity. All pilgrimages understood as good works of devotion "should be abolished" as "a devilish delusion"; the endowing of friaries should likewise end; members of religious orders should be free to come and go as they wish; the clergy should be allowed to marry; saints' days should be turned into working days; all the Church's fasting regulations and dietary restrictions should be left to individual discretion; pilgrimage chapels should be destroyed; the canonization of saints should cease; confraternities should be prohibited; the university teaching of Aristotle's ideas about human beings, nature, and ethics should stop; and canon law should be abolished. Implementing these changes would alter Christian life beyond recognition—which is exactly Luther's point. The drastic distortions of Christian faith and practice in the past demand dramatic corrections in the present.[79]

Underlying it all is Luther's furious rejection of papal authority, another teaching central to medieval Christianity. How far he has come regarding "the damnable canon law," the authority of which he still presupposed in late 1518! But now he says, "Nothing would be better than to make a bonfire of it." (These words will soon prove prophetic.) He sees canon law now as an oppressive instrument of papal tyranny, all the worse for the way in which popes abrogate it to serve their insatiable greed to cater to favor-seekers. "Let canon law perish in God's name, for it arose in the devil's name."[80] Repeatedly, relentlessly Luther hammers away at pernicious papal avarice.

And yet, remarkably, not all parties have given up on reconciliation. In late August, the papal envoy Miltitz appeals to Luther's mentor, Staupitz, to persuade Luther again to write to Pope Leo. In early September, Staupitz and an Augustinian colleague visit Luther in Wittenberg. Considering what Luther wrote about the papacy in *To the Christian Nobility,* it is somewhat astonishing he even agrees to send a letter. Though all three men know that *Exsurge Domine* has been issued, none has yet seen it.[81]

Luther's treatise strikes a deep chord, and his popularity is soaring. This makes it hard for Eck to get the papal bull publicly posted when, as instructed, he returns to Germany to oversee the distribution process. Disruptions accompany the public display of the bull in late September in the Saxon towns of Meissen, Merseburg, and Brandenburg. Eck has a go-between deliver the copy to Wittenberg, not daring to travel in person to Luther's own town. The bull arrives on October 10. Luther responds the next day, declaring in a letter that the bull has convinced him that the pope is the Antichrist. Nevertheless, one day later, he meets with Miltitz at Lichtenberg, on the road between Wittenberg and Leipzig, and agrees to keep his earlier promise to write to Leo. This time, however, he tells Miltitz that he'll add to his epistle another short work, *The Freedom of a Christian*.

Though Luther doesn't reject the established Church in principle, he rejects it because papal authority contravenes his understanding of God's Word. According to the terms of the bull, he can still change his mind and recant. But never since late 1517 has that been less likely, as his next treatise makes abundantly clear.

In October, Luther publishes in Latin *The Babylonian Captivity of the Church*. The title evokes the Babylonian captivity of the ancient Israelites recounted in the Old Testament: Luther argues that the papacy is holding present-day Christians, faith, the Church, and its sacraments in bondage. Just like the ancient Israelites, contemporary Christians have to be set free.

The Latin Church's seven sacraments have been in place since 1215, when the Fourth Lateran Council, building on earlier Christian practices and theological reflection, enumerated them: baptism, the Eucharist, penance, confirmation, marriage, ordination, and extreme unction. Luther evaluates each one based on his own theology. He concludes that some have been grievously misunderstood, distorted, exploited for material gain, or all of the above, while others were invented without biblical warrant or based on a misreading of scripture. Consequently, Luther reduces the number of sacraments to three—baptism, the Eucharist, and penance— although by the end of the treatise he says that, "strictly speaking," only baptism and the Eucharist count. As before, Luther's understanding of scripture is the foundation for his criticisms and bold imperatives, for "it is one thing to use the Scriptures wrongly, and another to understand them properly."[82] And with those criticisms and imperatives, Luther extends his rejection of many common Christian practices, just as he did in his treatise addressed to the Christian nobility.

Luther sets his own criteria for a sacrament: it must include a verbal promise from God plus a concrete sign of that promise. By these criteria, he thinks only two sacraments qualify: the bread and wine in the Eucharist and water in baptism. These promises and signs, received by Christians through faith, are what the sacraments are all about. They embody the faithful trust that grounds Christian life, provides consolation and peace, and inspires loving actions toward others. Any obstruction to the sacraments understood in this way robs Christians of the saving power of God's Word, subjecting them to tyranny. According to Luther's criteria, confirmation, marriage, ordination, and extreme unction do not qualify as sacraments and never should have been considered as such. They were mischaracterized due to dubious biblical interpretation, suspect pagan philosophy, wrongheaded scholastic theology, and the desire for clerical control over the laity—all that Luther has come to see as hallmarks of the medieval papacy.

Clerical ordination in particular is a poison antithetical to the priesthood of all believers. It subverts the baptism all Christians share by setting priests above laity and justifying clerical tyranny: "Here is the root of the terrible domination of the clergy over the laity.... Thus it arises that they make bold to command and demand, to threaten and urge and oppress, as they please." As with his vehement denial of papal authority and the discarding of so many widespread Christian practices in *To the Christian Nobility*, Luther dismisses long-standing sacramental practices in the Church. But as he pithily puts it, "The word of God is beyond comparison superior to the church."[83]

So drastically does Luther reinterpret the meaning of the

sacraments that it's misleading even to say that he keeps two (or three) of the Church's seven sacraments. He denies that the mass is a re-presentation of Christ's sacrifice. He insists that the Eucharistic bread *and* wine should be distributed to the laity, just as the Bohemian Hussites had done in the fifteenth century, because keeping the wine from the laity is just another expression of clerical domination. Luther insists on the mystery of Christ's real, corporeal presence in the Eucharist. But he denies the miraculous *replacement* of the bread and wine with Christ's body and blood—called *transubstantiation* in scholastic terminology—when the priest says the words of consecration: "This is my body." The mass is not a sacrifice offered by the clergy to God for recipients regardless of their spiritual state, according to Luther; rather, it is a recurring promise from God received only by Christians in faith. It "can benefit no one," Luther writes, it can "be applied to no one, intercede for no one, and be communicated to no one, except only to the believer himself by the sole virtue of his own faith."[84] So much for most of the literally millions of masses being said throughout Christendom. Offering masses for money or even for others was a perversion of the Eucharist, Luther now thinks, just as selling indulgences was a perversion of penance.

With canon lawyers and scholastic theologians as their lackeys, Luther believes, popes twisted the gospel of salvation into an unbiblical web of self-serving rules and oppressive regulations that ran roughshod over the clarity of God's Word. Christians need liberation from incarceration in the Church: "For what is there in common between liberty and a despotic Babylon?"[85] Luther pleads for Christian freedom in *The Babylonian Captivity of the Church*. Whereas in *To the Christian Nobility* he exhorted secular political leaders to perform a liberating, emergency rescue, now he extends his declaration of freedom. To wit, "It is not possible for either men or angels rightfully to impose even a single law upon Christians except with their consent; for we are free from all things." Or again, "It is mean, iniquitous, and servile for a Christian man, with his freedom, to be subjected to any regulations except the heavenly and divine."[86]

With *Exsurge Domine* newly complicating the diplomatic dance among papal, imperial, and Saxon officials, what Luther hopes will be church reform metastasizes into an imperative to resist and reject the Roman Church. During the autumn of 1520, driven by his own spiritual struggles, Luther now extends and deepens his message, and his popularity continues to grow. And public opinion matters. In late October, just after the coronation of Charles V as emperor in nearby Aachen, power brokers from the Holy Roman Empire gather in Cologne. Frederick of Saxony confers with Charles and, several days later, with Erasmus, who dislikes how things are unfolding. Soon thereafter Frederick meets with the papal nuncio (diplomatic representative) Girolamo Aleandro, who had accompanied the imperial retinue for the coronation. He implores the prince to avoid risking scandal and wants Frederick to imprison Luther or send him to Rome. Frederick again refuses, and for the same reasons: in his estimation Luther's case hasn't been fairly heard, nor have his writings been refuted by impartial judges.

Shortly after the coronation of Charles V, while Frederick continues to stave off Luther's imprisonment, his now-celebrity professor publishes his last major treatise of the year. Appearing in November and titled *The Freedom of a Christian,* it encapsulates the heart of his new theology, his total reinterpretation of Christian life, in both Latin and German, which guarantees the embattled Luther a wide audience. With a long dedicatory letter to Leo X, Luther finally satisfies his promise to write to the pope. Together, the letter and treatise testify to the personal and theological culmination of an improbable three-year trajectory.

In the letter, Luther distinguishes between Leo's person and the papal curia as an institution. He assures Leo he's never spoken ill of his actions, morals, or reputation. His concern has remained throughout with "ungodly teachings" and the tyrannical practices of the papal court, which "is more corrupt than Babylon or Sodom" and "is composed of depraved, desperate, and notorious godlessness."[87] Yet as pope, Leo has personally overseen the papal court for seven years, which makes him directly responsible for the custodianship and defense of doctrines Luther is attacking. How then can Leo hear Luther's vehement attacks against the curia—"the very gaping mouth of hell"—as anything but a personal insult from Luther, who has implicitly condemned his leadership as that of "an Antichrist and idol"?[88]

In *The Freedom of a Christian,* Luther changes his tone, laying out his understanding of the relationship between true Christian doctrine and authentic Christian life based on his own experience, reconfiguring the traditional understanding of the relationship between faith and actions (or "works"). According to Luther, human beings don't and can't contribute to their own salvation. He's felt this for years; he put forward dogged efforts and found only desperation in the Augustinian friary. If you look at yourself honestly, he's convinced, you'll see that "everything in you is completely blameworthy, damnable sins," as a result of which you "despair of your own powers" and "are then humbled and reduced to nothing in [your] own eyes."[89] God's law, the very *point* of God's commandments, is to induce just this despair, which readies the desperate "inner man" to seek help outside himself.

It's here that God's promises, his gospel, his saving Word, come to rescue the crushed sinner. Received in faith, the gospel not only provides the existential answer to God's deliberately induced despair but also utterly transforms your life: "Believing in him, you may become another human being by this faith, because all your sins are forgiven and you are justified by another's merits, namely, by Christ's alone." Then you're no longer held captive by spiritual struggle or despair but instead are liberated for genuine Christian life. Hence the first half of Luther's famous paradox about Christian life: "The Christian is a completely free lord of all, subject to none."[90]

Salvation isn't something you hope to receive at the *end* of your life as a Christian, provided you've been good enough to pass God's test. That's impossible—no one can live up to God's standards. Instead, salvation is something God gives you freely at the *outset* of Christian life *despite* your utter sinfulness, just as he gives you the faith to accept his promise of salvation. Hence "all things depend on faith," and "whoever has faith has everything and whoever lacks faith has nothing."[91]

It's here that Christian actions—"works"—enter the picture. Liberated by faith from the impossibility of trying to meet God's standard for salvation, you're no longer worried about it. God has already bestowed it, and your sense of certainty confirms it. Because you're no longer anxious about trying to be good enough for God, you're free to focus on your neighbors and their needs "so that all of our works may be ordered toward the advantage of others." And you're bound to do so, and will do so automatically, as it were, as an overflowing expression of your faith, fulfilling the second half of Luther's paradox about Christian life: "The Christian is a completely dutiful servant of all, subject to all."[92]

The purpose of actions in Christian life is not to make bit-by-bit contributions to your own salvation—again, that is not in doubt because you've already been saved by God's unmerited gift of grace. Gratefully saved sinners then discipline their bodies for the sake of Christian love: "The purpose of putting the body in subjection is so that it can serve others more genuinely and more freely." Genuine Christian love is the other-regarding fruit of God's freely bestowed faith. Christians "live in Christ through faith and in the neighbor through love."[93] You are *not* freed from having to act in loving, generous, merciful ways toward others; rather, you are freed from thinking that acting in this way contributes anything to your salvation—a blasphemous thought, in Luther's view, and superfluous as well, because God has already saved you.

The Freedom of a Christian is vastly less strident than Luther's other treatises of 1520, yet its new ideas about faith and works reinforce the dismissal of the same widespread religious teachings and practices. Abolishing them goes together with Luther's views about how God saves human beings and about what Christian life is. Luther's ideas translate his own experience into a new Christian theology that renders many inherited religious practices unnecessary if not dangerous. The shift is not a subtle one. Luther is no longer pursuing reform within existing institutions and assumptions; he's calling for a religious revolution in the name of God's Word and its transformative, liberating power.

Leo X denounces Luther as a raging boar and threatens him with excommunication. In turn, Luther pronounces the pope the pompous occupant of a tyrannical institution controlled by Satan. Incendiary deeds follow these inflammatory words: public burnings of Luther's books occur in Louvain on October 8, in Cologne on November 12, and in Mainz on November 28 and 29. Led by some of his colleagues, Luther responds in kind on December 10, exactly two months after *Exsurge Domine* arrives. In Wittenberg he leads a crowd of students and townspeople in burning the papal bull, books of canon law, and works by some of Luther's opponents.[94] As shocking as this act is, however, it is not the first time Wittenberg has witnessed such burning. Two years earlier, in March 1518, a group of zealous university students, most of whom studied under Luther, seized hundreds of copies of Tetzel's propositions against the *Ninety-Five Theses,* piled them in the city square, then set them on fire.[95]

A Double Severance Package

Following the terms of *Exsurge Domine,* Luther's refusal to recant leads to his excommunication. Without fanfare or drama, in early 1521 he is cast out of the Church as a heretic. He still wears his Augustinian habit and lives in the Wittenberg friary, but he no longer belongs to Leo's Church, rejecting its authority and many of its teachings and practices. His status as excommunicated heretic now jeopardizes the reputation of the University of Wittenberg and the standing of the city itself, thrusting Frederick more than ever into the spotlight. Without Frederick's continued protection, Luther is likely a dead man.

In late March, Luther receives a summons from Charles V to journey to Worms, where an imperial diet has been meeting for two months. Some of his friends and supporters urge Luther not to go, fearing for his life despite the emperor's promise of safe conduct to and from the city. There is reason for concern: a century earlier, at the Council of Constance, Hus received the same promise but was tried anyway and burned as a heretic.

In the first half of April, Luther and his small party travel by horse-drawn wagon three hundred miles southwest to Worms. When he arrives, Luther is treated like a rock star—or like a living saint and prophet, a hero—greeted and cheered by admiring crowds in city after city: Naumburg, Weimar, Erfurt, Gotha, Eisenach, Frankfurt. The crowds plead for him to preach; they clamor to see him; and they liken him to Christ on his way to Jerusalem before he was crucified. Luther accepts the parallel, acting as torchbearer for the gospel against forces of darkness.

On April 16 when they enter Worms, Luther and his companions enjoy a triumphant welcome. The "Luther affair" wasn't even on the diet's agenda when it opened in late January, but it has become the main event. On April 17, in the late afternoon, Luther is escorted into the local bishop's palace. Imperial princes and nobles from far and wide line the room, along with ecclesiastical officials, including a papal party led by the nuncio Aleandro, and in his finery the recently crowned Charles V.

Luther apparently expects a theological debate about specific issues related to his writings, similar to what occurred at Leipzig in 1519. Instead he confronts a stack of his works from the past three years. A spokesman for Charles V, speaking first in Latin and then German, asks two simple questions: Are the books his, and does he recant them? Luther acknowledges them as his own. But apparently caught off guard about the procedure—or afflicted by last-minute doubts?—he asks for time to consider his response. Charles grants his request, and the assembly adjourns until the next day.

On the following afternoon, in a larger hall to accommodate the crowd, the assembly reconvenes. The proceedings leave no doubt as to what Luther thinks or where he stands. Luther gives a speech of his own, accomplishing what Aleandro wants to prevent. Luther talks about his own writings, placing them in three categories and defending each one: expositions of the gospel and Christian life, criticisms of the papacy and its false teachings, and attacks on his detractors who defend the papacy. Pressed again by the imperial spokesman about whether he'll recant what he's written, Luther replies with famous words: "I have been subdued through the scriptures I have brought forth, and my conscience is held captive to the Word of God, as a result of which I cannot and will not recant anything, because to act against conscience is burdensome, injurious, and dangerous. God help me! Amen."[96]

The Word of God: scripture alone and the certainty that comes with it binds Luther's conscience and thereby frees it. He cannot and will not deny his own experience of many years, intensified and focused during his wild ride since 1517. Regardless of the consequences, he must defy the emperor, who continues to stand with the pope.

"Here I stand": Luther's reported words are apocryphal, but they capture his position well. Luther's words at Worms—in one of the many ironies of the Reformation—are the antithesis of modern views about the value of individual conviction. Luther stands by his own experience, not because as his it is valuable in and of itself—a modern position—but only because he believes it is an experience of the true, plain meaning of God's saving Word. God's law demolishes the sinner, then his gospel rescues the desperate from despair. This is how salvation works; according to Luther it is, in fact, how God works.

At Worms Luther stands not only boldly to condemn the papacy but also completely to repudiate individualism, autonomy, and subjective experience as such. To Luther, these are merely different ways people can resist the controlling liberation of God's Word rightly understood and rightly experienced. Luther's view of freedom is very particular, and very different from the sort modern people take for granted.

Despite Luther's stand on April 18, during the following week others are still trying to bring him around. Won't he reconsider? How can he be so sure he's right and countless theologians and saints, over hundreds of years, have been wrong? To no avail: Luther is certain and can't deny his own experience.

On April 26, Luther sets out with fellow travelers on the return to Wittenberg. The edict that formally condemns him won't be issued for another month, after the diet ends. Luther is now an outlaw as well as a heretic, and others fear more than ever for his life. Always canny, Frederick the Wise carries his princely protection to unprecedented lengths: on May 4, he arranges a preemptive "kidnapping" of Luther to shelter him from those who seek him with malign intent. Frederick begins harboring a condemned outlaw and heretic in defiance of the emperor.

Luther's sudden disappearance inspires speculation that he's been captured and killed. The great artist Albrecht Dürer is among those who think as much. Yet Luther remains alive and well, hiding in the Wartburg Castle, which overlooks Eisenach, where twenty years earlier he attended school as a teenager. There he spends ten months, as personally trying as they are productive. Among other writings and prodigious correspondence, he drafts his own German translation of the New Testament. Together with the Old Testament, a much more ambitious undertaking completed years later with assistance from colleagues in Wittenberg, Luther's translation of the Bible will become in subsequent decades—and indeed centuries—his most widely reprinted and influential work.

When a burdened Augustinian friar in Wittenberg in October 1516 lamented in a letter how busy he was, no Reformation was in sight. Only Luther's religious anxiety and his pastoral concern for Christian souls were present. By the summer of 1521, Martin Luther is Europe's most famous man and its all-time bestselling author. No one could have predicted it, least of all Luther himself, any more than he or anyone else could predict what would happen in the years to come.

However inadvertently, improbably, and unintentionally, Luther started the Reformation. But he never had control of it, any more than he had control of what took place in fits and starts between his first letter to Archbishop Albrecht of Mainz and his appearance before Charles V at the Diet of Worms. By the spring of 1521, Luther has taken his stand on principles—*sola scriptura* and the Holy Spirit's guidance—that all but guarantee the impossibility of anyone controlling the Reformation. The following few years will make this crystal clear. The Reformation will be uncoupled from the dramatic odyssey of a deeply religious man and will become the story of a no less dramatic and deeply contested movement.

CHAPTER 2

A FRACTIOUS MOVEMENT

THOUGH THE REFORMATION began with the forceful figure of Luther, it is incorrect to regard the Reformation as "his" and to see rival ideas and movements as "deviations" from Luther's views. That just favors Luther's position over those of others. Many of his contemporaries disagreed with Luther, who based his views on the authority of scripture confirmed by his personal experience. Many other Christians embraced the principle of scripture alone but rejected what Luther said about God's Word, just as he had rejected what defenders of the papacy said about it.

If everyone who rejected Rome had agreed with Luther about the Bible, the entire Reformation era and indeed the last five hundred years of Western history would have played out very differently. But already in the 1520s, the movement exploded radically beyond Luther's control, and as the contentious decade unfolded, he lashed out as fiercely against his new rivals as he had lashed out against his original enemies. Ideas were inspired and actions unleashed that he couldn't control, and some of them he condemned as harshly as he condemned the papacy. Though the Reformation started with one man, it quickly turned into a movement. Luther's insistence on scripture alone as the final authority for Christian faith and life cleared away long-standing obstacles to reform within the established Church by creating a principle and a position outside of it. Eventually the Western Christians who rejected Rome would be called *Protestants,* a term first coined in 1529. We might also call the earliest ones by a label they often used for themselves, *evangelicals*—from the Greek work for "gospel," *evangelion*—so long as we don't confuse them with (very different) evangelicals today in the United States and elsewhere.

The decade following the Edict of Worms repeatedly shows that it's much easier to denounce the Church as corrupt and unbiblical than it is to agree on how to understand God's Word and live according to it. Because religion shapes and, in Luther's Europe, is intended to influence every area of human life, the implications of this contentious disagreement are enormous.

What now is the right relationship between the Church and secular authorities? Does the freedom of a Christian extend to social, political, and economic concerns? What do proper Christian worship, sacraments, and ministry look like, and who has the authority to say so? How can you tell whether someone has the right understanding of the gospel or is really inspired by the Holy Spirit? Which prophecies about the world's end are trustworthy? The questions are nearly endless, and so are the answers put forward by divergent evangelicals.

The Reformation involves disagreements among Protestants no less than it assumes their repudiation of the Roman Catholic Church. Disagreement begins among evangelicals in the 1520s and never goes away. Instead of becoming a shared basis for reforming the Church, the Bible becomes a bone of contention *among Protestants* as well as between Protestants and Catholics. As a result, the Church becomes the churches.

The Reformation is not an initially coherent movement that only later fragments. Right from its start, the Reformation prompts divergent, conflicting claims about God's Word and God's will. Through abundant printed pamphlets and satirical woodcut images and mocking popular songs and salacious oral rumors, the Reformation spreads quickly and widely in the early 1520s, especially in the towns and territories of the Holy Roman Empire and nearby Switzerland. By the mid-1520s it inspires mass uprisings across much of central Europe in the so-called German Peasants' War, a startling revolt by downtrodden peasants and villagers demanding drastic changes in the traditional political hierarchy and socioeconomic realities they now consider unjust in light of the gospel as *they* understand it. To protect their territories, princes and their mercenary armies, whether allied with or antagonistic to Rome, put a swift end to these uprisings. Luther's defiant stand based on his understanding of God's Word inadvertently inspires armed conflict and threatens a society dependent on religion as the foundation for a shared social and political life. As a result, after 1525, wherever the Reformation survives and flourishes, it is able to do so only because of the political authorities who sanction and contain it under their watchful eye.

The decade after the Edict of Worms in 1521 critically influences the subsequent history of Protestantism. Basic patterns are established that will endure deep into the seventeenth century. Few patterns are more influential than the difference between forms of the Reformation that receive sustained political support and forms that don't.

Lutheranism and Reformed Protestantism—two expressions of the Reformation—receive political support. Despite condemnation from Charles V and other Catholic leaders, the patchwork character of the Holy Roman Empire enables these versions of the Reformation to take root. Starting in the 1520s, these "magisterial Protestants" (a term that refers to Lutherans and Reformed Protestants taken together) enjoy the political protection that allows them to begin to create new institutions, forms of worship, statements of faith, and ways of being Christian. Working together with clergy from newly established Protestant churches, many of whom are former Catholic priests, political authorities implement these measures, recognizing the importance of the inherited medieval view that subjects in any given city or territory should share the same religious beliefs and practices, provided in this case they aren't Catholic.

Unlike Lutheranism and Reformed Protestantism, all other expressions of the Reformation are outlawed. Lacking political patronage, these "radical Protestants" are often persecuted and punished by political authorities, whether these authorities are Lutheran, Reformed Protestant, or Catholic. Yet from the start radical Protestants demonstrate that God's Word is being understood in many different ways among Christians who reject the Roman Church. And the fact that these groups persist despite opposition is key to understanding the Reformation as a whole, as well as its abiding, complicated importance through the next five centuries. Their very existence makes clear that the Reformation cannot be reduced to Luther's theology or biography alone or to the theology or biography of any other individual Protestant reformer.

Moving from man to movement, then, let's see what the Reformation becomes in the years following the Edict of Worms, after Luther is cast out of the Catholic Church as a heretic. During these years, the Reformation escapes Luther's control and, in the process, scrambles religion, politics, and society throughout the Holy Roman Empire.

Karlstadt's Wittenberg

While Luther secrets away to the Wartburg Castle, life in Wittenberg goes on without him,[1] though his black-and-white portrayal of the restored gospel and the decadent papacy persists in his absence. In May 1521, Philip Melanchthon, author of the first systematic account of Luther's theology, teams up with Lucas Cranach, Frederick of Saxony's entrepreneurial court artist and wealthiest resident, to produce the *Passions of Christ and Antichrist*, thirteen pairs of satirical woodcuts with explanatory texts that sharply contrast the pope's showy pomp with Christ's humble simplicity.

Such images, which start to become more pervasive in and around Wittenberg, help reinforce Luther's rhetoric and inspire desires for concrete changes in religious practices, like the ones Luther previously attacked in his *Babylonian Captivity of the Church*. Similarly, preachers addressing students and townspeople play a part in the ongoing process, focusing their sermons on the mass, monastic vows, and religious images. *Images* here refer not to satirical depictions, like those found in Cranach's woodcuts, but rather to religious paintings, sculptures, woodcuts, and stained-glass windows with human or divine figures that play a role in Christian worship or piety. Religious images are everywhere in late medieval Christian culture, from the grandest cathedrals to the smallest chapels as well as in public squares and streets. But some evangelicals, on the basis of the Bible, now consider them not as helpful aids to prayer but rather as idols that violate the second of the Ten Commandments ("You shall not make for yourself an idol," as Deuteronomy 5:8 says), and destroying them turns into the sacred duty of iconoclasm.

Wittenberg's two leading preachers in Luther's absence are a zealous Augustinian named Gabriel Zwilling and Andreas Bodenstein von Karlstadt, Luther's colleague at the University of Wittenberg, who accompanied Luther to the Leipzig Disputation, where he too debated Johannes Eck. Inspired by Luther's idea of the priesthood of all believers, Karlstadt writes and preaches that the laity *must* be offered the consecrated wine at communion during the mass.

Withholding it, according to Karlstadt, is a sinful power play by the clergy, a practice unsupported by scripture. What's more, Karlstadt provides the liturgy in German, not Latin, so that everyone can understand it. Radicalized by Zwilling, Karlstadt publishes multiple treatises critical of established religious practices, further energizing lay Christians already influenced by Luther.

Karlstadt's ideas stir townspeople to action, and their actions in turn further embolden his ideas. Already in the summer and fall, some lay Christians are intimidating priests and attacking their homes. By November, Zwilling starts convincing his fellow Augustinians to leave the friary, and a month later, students and citizens start disrupting masses in the parish church of St. Mary's, where they pelt Catholic priests with stones. They also threaten the Franciscans at their friary and destroy one of their church's altars. During a clandestine visit to Wittenberg, Luther—sporting a beard he's grown during his exile—writes to George Spalatin, the secretary to Frederick of Saxony, that what "I hear and see pleases me very much," despite having been "disturbed" on his way to Wittenberg "by various rumors concerning the improper conduct of some of our people."[2] It's unclear just how much he knows about the disruptions. Before all but a few people know he's back in town, Luther returns to the Wartburg.

During the remainder of December, events move more quickly, though not everyone welcomes their direction. In sharp contrast to Karlstadt, most clergy from the Church of All Saints oppose any changes to the liturgy. For his part, Frederick insists on caution and consensus—the default of virtually all political leaders at the time, alert to the fragility of local political order. But neither caution nor consensus are forthcoming. Echoing the sermons of Zwilling and Karlstadt, some citizens present the city council with demands for evangelical preaching, an end to endowed masses, the reception of the Eucharistic cup by the laity, and a closure of brothels and a few local taverns. Frederick digs in his heels, forbidding any changes until further notice. But as Karlstadt continues to fortify his new role as Wittenberg's leading reformer, he announces that he'll celebrate his next scheduled mass at All Saints, on New Year's Day, in an evangelical fashion.

On Christmas Eve, however, protestors destroy religious images in St. Mary's, which apparently influences Karlstadt to move up his plans. Against Frederick's wishes, he celebrates a new worship service in German on Christmas Day, dressed as an ordinary layman. He offers the overflowing congregation the consecrated bread and the cup, a radically antipapal act reminiscent of the Hussites in Bohemia a century earlier.

Just days later, during the last week of December, three men appear from Zwickau, a small Saxon town on the other side of Leipzig, some 120 miles south of Wittenberg, who claim to be prophets directly inspired by God with a message of warning on the eve of the apocalypse. Luther's own apocalyptic sensibility has intensified with his increasing conviction that the devil has colonized the papacy, and in general, expectations of the world's imminent end have been widespread for years. In the heady atmosphere of Wittenberg in 1521, the arrival of the Zwickau Prophets make such beliefs more credible than ever. Time itself seems to be running faster, ticking more quickly toward the end of the world and God's coming judgment.

The Zwickau Prophets perturb Melanchthon. He writes to Luther and asks him to return. Luther tells him to wait, explaining at length how to test what the alleged prophets say and how they say it. While leaning toward skepticism, Luther doesn't dismiss them out of hand.[3] How can he? True to his personal experience, Luther insists on the necessity of being inspired by God's Spirit in order to interpret God's Word properly. It turns out that the Zwickau Prophets have little effect on happenings in Wittenberg, but in subsequent years others like them in the Holy Roman Empire will have a greater impact.

The new year brings more actions and writings against the old ecclesiastical order. Karlstadt gets married, literally practicing what he preaches about clerical marriage. Extending earlier actions by townspeople, the remaining Augustinians in the cloister become image-destroying iconoclasts in their own chapel. They remove the religious images from their chapel and, in a public display, demolish them. Karlstadt stands with the citizens pressing for religious changes. He plays a key role in drafting the new ordinances for alterations in religion, and on January 24, 1522, the Wittenberg city council approves them. Prompted partly by popular pressure from below—and against Frederick's wishes—Wittenberg institutionally approves the Reformation.

Just days after this triumph, Karlstadt publishes a treatise titled *On the Removal of Images*. It condemns religious sculptures and paintings as inherently idolatrous and directly opposed to the Old Testament. "I say to you," Karlstadt writes, "that God has forbidden images to no lesser degree and no less expressly than murder, theft, plundering, adultery, and the like."[4] Though Karlstadt stops short of calling for iconoclasm, during the first week in February, Wittenbergers destroy more religious objects from the parish church of St. Mary's.

Informed of what's afoot in Electoral Saxony, Charles V issues a mandate prohibiting religious innovations and ordering restoration of the status quo. He empowers Catholic bishops to conduct a visitation (an official inspection) in Wittenberg. In response, some of Luther's colleagues and members of the city council ask Luther to return, although Frederick worries that might make matters worse.

Luther arrives in Wittenberg on March 6, 1522. He dons a freshly made Augustinian habit—in contrast to his confreres, who cast theirs off when they left the friary—and for the next eight days he preaches a series of sermons in St. Mary's, one a day from March 9 through March 16. He blames Karlstadt and Zwilling for inciting disruption, even though other clergy, students, townspeople, and members of the city council all actively participated in what transpired.

In Luther's estimation, Karlstadt has made crucial mistakes based on theological misunderstandings. Through the city council, Luther argues, Karlstadt has forced citizens to accept changes in religious practices before they are ready. Insisting that images are idols and therefore *must* be removed from churches compromises evangelical freedom, as does insisting that laity *must* receive the communion cup. Whereas Karlstadt believes he's obeying God's Word, Luther sees him insidiously reimposing the law with his rhetoric of liberation. In Luther's view, once lay Christians understand faith and freedom properly, they'll quietly see they don't need images, and communion in both kinds can proceed without incident. Until then, Luther advocates temperance and patience.

The former allies disagree about more than simply the *pace* of religious changes. They also differ on the substance of *what* should be changed. While Luther and Karlstadt are both deeply committed to scripture as the only legitimate foundation for Christian teaching and practice and are convinced that scripture is clear, they disagree about its meaning. By March, they openly disagree about practices related to the Lord's Supper, the permissibility of religious images, the oral confession of sins, and the character of the Old Testament.

Luther's return to Wittenberg ends the fast-moving, communal character of the Reformation there. In the future, it will proceed more incrementally without unsettling Frederick, who despite protecting Luther also has to worry about upsetting Charles V. After Luther returns, for years the mass is again celebrated in Latin, until Luther's liturgy in German is instituted in Wittenberg following Frederick's death in 1525, four years later.

Karlstadt gets shut out. Just weeks after his triumph as Wittenberg's newly married, vocal leader of the Reformation, inspiring the townspeople and negotiating religious changes with the city council, he is marginalized after Luther's return—defeated, prohibited from preaching and publishing, and in effect publicly silenced and humiliated.

Luther, however, hasn't seen the last of Karlstadt, who grows disaffected with academic life and in 1523 leaves Wittenberg to become a rural pastor in Orlamünde, a small town more than a hundred miles to the southwest. There he shepherds changes like those that were undone in Wittenberg after Luther's return. Karlstadt also develops further his own views about the Eucharist, denying not only transubstantiation (as Luther had) but also any real, corporeal presence of Christ in the consecrated bread or wine. This idea will turn out to be deeply influential among many Reformed and radical Protestants. But it enrages Luther, who rails against it as nothing less than a satanic attempt to deprive Christians of Christ's consoling presence in the sacrament. The acrimony between Karlstadt and Luther is palpable when they meet face-to-face in the town of Jena in August 1524. A few weeks later, Frederick of Saxony informs Karlstadt that he is not only being removed from his position in Orlamünde but also being banished altogether from Electoral Saxony. There's little freedom for this Christian, at least not in Frederick's lands.

The restoration of order in Wittenberg that follows Luther's return from exile does not indicate a consensus. The lingering dispute between Karlstadt and Luther is a harbinger of much more to come not only in the early German Reformation but also throughout Europe in the Reformation era as a whole. Only reformers who successfully negotiate political challenges have a chance to realize their religious aims, at least in ways that affect large numbers of people over extended periods of time. Those who fail politically find themselves marginalized religiously: this is what separates the magisterial Reformation from the radical Reformation. The issues that arise in Wittenberg about how the interpretation of scripture relates to the exercise of authority, the articulation of Christian truth, and the exertion of political power will accompany the Reformation everywhere.

Zwingli's Zürich

More than four hundred miles to the southwest in the German-speaking Swiss city of Zürich, Reformed Protestantism emerges in the 1520s as a distinct form of the Reformation, different from Lutheranism.[5] Zürich is one of several city-states and other small territories, called cantons, that together make up the Swiss Confederation (more or less modern-day Switzerland). Each canton exercises jurisdiction over its own territory and people, and the Swiss Confederation as a whole is independent of the Holy Roman Emperor. Swiss cities therefore enjoy even more political independence than the imperial free cities, to say nothing of towns such as Wittenberg, which are subject to their territorial princes.

In Swiss communities, city magistrates—not princes, electors, or even Charles V—hold the reins of power. If city magistrates, for instance, decide to reject the authority of the local Catholic bishop, they become the authorities who decide what religious changes will be introduced, in what manner, and by what means. Although Luther's writings are published in Basel and his ideas influence Swiss reformers, no Swiss city adopts his version of the Reformation. In fact, Swiss reformers prove far more influential than Luther in introducing the Reformation in many cities in some parts of the Holy Roman Empire. Among these reformers is Huldrych Zwingli (1484–1531), the most important leader of the early Reformation in Zürich.

Like Luther, Zwingli was initially schooled in scholasticism, attending university in Vienna and Basel. Unlike Luther the Augustinian friar, though, Zwingli is a parish priest; he does not agonize within the rigors of monastic life. Much more formative for Zwingli is Christian humanism: he pursues Greek (and then Hebrew) with alacrity and becomes an enthusiastic fan of Erasmus, applying his linguistic skills to the study of the Bible and church fathers, as Erasmus did. While Zwingli reads Luther, as do so many others in central Europe who care about religious reform, he never considers himself an acolyte of Luther. In fact, he becomes Luther's determined adversary, especially over the interpretation of the Eucharist. Even aside from this sundering disagreement, though, the character of Zürich's Reformation differs from Wittenberg's.

By the time the Zürich city council hires him as the regular preacher for the city's main church, the Great Minster, in January 1519, Zwingli has already earned a reputation as a good preacher. From the start of his ministry in Zürich, Zwingli preaches in a way that reflects his humanist study. Instead of expounding on the scripture verses prescribed for each mass, as is usually done, he starts at the beginning of a biblical book (the Gospel of Matthew is his first) and works his way through each book steadily and systematically, week by week. Frequently, Zwingli uses scripture to criticize traditional religious beliefs and practices.

Like the residents of other Swiss cities, Zürich's citizens share a strong sense of community identity rooted in their political independence. Zwingli combines this civic pride with his own vision of the Reformation, one that emphasizes the duty of magistrates to govern citizens' behavior along evangelical lines.

Enthusiasm for evangelical ideas accelerates in Zürich in 1522. Early in the year Leo Jud, another ardent preacher and priest, arrives in the city and becomes Zwingli's close ally. Jud is among those who conspicuously eat sausages during the early days of Lent, willfully violating the Church's fasting regulations as an expression of gospel freedom, at exactly the same time Luther is preaching his sermons against Karlstadt's reforms in Wittenberg. Zwingli defends Jud's actions first from the pulpit and then in print. In the ensuing months, in and around Zürich, as well as in other cities of the Swiss Confederation, members of the clergy and laity alike disrupt sermons, stage protests, break fasts, and refuse to pay tithes, the ecclesiastical taxes that support the clergy.

In the summer Zwingli petitions the Bishop of Constance to allow the clergy to marry, and more shockingly, it becomes known that he himself has already secretly married, breaking his vow of celibacy. He sends a published statement of his faith to the bishop, Hugo von Hohenlandenberg, in August and the following month preaches a sermon later published as a treatise titled *On the Clarity and Certainty of Scripture*. Bishop Hugo shows no signs of sympathy for Zwingli's preaching or teaching or breaking of vows. But the city council takes matters into its own hands. The council releases him from these vows and creates a new preaching office for him. In effect, the city magistrates assert their own religious authority above that of the bishop and indeed above that of the Roman Catholic Church.

It's not entirely surprising, then, that in January 1523, when the bishop accuses Zwingli of heresy, the Zürich city council again asserts its authority. Before an audience of six hundred in the city hall, in proceedings held in German rather than in Latin, Zürich's lay magistrates implicitly claim authority over the bishop. They side with Zwingli against the bishop's representative. In the sixty-seven propositions Zwingli draws up, he defends *sola scriptura*, denies the mass is a sacrifice, rejects prayers to the saints, spurns dietary restrictions, and advocates clerical marriage, among other things. Many of his points overlap with Luther's criticisms from his treatise *On the Babylonian Captivity of the Church*.

Most astounding here is the reversal of clerical and lay roles: local magistrates are asserting religious authority—and not just in matters of jurisdiction, as in the late Middle Ages, but in matters of doctrine. Following Zwingli's lead, *they're* deciding what Christian truth is, and *they're* saying what scripture means. It's like Wittenberg's short-lived ordinances of January 1522, except there's no Charles V, Frederick of Saxony, or Luther returning from the Wartburg Castle to pressure them to stop. The Zürich city council determines that none of Zwingli's propositions are heretical and that all preaching in the city and the canton should be based on scripture. Small wonder, since by now members of the city council have been listening to Zwingli's sermons for more than four years. Zwingli has become their trusted guide to God's Word and Christian life. The implications are astonishing: apparently, every local council of secular authorities is now free to decide for themselves what is and isn't Christian truth.

The politically savvy Zwingli knows what he's doing. He's got a different understanding of what Luther calls law and gospel, one that meshes with the sense of civic responsibility and community pride shared by Zürich's magistrates. For Zwingli, law and gospel are not opposed to each other; rather, the restored gospel also serves as God's true law, religiously and politically. Biblical law is not only God's hammer to demolish pride and deliver human beings to saving grace, it is also a divine guide for properly ordering all of human life. "No teaching serves a government and magistrate better than the teaching of Christ," Zwingli writes in 1523, because "it teaches what is good and what is evil."[6] Civic magistrates and evangelical clergy are to oversee Christ's teaching in action, with the urban community and the church cooperating and complementing each other as two sides of the same coin.

In the ensuing months, agitation and unrest escalate. Multiple acts of iconoclasm occur, many publications criticizing images and the mass appear, and some villages around Zürich determine Christian truth and practice for themselves and, taking a step Zürich did not, refuse to pay tithes. In one of them, Witikon, village magistrates kick out the incumbent priest and choose their own, Wilhelm Reublin. Like Zwingli, he marries, only he does so publicly, which helps to keep questions about clerical marriage and celibacy on the boil.

In October, the Zürich city council hosts a second disputation, and even more people attend. The disruptions of recent months have put controversy about the mass and religious images front and center. The focus of the meeting this time is on conflict between Zwingli and some of his reforming colleagues, who, like Karlstadt in opposition to Luther, insist on pressing the demands of scripture as *they* understand it. These colleagues, who are fast turning into antagonists, include Balthasar Hubmaier, who earned his doctorate in theology with Johannes Eck in Ingolstadt, and the learned humanist Conrad Grebel.

For Hubmaier and Grebel, religious images and the mass contradict God's Word, so they have to be eliminated. Period. Zwingli agrees that religious images are idols and the mass is not a sacrifice. Central to his reforming ideals are pure, biblical worship and a hatred of idolatry. But, much like Luther in Wittenberg, Zwingli wants to slow things down. He insists that more instruction and preaching are needed to prepare the way for reforming worship and for eliminating religious paintings, sculptures, and stained glass. Predictably, the city council agrees. Until further notice, images are to remain in place and the mass is not to be altered or maligned. The council also orders preachers to continue preaching "according to the gospel"—without specifying exactly what that means.

Zwingli's position as preacher in the Great Minster depends on the city council. Because he understands this, he skillfully mediates between public agitation for religious changes and the decisions of

Zürich's magistrates, who step by step come to approve Zwingli's version of the Reformation. Sometimes Zwingli rails against traditional teachings and practices, in effect pushing for religious change; at other times, as in the disputation of October 1523, he holds back, essentially functioning as the spokesman for the council's incremental approach. The eventual outcome is a successful Reformation that drastically remakes Zürich's religious life yet at the same time alienates other men and women who reject Zwingli's version of the Reformation. They see him as an objectionable pragmatist willing to sacrifice the radical challenges of God's Word for the sake of political expediency, in much the same way that Karlstadt came to see Luther.

Partly because of Zwingli's astute political maneuvering, matters in Zurich quickly begin to change. Before long the city council starts to implement the changes it initially prohibited, along with many more. Within a year and a half, by mid-1525, council members order all religious images removed from the city's churches. They shut down the city's many male and female monasteries and prohibit the taking of religious vows; they abolish the mass and create a new liturgy in the vernacular; and they institute regular scholarly discussions about scripture for clergy and those in clerical training. And to oversee a wide range of matters pertaining to marriage and morals, they establish a new court under the jurisdiction of the city, not the bishop.

In Zürich's radically altered worship after 1525, married clergy expound God's Word, their sermons echoing off whitewashed church walls. Gone are the mass, the priests, monks, friars, nuns, and countless religious paintings and sculptures and panes of stained glass. Gone too are fasting and processions and candles, pilgrimages and prayers to saints, and celebration of saints' days. Zürich has become a godly city, a biblical city, and in partnership with Zwingli the city council has made it happen.

But the city council's authority also alienates other evangelicals.

Already visible in the disputation of October 1523, the disaffection persists and spreads, deepens and coalesces. Behind the issue of community self-determination lie more fundamental concerns about what scripture says and what the Church and Christianity are supposed to be. For evangelicals such as Hubmaier, Grebel, and Reublin, displeased with the content and politically enforced character of Zürich's new church order, Christian commitment can't and shouldn't capitulate on the tithe or the baptism of infants, because in their view neither one is based in scripture. To impose them means nothing less than a new tyranny in gross violation of Christian liberty as found in scripture.

These convictions lead to yet another form of the Reformation: Anabaptism. As in Wittenberg, in Zürich the Reformation's cornerstone of scriptural authority quickly becomes the source of acrimony. Like the Reformation in Zürich, Anabaptism emerges out of the swift spread of the evangelical movement in the Holy Roman Empire and Swiss Confederation in the early 1520s. We'll meet it again shortly.

Reformation as Urban Disruption

Wittenberg and Zürich are examples of how appealing to God's Word in the early 1520s provides *both* justification for rejecting the Roman Church *and* a shared foundation for disagreeing about the meaning of scripture. Neither town is a free imperial city, a political community in the Holy Roman Empire answering only to Charles V, the emperor. Such communities are critical to the spread of early evangelical ideas and actions. In the 1520s, dozens of free imperial cities are the sites of an aggressive, disruptive Reformation movement as unexpected as an Augustinian friar becoming a publishing sensation and celebrity papal critic.[7]

This unfolding movement, unwieldy and unsettling as it is, places civic magistrates in a bind. In the face of popular agitation, will they obey the Edict of Worms and suppress evangelical ideas and actions? Or will they accommodate a movement that rejects the religion of their forebears and threatens the urban order they have sworn to maintain, in defiance of the emperor?

Civil strife is a plague to densely built sixteenth-century cities, none of which has professional police forces as we know them. These are communities held together by ties of family, kinship, friendship, and professional relationships. Because they are compact centers of commerce, artisanal manufacturing, education, and political influence, the stakes are high. Soon some magistrates as well as territorial princes also approve of the new religious ideas, which complicates their conundrum. Unable to avoid the situation or defer their duty indefinitely, they have to act.

In many German and Swiss cities, the eventual acceptance of the Reformation depends on local political authorities making calculated decisions. With the notable exception of Cologne, where an alignment of antievangelical institutions effectively stymies the Reformation, magistrates in most of the major free imperial cities choose to defy the emperor rather than suppress the evangelical movement. They're pressed to resist the emperor by clergy who are sympathetic to reform and who see the urban laity inspired by Reformation preaching, publishing, exhortation, and example. Without any clear blueprint, activist clergy and townspeople, together with political authorities, transform the Reformation message into a movement for religious, social, and political change.

Most of the important leaders in the early Reformation are members of the clergy. Whether parish priests like Zwingli or members of religious orders like Luther, they criticize the papacy and the established Church. They are crucial in spreading the Reformation. But it also spreads in the early 1520s because their sermons, pamphlets, and counsel strike a chord with listeners and readers, resonating in ways that prompt laypeople to act.

Luther's pioneering approach of appealing directly to the laity about religious matters is in some ways the most astonishing aspect of the movement. In their preaching and pamphlets, evangelical clergy repeatedly address "the common man." Their words tap in to generations of widespread anticlericalism; almost all urban people resent something about the shortcomings or privileges of priests, monks, friars, nuns, bishops, or all of the above. In their intimate communities enclosed behind protective city walls, evangelical clergy and laity together make "the gospel" into a problem that forces political authorities to respond.

In the early 1520s, the specific content of scripture matters less than zealous hostility to an old regime. Clergy hot for reform in cities such as Strasbourg, Nuremberg, and Magdeburg rant against papist idolatry, tyranny, and corruption. Because they believe that nothing less than eternal salvation is at stake, their urgency is palpable; this is a matter of literally more than life and death. Clergy convinced of the evangelical cause attack established institutions in countless sermons, in a profusion of pamphlets, and in a flood of woodcut images. The scales have fallen from their eyes; now they see clearly. These are men who were ordained as priests and took vows of obedience in a Church they now believe has been colonized by Satan as a prelude to the Last Judgment. They've been tricked, and so has the laity.

So they rail against priestly greed and monastic orders and clerical celibacy. They condemn the mass and indulgences and religious images, and they satirize prayers to the saints and pilgrimages and processions. None of this is tolerable, they're now convinced, and none of it is Christian. And good Christian laypeople shouldn't stand for it, even though it's the religion that they and their parents and grandparents and great-grandparents before them grew up with and practiced all their lives. Indeed, it's the religion that the evangelical clergy themselves practiced, preached, and promoted just a few short years before.

Townsfolk listen, and significant numbers of them spring into action, including members of guilds, apprentices, shopkeepers, low-ranking officials, and servants. Some of them even preach and write and publish their own pamphlets.[8] A few women take active roles, such as Argula von Grumbach, a Bavarian noblewoman who audaciously pens a pamphlet criticizing the theology faculty (which includes Johannes Eck) at the University of Ingolstadt. Attacking clerical greed and appealing to secular rulers, as Luther did in his appeal to the German nobility, Grumbach writes, "God grant that the princes and lords will no longer let themselves be led along like monkeys on a chain by these so-called spiritual rulers," for "the sweat of the poor is used in the service of the devil."[9] The middling ranks of townspeople ordinarily have little influence in politics, but they can pressure magistrates if enough of them make trouble. Which is just what they do: in multiple German cities in the early 1520s, they foment civil disobedience and sometimes engage in violence in the name of the gospel.

Laypeople disrupt masses and attack clergy, often verbally and sometimes physically. They devour the propaganda of vernacular pamphlets. They laugh at wildly popular woodcuts that satirize the old Church, images that serve as the sound bites of the Reformation.[10] They publicly mock the Church by appropriating the festive rituals of Carnival, the days in the Church's calendar just before Lent. Gathering in pubs and on the street, they stage protests and, together with reforming clergy, issue demands to city officials: clergy must be allowed to marry, monasteries must be shuttered, and the mass must be abolished and replaced by evangelical worship. As in Wittenberg and Zürich, they smash religious images, for centuries regarded as devotional aids but suddenly, shockingly, unmasked as idols prohibited by God's command in scripture.

It's remarkable enough that so many priests do an about-face on so much of what they thought God sanctioned. Even more remarkable is their appeal to the laity to decide religious matters for themselves. But then again, what is the risk? Evangelical clergy are confident that the laity will follow their lead, becoming righteous rebels initially within—but increasingly outside—the ranks of a reeling Church.

The spoken words of sermons and printed words of pamphlets mesh with the Word of God in a confluence of media and message. Between 1520 and 1525, more than seven thousand pamphlets are published in Germany, the vast majority of which criticize the established Church and promote the Reformation.[11] Such a proliferation of print has no precedent in European history. It matters little that most people can't read, because almost everyone knows someone who can, and who can read aloud to others, whether in someone's house or in a city square or marketplace. In this way print is combined with oral communication, just as texts and images are combined in many of the woodcuts produced for the cause.

Luther remains far and away the most widely published author.[12] Yet his understanding of justification by faith alone, salvation by grace alone, and law and gospel likely goes over the heads of many who oppose the traditional Church. Almost none of them have spent years studying biblical languages, meditating on and teaching scripture, sharpening their argumentative skills through scholastic debate, or reading the church fathers. What reformers say and how their message is received are two different things.

By and large, those who maintain their allegiance to the traditional Church are caught off guard by the early Reformation movement, just as they were by Luther's out-of-nowhere ascent. Still, some political authorities can and do take action against it. For instance, in Cologne, a free imperial city of the first rank, city officials cooperate with the clergy and university to shut down the Reformation straightaway.[13] Similarly, Duke George of Saxony staunchly opposes the movement in his territories and stifles the printing of evangelical materials in Leipzig.[14] As early as 1524, several of the Swiss cantons near Zürich start banding together against Zwingli's innovations.

In the early 1520s, dozens of Catholic clergy publish denunciations of Luther and his supporters as dangerous heretics intent on condemning the Church and bent on subverting all authority. Catholic clergy insult and satirize the evangelicals right back. They warn that the evangelicals' blasphemous attacks on the faith will provoke God's wrath and undermine political authority as well. Their efforts, however, are dwarfed in quantity by evangelical publications, and they receive less attention because Catholic authors typically write at greater length and proportionally more in Latin than their adversaries.[15] But fundamentally, Catholic writers don't *want* a public dispute about religion. Part of their point is that Christian doctrine *isn't* something you can decide for yourself based on scripture alone, as Luther and other evangelicals insist—especially if you're a lay artisan who has never studied theology, probably can't read, and almost certainly can't read Latin, the language of scholastic theology. Urging an average layperson to determine Christian teaching from the scriptures is like asking someone who's never worked a blacksmith's forge or operated a bellows to hammer out some horseshoes.

But cities such as Cologne and territories such as Ducal Saxony, which take early and decisive action against the evangelical movement, are exceptions. In most German cities, local agitation prompts city councils to act in favor of the agitators, although not all at once. The authorities see that social and political unrest over religion cannot be tolerated because it will tear apart their already fragile and often fractious urban communities. Their duty to maintain order makes most of them temperamentally suspicious of change. Yet agitation persists and grows because clergy who preach "according to the scriptures" based on the "pure Word of God" have the permission they need to continue. Significant numbers of magistrates themselves are won over to the evangelical cause and become its supporters on city councils. The Reformation gives them the opportunity to extend their jurisdictional control over the Church, an oversight that has already increased in the late Middle Ages. Only now they will do it *against* rather than *in support of* traditional religious practices and institutions, persuaded that authentic Christianity is actually something different from the faith they've known all their lives. Closing down monasteries and seizing the property and possessions of religious orders is a coup for urban magistrates; monastic holdings can be put to alternative useful ends, such as education and poor relief. Reading the writing on the wall, urban officials move in favor of the Reformation despite defying the emperor. One step at a time, as in Zürich, they begin acting on evangelical demands, undoing established religious practices and implementing substitutes.

In large cities such as Nuremberg and smaller ones such as Nördlingen, secular authorities close down monasteries and permit priests to marry, thereby folding the clergy into urban life and keeping them bound by civic laws under their control. New-order clergy are now citizens with no special legal exemptions, and they preside over worship services approved by magistrates, in which laity receive communion with both bread and wine. The same magistrates remove images from churches and abolish fasting regulations.

Turning a message into a movement involves disruption, but urban magistrates manage the militancy of the early German Reformation in their cities. Yet the movement quickly proves to be bigger even than the cities, growing with its own momentum, outpacing urban magistrates. As it spills over into hundreds of villages across central Europe, it grows more radical and threatens revolution.

Reformation as Revolution:
The German Peasants' War

"The freedom of a Christian": what does it mean in the early 1520s? For adherents of the early Reformation, it means rejecting the authority and many of the teachings and practices of the corrupt, self-serving, greedy papal Church. But what else does it mean?

Luther's answer focuses on justification by faith alone. In a hierarchical society built on assumptions about dutiful deference and obedience to authority, Christian freedom, in Luther's view, has nothing to do with altering political institutions or socioeconomic realities. Those concern merely the "outer man," not the inner man, where God works in the heart and implants faith and saves by his grace. Anyone who thinks the gospel implies political or socioeconomic change misunderstands the gospel. Luther articulates the difference between faith and politics in a pamphlet he publishes in 1523 titled *On Secular Authority: How Far Does the Obedience Owed to It Extend?* "Secular government has laws that extend no further than the body, goods, and outward, earthly matters," he writes. "But where the soul is concerned, God neither can nor will allow anyone but himself to rule," for "by what right does secular authority, in its folly, presume to judge a thing as secret, spiritual, hidden as faith?"[16]

Jesus was a humble carpenter, not a university professor; he was a simple worker, not a scholar. Again and again in the Gospels Jesus announced the good news of "the kingdom of God" to the poor and marginalized. He said God will judge you based on whether you respond to people's material needs—feeding the hungry, clothing the naked, sheltering the homeless. Human beings are *embodied* souls, which is why the medieval Church emphasized both the spiritual *and corporal* works of mercy, all of which are taken straight from scripture—including burying the dead, from the apocryphal

Book of Tobit. Rather than ignoring Christian works of mercy, Luther seeks to reconfigure the place of such actions in Christian life: they *result from* your salvation by God; they do not contribute to it.

But for other evangelicals, such a reconfiguration is mere tinkering. It runs the risk of luring the "saved" into complacent inaction. It leaves the "common man" at the mercy of all the same injustices and exploitation ordinary Christians have always experienced in the grinding agricultural life of peasants in which most men and women toil. It misses the real point of Christian freedom, and it sells short the real point of the gospel.

In 1525 the early Reformation peaks as a popular movement in the so-called German Peasants' War, the largest mass uprising in European history before the French Revolution of 1789.[17] The term is something of a misnomer, because the conflict also involves sympathetic townspeople and clergy as well as rural villagers, farmers, miners, and servants. For these men and women, full Christian freedom means more than just being liberated from the unbiblical teachings and practices of the established Church. It means being liberated as well from oppressive, hierarchical, unjust socioeconomic relationships in society at large. The previous generation already saw a series of rural uprisings in southwestern Germany. Rebellious peasants regularly seek redress of grievances about taxes and fees, labor demands, and the administration of justice. When this tradition meets the intoxicating spread of the early Reformation in an atmosphere of apocalyptic expectation, layfolk in the countryside take action that is more ambitious and potentially revolutionary than the actions of laypeople in cities.

The Peasants' War begins in the summer of 1524 in southwestern Germany, in the Black Forest just north of Zürich and its surrounding villages. That's significant, because Zwingli is convinced that the gospel ought to serve as a template for all of human life,

including politics and social relationships, and his conviction reso-
nates with the region's ordinary folk. But in their view the changes
have to go deeper; they have to encompass whole territories, not
just individual cities. And when established institutions contradict
the gospel, you can't just leave them alone. The authentic Word
of God calls for a different *kind* of society, one built on Christian
brotherhood, egalitarian cooperation, and the just exercise of
power to replace a world in which the rich and powerful exploit
the poor.

Throughout the fall and winter, the Peasants' War continues to
gain adherents and momentum. At its peak in the spring of 1525,
it encompasses multiple armies, or "bands," that stretch from what
is now eastern France through southern and central Germany and
northern Switzerland and into Austria. The bands are not centrally
coordinated, and even if they had shared the same aspirations, the
difficulty of communicating and traveling over such distances would
have made such coordination impossible. By April 1525 nearly three
hundred thousand persons are involved. None of the previous rural
rebellions were anywhere near as large. Neither were they motivated
in the same way. The Reformation, by appealing to the common
man, the gospel, the Word of God, and Christian freedom, makes
the difference. The Reformation now takes shape as a militant mass
movement, an unexpected escalation in 1524 and 1525.

Common people draw up many lists of grievances, aided sometimes by like-minded clergy. They present these grievances to city
magistrates or members of the nobility who wield political authority.
Generally speaking, these Christians want basic changes inspired
by the gospel to infuse their traditional, broader understanding of
"divine law." They want the right to choose their own clergy. They
want an end to feudal taxes and fees they consider burdensome and
unjust. They want access to shared woods, fields, and streams for
their use. And they want the abolition of traditional serfdom and

the oppressive conditions it entails. Because the gospel is just as relevant for material concerns as it is for spiritual ones, their demands encompass economic as well as religious matters. Commoners have souls *and* bodies, just as do the rich and powerful.

The most popular list of grievances during the uprisings, *The Twelve Articles of the Swabian Peasants,* is written by the furrier Sebastian Lotzer and the Memmingen priest Christoph Schappeler. Amazingly, it's published more than twenty times in less than two months during March and April 1525. Lotzer and Schappeler state the matter clearly: "Until now it has been the custom for us to be regarded as a lord's personal property, which is deplorable since Christ redeemed us all with the shedding of his precious blood—the shepherd as well as the most highly placed, without exception. Thus, scripture establishes that we are and will be free." They are willing to obey legitimate authorities "in everything that is proper and Christian"—a crucial qualification because it does not include feudal servitude: "Without a doubt, as true and just Christians, you will also gladly release us from serfdom, or show us from the gospel that we should be serfs."[18] Cleverly, the authors adopt Luther's strategy of challenging adversaries to use scripture to prove them wrong, confident that it cannot be done.

The commoners' aims deeply threaten the established political and social order. Virtually all secular authorities, whether urban magistrates or princes, are predictably appalled. They are not about to turn the world upside down and give up their privileged positions. This is doubly true for the many who believe that political and socioeconomic hierarchy is part of God's natural order. Yet in some cases, before the late spring of 1525, the authorities cannot galvanize their own troops fast enough to put the commoners down, so they negotiate in order to buy time, acceding to certain demands. But the peasant bands, moving from place to place, cannot enforce what they pressure authorities to accept. More successful—and more destructive—is their capture and pillage of literally hundreds of noble castles and dozens of monasteries.

Other aspirations during the Peasants' War are more extreme. Some are set forth by Thomas Müntzer, an apocalyptic preacher and leader during the uprising in Thuringia in central Germany. Like Karlstadt, Müntzer is originally keen on Luther but then falls out with him. Luther thinks that guidance by the Holy Spirit is essential for understanding God's Word, but like the Zwickau Prophets who showed up in Wittenberg, Müntzer thinks that without a stronger, more direct inspiration of God's "inner Word" by the Spirit, the "outer Word" of scripture is worthless, even if someone has "devoured a hundred thousand bibles."[19]

In Müntzer's view, Luther doesn't understand God's Word at all, which is why he's so blind to the plight of the peasants and how they're oppressed by the clergy and secular authorities, "like eels and snakes copulating together in a heap."[20] The extraordinary events unfolding all around are indeed signs of the rapidly approaching end of the world, but God is on the side of the peasants, and the Spirit calls for holy and violent resistance. Yet Luther—"Brother Fattened-swine and Brother Soft-life," "Doctor Liar" and "the spiritless, soft-living flesh at Wittenberg"—sides with the authorities against ordinary folk.[21]

Luther is convinced that the gospel, faith, and salvation are not to be combined with politics, social realities, or the economy. In his view, rebellion against political authorities disobeys God's command, as the apostle Paul explicitly says: "Let every person be subject to the governing authorities, for there is no authority except from God, and those authorities that exist have been instituted by God" (Romans 13:1). Without the stability provided by these divinely instituted rulers, society would quickly collapse into a chaos of sin and destruction. The peasants' claims about the gospel are intertwined with their subversive actions, and together they imperil

Luther's own reforming efforts. Luther's Catholic critics gloat with told-you-so glee; the Peasants' War is a confirmation of everything they warned Luther about. Rejecting the Catholic Church will lead to a meltdown of the social and political order.

Luther initially counsels restraint, chiding authorities and the disgruntled commoners, but in May 1525 he denounces the rebellion in a pamphlet titled *On the Robbing and Murdering Hordes of Peasants*. Like many of his other works, it's a bestseller, with more than twenty editions printed by the end of the year. His exhortations shock even some of his friends. "Let everyone who can smite, slay, and stab, secretly or openly, remembering that nothing can be more poisonous, hurtful, or devilish than a rebel," Luther writes. "It is just as when one must kill a mad dog; if you do not strike him, he will strike you, and a whole land with you."[22]

By the time Luther's pamphlet appears, most of the peasant bands are well on their way to defeat. They're hugely overmatched once princes get their armies in order, and they suffer enormous casualties. On May 15, Müntzer eagerly leads his band into battle at Frankenhausen, where they're utterly routed. More than six thousand of them die, while they kill only six men in the army opposing them. Müntzer himself is captured, tortured, and soon thereafter executed.

The unrest continues in parts of Austria into 1526, but there too it is suppressed. Altogether, probably a hundred thousand peasant combatants are killed in the field or executed during the two years of conflicts. If the Reformation's calls for Christian liberation are the crucial catalyst that makes these uprisings unlike any before them, then the Peasants' War is the first war of religion in the Reformation era. Or rather, it is the Reformation era's first war of more-than-religion, because the commoners' aims reflect Christianity's traditional emphasis on making faith shape the rest of human life.

The German Peasants' War is also the most important watershed of the early Reformation. It signals an attempt to realize the gospel in ways that will remake socioeconomic and political hierarchies. It fails, and political rulers win. The Reformation will undermine the authority of the old Church but not the authority, power, or control of political rulers. Indeed, the Reformation, wherever it begins to transform Christian life, as in Wittenberg, Zürich, Strasbourg, Nuremberg, and other cities and territories, will do so only and always under the watchful eye of the political authorities.

After 1525, following the Peasants' War, the number of pamphlets being published drops off dramatically. Magistrates and princes are now alert to any hint of social or political radicalism in the Reformation. Working together with cooperating clergy, they approve what scripture means and they suppress anything they consider disruptive. A consequence of this is that Christian life becomes a trial for anyone with a different view of the gospel.

The Gospel Against the World: Anabaptists

In the wake of the Peasants' War, Anabaptists—who belong to the early Reformation as much as Luther, Karlstadt, Zwingli, Müntzer, and the thousands of rural and urban men and women enthusiastically applying the Word of God in their own ways—feel the force of political authorities newly sensitized to religious radicalism. Anabaptism first emerges in the villages around Zürich at the same time the Peasants' War rages in the region. Those who become the first Anabaptists are also concerned about tithes and socioeconomic justice.[23]

After the efforts to transform the whole society are crushed, Anabaptists seek to preserve the impulse on a much smaller scale: theirs will be a socially realized Reformation of Christians who follow Christ in concrete discipleship. If the world rejects the truth, then the truth must reject the world. As one of the peasant manifestos from late 1524 puts it, "We would much rather have God as a friend and people as enemies than have God as an enemy and people as friends."[24] Their commitment will be tested by persecution, as they form communities that reject both Roman Catholicism and the Reformation of Luther or Zwingli.

Anabaptism means "rebaptism"—an abusive slur foisted on Anabaptists by their critics. Like other evangelicals, Anabaptists condemn the inherited view of the sacraments, the mass, religious images, clerical celibacy, papal authority, and more. What sets them apart is their rejection of infant baptism and their insistence on adult (or believers') baptism. In their view, believers' baptism isn't *rebap-tism* at all because infant baptism is meaningless in the first place—just another invented Roman practice with no basis in scripture.

In rejecting infant baptism, early Anabaptist leaders, such as Balthasar Hubmaier, Conrad Grebel, Felix Mantz, and others, are simply following principles laid down by Luther and Zwingli. If justification takes place by faith alone, and newborn infants don't and can't have faith, what sense does baptizing them make? It's nothing but another empty ritual—though it subjects everyone to the clergy's control. Infant baptism also helps to explain why Christendom has arrived in such a dire state: thinking that sprinkling babies with water makes them Christians, and later pleading with those grown-up babies actually to live as Christians should? That's exactly backward! In real Christianity faith comes *first,* then baptism follows as an outward sign of your inward faith. Mark's Gospel is plain as can be in laying down the order: "The one who believes and is baptized will be saved" (Mark 16:16).

Luther and Zwingli and their allies are wrong too about human capacities in matters of salvation, exaggerating the depths of our sinful depravity. In this respect, Anabaptists resemble their Catholic contemporaries and predecessors more than Luther or Zwingli. Faith requires your free, self-conscious response to God's interior call: it is God's gift, but *you* have to accept it with a deliberate choice. Then baptism follows as the exterior sign of your commitment to follow Christ in discipleship. Christ asked his own disciples, "Why do you call me 'Lord, Lord,' and not do what I say?" (Luke 6:46). Anabaptists ask: Why is the sixteenth century any different from the first century? Christianity is most importantly about *living* a certain way, not about the justification of wretched sinners prior to all Christian action. Baptism is also your entrance into a community of other Christians—the Church—who make the same commitment.

Infant or adult baptism—what's the big deal in the 1520s? For many centuries, infant baptism has performed double duty: it initiates you into your local parish *and* into your community just days after your birth—another manifestation of religion as more-than-religion. Christianity is not separate from community social relationships; it rather informs them. To reject infant baptism drives a wedge between the two, implying that the Church might not include the whole community. Rejecting infant baptism is also an act of defiant disobedience against political authorities who make and enforce the laws, because Christianity is not separate from politics either. During the Peasants' War and its aftermath, defiance like this is the last thing magistrates and princes want to see. Yet for most Anabaptists, the large-scale, bloody suppression of humble folk in the Peasants' War demonstrates that the established authorities are morally bankrupt and indeed diabolical.

Anabaptists turn the Reformation principle of *sola scriptura* against Luther and Zwingli, much to the irritation of these two reformers. Infant baptism can't be justified on the basis of scripture alone because nowhere does the Bible explicitly mention it. Luther thinks it prefigures justification by faith alone as something done completely for and to you by God and so is a legitimate practice. Zwingli argues for it as a Christian parallel to the Old Testament practice of circumcision (which of course applies only to boys, not girls). Anabaptists are unconvinced, just as Luther is unconvinced by his critics who defend papal authority and the Roman Church's interpretation of scripture against his own. As far as Anabaptists are concerned, neither argument amounts to a genuine biblical grounding for infant baptism.

But in Zürich, Zwingli has the city magistrates on his side. In January 1525, the Zürich city council makes Anabaptism punishable by death. Not long thereafter, the first executions take place—often by drowning, a grim public display in which authorities use water, which is central to baptism, as an instrument of execution, a brutal and carefully orchestrated act of judicial theater intended to deter the spread of Anabaptism. In the next few years, however, Anabaptism grows in the same areas where the Peasants' War raged most intensely—parts of Switzerland, southwestern and central Germany, and parts of Austria. Other cities and territories, including those ruled by Charles V's brother Ferdinand, also pass capital legislation against it. Here is something on which evangelical and Catholic authorities agree.

Hundreds of Anabaptists are executed in the decade following the Peasants' War. For Anabaptists, this confirms Christ's words about those martyred for his sake: "Blessed are those who are persecuted for righteousness' sake, for theirs is the kingdom of heaven" (Matthew 5:11). They preserve the memory of their martyrs in hundreds of songs and stories, which in addition to celebrating their sacrifice also encourages beleaguered Anabaptists to persevere.

Some Anabaptists meet persecution with pacifism. For Conrad Grebel, Zwingli's colleague, discipleship means specifically turning the other cheek in the face of threats: "True Christians," writes

Grebel, "use neither the worldly sword nor war, for among them killing has been totally abolished."[25] He's writing to Thomas Müntzer, the advocate of apocalyptic violence in the Peasants' War. For Grebel and others like him, Anabaptist discipleship is a radical, transformed expression of the medieval imitation of Christ, enacted under the most difficult of circumstances.

Many Anabaptists also practice separatism, worshipping as much as possible apart from the politically mandated forms of Christianity, whether Protestant or Catholic. This practice is an outgrowth of their rejection of infant baptism. Often this means dangerous, clandestine gatherings in woods, fields, or caves to read scripture, pray, sing, and celebrate the Lord's Supper. If the situation is not too dangerous, they sometimes cautiously meet and worship in a believer's house. They are not permitted anywhere in these years to have churches of their own.

Yet there's nothing intrinsically separatist about Anabaptism. If enough evangelicals in a village or town choose to be baptized as adults, as a witness to their faith and a sign of their commitment to Christian discipleship, Anabaptism can become the community's form of the Reformation. In the small town of Waldshut near Zürich, Balthasar Hubmaier baptizes over three hundred adults in April 1525, at the same time the town is supporting local peasants in their rebellion. Anabaptism is briefly the dominant expression of the Reformation in Waldshut, prior to persecution.

It's the large-scale crushing of commoners in the Peasants' War that turns Anabaptists, many of whom were involved in the uprisings, into separatists. And their own treatment by the authorities reinforces their us-against-them view of the world. As a former Benedictine monk turned Anabaptist leader named Michael Sattler puts it in 1527 shortly before he is captured, tortured, and executed: "There has never been anything in the world and among all creatures except good and evil, believing and unbelieving, darkness and light, the world and those who are out of the world, God's temple and idols, Christ and Belial, and neither may have anything to do with the other."[26] This is much like Luther's harsh language against the papacy, only deployed against those whom Sattler views as enemies of the gospel.

Severe early persecution of Anabaptists eventually takes its toll, eliminating many early leaders, including the most learned among them. Unlike Catholics, Lutherans, and Reformed Protestants, the Anabaptists and most other radical Protestants do not have access to university education until much later. They lack training in humanist scholarship or the study of Latin, and so they do not stand on the same footing as those who do when it comes to arguing about biblical interpretation and Christian doctrine. But as Anabaptists see it, being a Christian and following Christ properly depend on none of these things. Advanced education, according to Anabaptists, easily leads to the deadly sin of pride—again, Jesus was a simple carpenter, not a scholar.

Though Anabaptists share a commitment to believers' baptism and *sola scriptura,* they disagree about many other issues. The Bible proves no more capable of providing a cohesive community among early Anabaptists than it does among early evangelicals in general. And just as among evangelicals as a whole, disagreement among Anabaptists proves socially divisive.

Anabaptists dispute how discipline should be exercised among members who fail to live up to their high standards as visible saints. Those in central Germany are influenced by Müntzer, which creates tensions with Anabaptists elsewhere. Hubmaier's approval of coercive violence distinguishes him sharply from Grebel and his colleague Felix Mantz, both of whom are principled pacifists. Starting at the end of the 1520s, followers of Jacob Hutter, an Austrian hat maker and Anabaptist leader, insist that believers must follow the example of the earliest Christians as stated in scripture (Acts 2 and

4) and not own private property, holding all things in common instead. This practice of communal ownership puts the Hutterites at odds with nearly all other Anabaptists.

It's perhaps not surprising that self-consciously committed Christians who are willing to separate from the world will be willing to separate from each other as well, whenever they think others are wrong about something important. That's precisely what Luther did in becoming a reluctant rebel in the first place. The Anabaptists simply extend this principle and practice of the Reformation itself.

For and Against Free Will

In 1524 and 1525, as the early Reformation culminates in the Peasants' War and the first Anabaptist communities are emerging, Luther and Erasmus fight their own battle, one about free will. Do human beings have it or not in their religious lives? Their answers reflect two dramatically different conceptions of human capacities, God's relationship to human beings, and the nature of Christian faith itself. Erasmus argues that we possess free will and that except for a few scriptural passages that seem to suggest otherwise, the Bible implies as much. He publishes his views in 1524 in a politely written treatise titled *On the Freedom of the Will*. Luther counters in late 1525 with a vehement criticism of Erasmus's views in a treatise five times as long titled *On the Bondage of the Will*. It's a showdown between the leading Christian humanist and the most influential early Protestant reformer. Far from an abstruse academic debate, their dispute reflects essential differences about the interpretation of the Bible and the very character of Christian life and experience that apply to everyone.

Luther has been tangling with Catholic critics since 1518, but this is different. Most of his other adversaries are professional theologians. But Erasmus, northern Europe's most distinguished Christian humanist, was seeking reform in Christendom for years before Luther became a public figure. His edition of the New Testament in 1516 and his call to return to scripture and the church fathers as a basis for Christian renewal inspired Luther and many other leaders, including Zwingli, in the early Reformation. Erasmus doesn't join the Reformation, but neither does he publicly condemn it from the start.

Erasmus values civility and peace as expressions of genuine Christianity. He deplores the disruptions that are roiling Christendom in the early 1520s, the polemics and hostility on all sides. He doesn't want to add to them, and he seeks instead to remain above the fray. Yet in 1524, he's persuaded to write against Luther on a topic on which he thinks scripture is clear—and clearly against Luther. And he does so in a manner that models the measured civility he thinks belongs to charitable Christian dialogue, even when it involves parties that disagree: "We are not two gladiators incited against each other," he writes in his treatise.[27]

Luther's strident manner perturbs Erasmus as much as does Luther's position on free will, so in his treatise Erasmus addresses both tone and substance. In Erasmus's view, Luther mistakenly thinks we have no free will in our salvation. Luther further compounds his position by acting as though questions about God's will and human actions have simple and straightforward answers. He makes things worse still by emphasizing our unfree sinfulness at the expense of scripture's clear "precepts for a morally good life," which articulate what it really means to be a Christian. Averse to divisive anger and conflict, Erasmus also regards the issues involved as difficult. So he takes a cautious, minimal stance about our free will in religion: "All I am willing to assert is that the will enjoys some power of freedom."[28]

Luther will acknowledge no other authorities but scripture, so Erasmus accepts the terms and makes his case on the basis of the Bible. He says the two of them are at odds not about the value of scripture, which is "loved and revered by both parties," but rather about its sense, its interpretation.[29] How scripture should be understood is the key question underlying all the religious initiatives and conflicts of the 1520s. What justifies the rejection of the Roman Church is the belief that its understanding of scripture is wrong and one's own understanding of scripture is right, whether it comes from Luther, Karlstadt, Zwingli, Grebel, Müntzer, or any other evangelical.

Erasmus anticipates that Luther and his allies will argue for the clarity of scripture, so he challenges their conviction: "If it is really so clear, why have all the excellent people here acted like blind men for so many centuries, especially in so important a matter as my opponents hold it to be?" The very fact that scripture has been the subject of so much complex, sophisticated commentary for more than a thousand years implies that it's less than clear, not to mention the fact that evangelicals disagree among themselves about its meaning. Erasmus also anticipates and critiques appealing to the Holy Spirit as a guarantee of the correct understanding of scripture: "What can I do when several persons claim different interpretations, but each one swears to have the Spirit?"[30] This vexing problem of the early Reformation will last long beyond the 1520s. Indeed, it will never disappear or be resolved.

Erasmus models his own approach of respectful restraint, and he suggests, rather than insists, that human beings must make some contribution, however minimal, to their salvation. The many biblical passages with God's commandments and exhortations make no sense without genuine human responsibility. "What is the purpose of all the commandments, if it is impossible for anybody to keep them?"[31] Without human responsibility, there can be no culpability for sins: God's condemnation of sinners would be arbitrary, tyrannical, and unjust.

According to Erasmus, the handful of biblical passages that seem to imply we have no free will must be interpreted figuratively. Though we're certainly inclined toward evil, we're also able to resist it. We can and must retain some capacity for good, in cooperation with God's grace, however small. "It would be ridiculous to command one to make a choice, if he were incapable of turning in either direction."[32] Luther's view, Erasmus argues, exaggerates the effects of original sin on human capacities in insisting that our faculties are not simply weakened but obliterated. And his strident rhetoric undermines Christian solidarity: "The whole world is now shaken by the thunder and lightning born of the collision of such exaggerations."[33]

Luther vehemently disagrees. He gives Erasmus high marks for his excellent Latin and commends him for having "attacked the real thing, that is, the essential issue" by zeroing in on free will, which is more important than papal authority, purgatory, or indulgences.[34] Yet in Luther's view, Erasmus is dead wrong in what he says and how he says it, because acknowledging human beings' impotent sinfulness before God is a necessary precondition for God's grace and his gift of faith.

An assertion of *any* human contribution to your own salvation—which in this context is what free will means—undermines the whole process. It leaves arrogantly self-righteous human beings trying to save themselves through their own efforts. And Erasmus only makes it worse by affecting a tone of measured moderation and skeptical distance about the cornerstone prerequisite for eternal salvation. Luther proclaims his "disgust, disinclination, and distaste" for Erasmus's views and stance, mocking him with scolding sarcasm and incredulous insults: "You command fine, elegant analogies and epigrams; but the way you apply them when you treat of holy things is childish—indeed, perverse."[35]

Luther denigrates at length every one of Erasmus's main points. Scripture is clear about important matters, including free will. Those who don't see this lack the Spirit and are blinded by Satan. According to Luther, God's commandments don't imply that we have any ability to follow them; they're intended to break us down with the painfully humiliating awareness that we are incapable of doing so. Because as long as we think we "can make even the smallest contribution" to our salvation, we resist admitting our total dependence on God. Without God's grace, even our seemingly good actions are sinful and vainly self-regarding, a point Luther also made in his *Treatise on Good Works* in 1520. There is no free will *at all* in religious matters. We are moved either by God or by the devil: "So man's will is like a beast standing between two riders. If God rides, it wills and goes where God wills.... If Satan rides, it wills and goes where Satan wills. Nor may it choose to which rider it will run, or which it will seek; but the riders themselves fight to decide who shall have and hold it." [36]

Appallingly, in Luther's view, Erasmus cares more about avoiding disturbances than proclaiming the gospel. Of course the Word of God provokes opposition and resistance! Disruptions inevitably ensue, because "the world is the kingdom of Satan" and so "the Word of God and traditions of men fight each other in implacable opposition."[37] The devil hates the gospel and opposes it, unleashing the Antichrist as his agent of destruction. All the uproar and unrest of the early 1520s, including the Peasants' War, are signs that Luther is indeed boldly daring to proclaim the gospel, and the greater the resistance, the more obvious is this the case.

The dispute between Erasmus and Luther, like the contentions of the 1520s in general, reveal implacable differences over interpreting the Word of God *within* the Reformation as well as *between* its various proponents and defenders of the Roman Church. Erasmus is hardly a neophyte when it comes to the Bible. He's spent years steeped in scripture and is no less devoted to it than Luther or any other evangelical: "I know for certain that I am not resisting the truth," he writes, "that I love from the bottom of my heart true evangelical liberty, and that I detest everything adverse to the Gospels."[38]

In the 1520s, all who care about Christian truth and the reform of Christendom agree with this, loving Christian freedom and detesting everything at odds with the Gospels. But they disagree with each other about what evangelical liberty and the Gospels *mean*. Harsh polemics drown calls for moderation, with some protagonists, like Luther, justifying their ruthless rhetoric because so much is at stake. And doesn't their severity make sense if eternal salvation and damnation really depend on getting things right?

The dispute between Erasmus and Luther signals the end of Christian humanism as a reforming initiative aiming to renew Christendom as a whole. As the sixteenth century unfolds, Protestant and Catholic humanists will marshal their knowledge of languages and scholarship *against* each other in the service of rival theological commitments. Like Catholics and magisterial Protestants more generally, Erasmus and Luther believe in original sin but remain deeply divided about the extent and the range of its effects. Ultimately, this divide implies very different views about human nature. On one side are those convinced that only if utterly sinful human beings acknowledge their inability to contribute to their salvation can they be saved by God's grace. On the other side are those who agree that human beings cannot be saved without God but that we retain some goodness and capacity to freely cooperate with God's grace as a necessary precondition for our salvation. Different views of human nature go together with different views of God and of how God interacts with human beings. And through all the rancor eternal salvation is hanging in the balance.

Broken over the Bread:
The Eucharistic Controversy

Early evangelicals embrace Luther's condemnation of the traditional Latin mass, which has been the center of Christian worship for centuries. In their view, the mass is not a sacrifice, celebrated by the clergy, that ritually reenacts Christ's passion and crucifixion. Everywhere the Reformation is established, the mass is abolished.

Scripture clearly attests that Christ ate a final meal with his disciples just before his death and told them to "do this in remembrance of me" (Luke 22:19). The Gospels recount the story: "Take, eat; this is my body," he said after he blessed and broke bread with them. Then he did likewise with a cup of wine (which is why Protestants insist that the laity too should receive wine as well as bread at communion). But what did his words and actions mean? What are sixteenth-century Christians doing—and what is God doing—when they follow Christ's commandment to eat in remembrance of him?

So the Eucharist too becomes yet another socially and politically divisive issue emerging from rival interpretations of scripture.[39] Though the schism begins in the 1520s, it persists in various forms throughout the Reformation period and long after. Just as baptism divides all Anabaptist groups from the magisterial reformers, so too does the Lord's Supper—the other sacrament retained in some way by nearly all Protestants—set magisterial reformers at odds among themselves.

For most evangelicals, often collectively called "sacramentarians," the Lord's Supper, which replaces the mass, no longer involves Christ's material, miraculous presence. The notion of Christ's physical presence, in their view, is an unbiblical superstition, like belief in the power of saints' relics, and the papist clergy uses and abuses it in the same way: to assert privilege and control over laypeople. It conflates and confuses the material with the spiritual. After his resurrection, Christ ascended into heaven and, in the words of the Christian creed, "is now seated at the right hand" of God the Father. How then could he be repeatedly, simultaneously present in small pieces of bread in thousands of churches? "This is my body" means "this *signifies* my body." Christ surely didn't mean he really was bread when he celebrated the Last Supper with his disciples any more than he meant he really was a vine when he told them, "I am the vine" (John 15:5). Though not physically present in the Eucharistic bread, Christ is present spiritually in communion if you have faith (but not if you don't). The Lord's Supper is a memorial meal that recalls Christ's sacrifice and your salvation by faith alone.

This is Zwingli's position. Some evangelicals share it; others, including Karlstadt and all Anabaptist groups, deny Christ's corporeal presence in the Eucharist but in ways that differ from Zwingli's beliefs. Regardless of how it is specifically understood, in their view the Lord's Supper has nothing to do with Christ's material presence. It merely commemorates Christ's sacrifice, spiritually strengthening individual Christians who have faith and share bonds of Christian community with one another.

Against these sacramentarians stand Luther and his allies. For Luther, to deny Christ's corporeal presence in the Eucharist is to deny what the Lord's Supper *is* and what God *does* in it: nothing less than miraculously offer Christ to Christians, really and fully, for their consolation and communion with him. Rome is wrong about transubstantiation (who could fathom *how* God does it?) and about the mass as a sacrifice, but it is correct on this critical point against the "fanatics," as Luther repeatedly calls them. Such fanatical sacramentarians empty the sacrament of the savior, leaving them with nothing but a "spiritual" presence that actually remains just bread. And as with so much else that he opposes, including the papacy and the rebellious peasants, Luther rails against them as inspired by the devil.

Numerous pamphlets about the Lord's Supper appear in the early 1520s, but the real beginning of the public controversy comes in late 1524 when Karlstadt, writing from the town of Jena, publishes two treatises on the subject in German. Luther responds in his treatise *Against the "Heavenly" Prophets*. In the spring of 1525, Zwingli joins the fray, and others soon jump in, back and forth, on the Lutheran and sacramentarian sides, in both German and Latin. Sometimes with great sophistication, evangelical leaders use philological and philosophical and rhetorical arguments, dissecting and comparing relevant scriptural passages and literary devices and biblical metaphors. They defend and attack, cajole and accuse, but neither side succeeds in persuading the other. The sacrament that symbolizes Christian unity has become and will remain a source of division among evangelicals.

From Strasbourg, Martin Bucer, the former Dominican priest turned evangelical leader, whom Luther first inspired back in 1518 at the Heidelberg Disputation, tries his best to make peace between the two sides. But his efforts achieve little. For the parties involved, the Lord's Supper obviously is a matter of primary importance. In Luther's view, Zwingli's stance on the Eucharist renders him "un-Christian," discrediting everything else about him and making him "seven times worse than when he was a papist."[40]

Others draw conclusions that set them apart from Lutherans and Zwinglians as well as at odds with Anabaptists. The lay nobleman Caspar Schwenckfeld begins as a follower of Luther and helps to establish the Reformation in Liegnitz, Silesia, east of Saxony. But the Eucharistic controversy leads him to his own sacramentarian understanding of the Lord's Supper. He believes Christians should refrain from receiving the Eucharist until a visible moral improvement in their lives makes them worthy of the sacrament. Schwenckfeld stops receiving the Eucharistic bread in early 1526 and, as it turns out, never receives it again before his death in 1561. Schwenckfeld and others, collectively known as "spiritualists," simply take an either-or distinction between matter and spirit and the interior nature of faith to their logical extremes. In various ways, they emerge from the evangelical movement of the 1520s as yet another expression that shows the diversity of the early Reformation.[41]

The Eucharistic disagreements between Lutheran and sacramentarian reformers are intellectually complex, involving difficult philological questions about the interpretation of scripture and vexing philosophical issues about God's relationship to the world. But they're far from abstract or divorced from the rest of life because this controversy, like religion in general, is not separate from social relationships or politics. Lutheran and Zwinglian churches are established in socially exclusive ways. You belong to one or the other because Christian worship is the collective public expression of shared beliefs. Worship is a shared religious ritual meant to inform and bind together the members of a community. And you don't pretend you agree with others about something so important, even if it means sacrificing real-world political advantage at the highest levels.

The height of the Eucharistic controversy comes at a bad time for evangelicals. In the later 1520s, they're religiously and socially divided at a moment that requires unity. Since the Diet of Worms in 1521, Charles V has been engaged in war against the king of France on the Italian peninsula, concerned about Turkish invasions to the east, and attentive to Spain and its expanding overseas colonies. But as the decade turns, he summons a diet to meet in Augsburg, the empire's wealthiest city. Charles is exasperated with the repeated excuses for disobeying the Edict of Worms, and he means to put an end to the Reformation in the heartland of Europe.

Though the Reformation has spread like wildfire in the 1520s, it has not burned clean through the Holy Roman Empire. The fundamental religious rift remains between those opposed and those loyal to Rome. A majority of political representatives that convene at the Diet of Speyer in 1529 vote to undo the changes in religion and enforce the Edict of Worms. A minority of five evangelical princes and fourteen cities protest this vote—the origin of the term *Protestants*. Talks ensue about forming a defensive alliance against Charles V, an association that will be stronger if evangelicals embroiled in the Eucharistic controversy can set aside their differences and unite to stand against the Catholic emperor. To this end, Philip of Hesse, a ruling prince who started dismantling the old religion in his central German territory in 1524, invites Zwingli, Luther, and their respective allies to meet in Marburg in the fall of 1529. Because of their shared desire for reconciliation, Philip of Hesse also invites Bucer and some of his Strasbourg colleagues to Marburg.

Between October 1 and October 3, these groups meet during the Marburg Colloquy. This is the only time Zwingli and Luther meet in person. They agree on fourteen of fifteen propositions Luther has drawn up for discussion. But on the question of the Lord's Supper, neither reformer yields. In person no less than in print, they preserve the schism over the sacrament of communion. Despite his admiration for Luther, Zwingli thinks him hopelessly stubborn, while Luther refuses even to shake Zwingli's hand at the end of the proceedings, a rebuff that reduces Zwingli to tears. Because these emerging Protestant groups cannot find accord, they are unable to present a unified front against Charles V.

When Charles V arrives in splendor and presides over the Diet of Augsburg in the summer of 1530, the Lutherans present their statement of faith—the "Augsburg Confession," which becomes a cornerstone document of Lutheran doctrine. An alliance of four southwest German cities led by Strasbourg presents a separate statement of faith. But, despite the influence of the Zwinglian reformers outside the Swiss Confederation in the empire, Charles V refuses to grant a hearing to the Zwinglian cities of Zürich, Basel, and Berne. Catholic theologians write and present formal condemnations of Luther's and Strasbourg's statements of faith, and Charles V demands that both groups comply with the Edict of Worms. In response, at the very end of 1530 and early in the new year, multiple Protestant cities and princes from both groups organize the Schmalkaldic League, which proves crucial to the spread and strengthening of the Reformation in the Holy Roman Empire during the 1530s, but the Reformed Protestant cities do not take part in it.

There will be no unified Protestant political front against the emperor, just as there will not be—and never was—any unified evangelical front against Rome. *Sola scriptura* attracts those who believe it opens long-blocked doors to salvation and gives them a basis for rejecting the Roman Church not just as sinful or corrupt but as gravely mistaken in its teachings. To the exasperation of evangelicals, however, their shared commitment to scripture's sovereign authority is also the basis for their divisions doctrinally, socially, and politically. This includes the standoff between Reformed Protestants and Lutherans, both of whom work with rather than against political authorities, especially in the wake of the Peasants' War. By 1531, when Zwingli is killed in battle fighting alongside fellow citizens against Catholic forces in the Swiss Confederation, Reformed Protestantism and Lutheranism have essentially become two distinct traditions.

Münster: An Apocalyptic Anabaptist Kingdom

From about 1530, the evangelical preacher Bernhard Rothmann denounces Catholic practices and exalts the Word of God in Münster, a city of around nine thousand people in Westphalia,

a region in western Germany.⁴² He wins adherents among some
citizens. In the spring of 1532, over the objections of the Bishop
of Münster and most of the city's clergy, the Münster city council installs Rothmann in St. Lambert's, the primary parish church.
The next year, under the protective umbrella of the Schmalkaldic
League, a more solidly Lutheran city council approves the abolition
of the mass and the removal of side altars from churches, the reduction of religious images, and an end to other Catholic practices.
Hardly a card-carrying Lutheran, Rothmann favors sacramentarian views of the Lord's Supper, which creates tension with members of the city council. What's more, in 1533 Rothmann rejects
infant baptism in favor of adult baptism, breaking imperial law.
The volatile situation becomes more difficult when some Dutch
Anabaptists, inspired by an apocalyptic preacher from Strasbourg
named Melchior Hoffman, arrive in Münster in January 1534 and
begin to baptize large numbers of citizens. Outraged, the bishop
orders their arrest, but the city council ignores him.

Rothmann's preaching further reinforces the baptizers' conviction that the end times are just around the corner and that Münster
has a key role to play in the apocalypse by reinstituting baptism as
Christ's apostles practiced it. In early February strange phenomena
in the sky appear and are interpreted as God's providential confirmation that the end of the world is near: multiple suns, a man with
bloodied hands, and a sword-wielding rider on a white horse. When
the city council decides to tolerate the adult baptisms, the bishop prepares to besiege the city with an army, which causes Lutherans and
Catholics to evacuate. As word spreads of happenings in Münster,
hundreds of Anabaptist immigrants begin pouring into the city, in
effect shifting the makeup of the city's population. In late February,
the newly elected city council approves Münster as an Anabaptist
city—echoes of Hubmaier's short-lived success in Waldshut outside
Zürich in 1525 but on a much larger scale.

Among the town's new arrivals is a charismatic Anabaptist leader named Jan Matthijs, a baker from Haarlem in Holland. He proclaims Münster the New Jerusalem and warns that God's apocalyptic wrath will descend on the world at Easter in 1534. According to Matthijs, only the baptized will be spared. The city is becoming more thoroughly Anabaptist, its residents inspired by Matthijs and bound together by a common apocalyptic hope. The bishop's siege further strengthens their shared sense of purpose as they organize militarily and prepare to defend their city.

In early March, Matthijs proclaims an end to traditional ranks and roles, and the city council abolishes private property, another version of scripture in action, similar to that affirmed by the Hutterites in Moravia, who also hold possessions in common. Inspired by Christ's earliest followers as recounted in the Acts of the Apostles, brothers and sisters in faith are to share all things as they wait for the end of the world. But instead of the apocalypse, Easter Sunday—April 5, 1534—brings only the death of Jan Matthijs, who is killed when he rides outside the walls of the besieged city.

After his death, another charismatic leader takes over: Jan Beukels from Leiden, or "Jan van Leiden," a tailor turned prophet. He dissolves the city council and in its place appoints twelve elders, echoing the twelve tribes of Israel from the Old Testament and Christ's twelve apostles. Following Matthijs's lead, Beukels revises the apocalyptic expectations energizing the city. But unlike Matthijs, Beukels, who is also known as King Jan, wants to establish the true order of salvation, which he prepares his followers to spread outside of Münster when the time is right. They mint silver coins with brief biblical quotations: "The Word has become flesh, and dwells among us—1534," and "Unless a person is born again, he cannot see the Kingdom of God."[43]

As Beukels prepares to expand the kingdom, the Münster Anabaptists successfully repel two attempts by the besieging army to take their New Israel, once in May and again in August. The mercenary force now circling the city includes the bishop's soldiers and soldiers fighting for Philip of Hesse—a Catholic and Lutheran cooperation against a common foe that bespeaks their outrage at what is going on in Münster. Their horror only increases when Beukels institutes polygamy, a practice with biblical precedent among Old Testament patriarchs. In accord with scripture's teaching about the marital subordination of wives to husbands, this move endeavors to bring the much more numerous adult women in the city (around 5,500) under the control of the men (only around 2,000). It also seeks to provide for crucial procreation in the new order, which suggests that the apocalypse Beukels promises is not imminent. His embrace of polygamy provokes opposition, as forty-seven conspirators try to overthrow the regime from within at the end of July 1534. Beukels orders their execution.

Though Beukels's power is considerable, it is locally circumscribed and short-lived. Besieging forces tighten their hold on the city, which limits the spread of the Anabaptist Kingdom beyond its own walls. From late 1534 on, the apocalyptic tone of Rothmann's writings shifts. The end is near, but he now focuses on sacrifice and suffering rather than triumph. In the early months of 1535, food shortages become more acute. A deserter helps soldiers breach the city's defenses on July 25, and after considerable bloodshed the reign of King Jan is over and with it the Anabaptist Kingdom. Beukels and other leaders are imprisoned, interrogated, and tortured. In January 1536, they're executed in front of the city hall. The mutilated corpses of the disgraced leaders are suspended in iron cages from the tower of the St. Lambert Church. The cages, which are left in place as a reminder of the authority of civic political order over religious radicalism, remain today.

The Anabaptist Kingdom of Münster is as much a biblically inspired city as Zwingli's Zürich or Luther's Wittenberg. It's just differently inspired because its leaders understand God's Word and follow the Holy Spirit differently. What the early Reformation shows so clearly is that scripture and the Spirit can be interpreted and applied in radically divergent ways. Once the papacy and the Catholic Church are thrown off, there are no shared authorities to adjudicate disagreements. And as the Peasants' War and the Kingdom of Münster make clear, some ways of understanding God's Word are themselves socially and politically radical.

What happens in Münster in 1534–1535 shocks political and ecclesiastical authorities throughout Europe. If any further confirmation is needed after the Peasants' War about the potential dangers contained in scripture, Münster provides overwhelming evidence. For their part, Lutheran and Reformed Protestant leaders condemn what happened and try to distance themselves from Münster. Catholic propagandists, by contrast, interpreted the Anabaptist kingdom, like the Peasants' War, as the logical extension of the Reformation's attack on the established Church. Those who condemn the Church are bound to condemn authority, whoever exercises it.

Brave—and Troubled—New World

The early Reformation in the Holy Roman Empire and Swiss Confederation is a story of unintended consequences, and as we shall see in the following two chapters, those consequences not only changed their world but also still affect ours. At Worms in 1521 Luther deliberately defied the command to reject heresy as Rome defined it. Instead he rejected the papacy, clinging to Christ and the gospel for dear life—and for eternal life. The ensuing rift endures to this day, and the subsequent divergences and conflicts between Protestants and Roman Catholics deepened in the 1520s, with consequences that would remain for hundreds of years to come. But the divide between Protestantism and Catholicism is only part of the story.

The early evangelical movement was a dynamic, diverse, and creative outpouring of Christian commitment in the cities and villages of central Europe. It turned out that the Word of God, liberated from the prescriptions of the Roman Church, could be understood in many different ways. Different assertions and priorities followed—about the Church, political authorities, worship, the sacraments, and more—depending on how you understood scripture and the Spirit or whose interpretation of them you decided to follow.

Before 1526, hundreds of thousands of Christians acted on the view that gospel freedom means correcting social injustices or even drastically leveling a hierarchical society. After the Peasants' War, German princes in Saxony, Hesse, and other territories continued building Lutheran communities through new practices and institutions. Following Zürich's example, Swiss magistrates in cities such as Basel and Berne simultaneously constructed Zwinglian communities. At the same time, Swiss Anabaptists formed distinct communities of their own, as did Anabaptists from southern Germany and Austria, some of them leaving these regions and journeying east to join the Hutterites in Moravia. Other creative evangelicals, such as Schwenckfeld, attracted spiritualist followers, including a disproportionate number of women.[44] Inspired by God's Word and the power of the Holy Spirit, these different Protestant groups formed communities based on their competing interpretations of scripture.

But conflict wasn't the goal, even if many contemporaries regarded the chaos as a sign of God's imminent Last Judgment. Luther saw things this way, though it certainly wasn't what he wanted. Throughout the decade, Luther consistently denounced his opponents, whether Karlstadt, Zwingli, Müntzer, or others, as possessed by the devil, just like the papacy. No one else who rejected Rome wanted the conflicts and divisions to happen either. They wanted to reform the Church and make society more Christian, not get mired in all sorts of conflicting claims among antagonistic groups. Yet this is exactly what happened, the unintended outcome of all their experiences, convictions, decisions, and actions. Instead of reforming one Church, they inadvertently created mutually exclusive churches in the first decade of the Reformation.

Today, many people celebrate religious diversity or at least "agree to disagree." But virtually no one held this view in the early sixteenth century—and for good reason, because their hope of eternal life depended on the fit of their faith, and all that implied, with God's truth. That's why, starting in 1523, evangelicals, the large majority of them vulnerable Anabaptists, began undergoing martyrdom rather than renounce their faith and its real-world practices.

Many who thought Luther was right about Rome denied he was also right about the gospel. After all, he too was just a man. Different churches reflected different readings of scripture, different experiences of God, and different openness to the Spirit. Rival evangelical claims arose immediately—so obvious, so maddening, and so unwelcome from the very start of the Reformation. What seemed in the heady exhilaration of 1520 a cure for Christianity's problems unintentionally created a new one: How could you now discern what true Christianity was?

In Luther's estimation, "scripture alone" was the solution, but in reality it only created another problem. Though it liberated evangelicals from the Roman Church, it also plunged them into the beginning of an unwanted Protestant pluralism. What lay behind these church-dividing disagreements was the very thing that had launched the Reformation in the first place: Luther's insistence on scripture as the singular authority for Christian faith and life.

If religion had been just religion, these fissures might not have mattered too much. But in the sixteenth century religion was never just religion, so the ruptures and rifts made worlds of difference. Religion wasn't separate from the exercise of power or one's duties to others or the buying and selling of goods; it wasn't separate from education or morality. It touched everything, which meant disagreements about it threatened to disrupt everything. Frictions between evangelicals and those who resisted them in defense of the old religion were bad enough. But expressions of the Reformation such as the Peasants' War and the Anabaptist Kingdom of Münster showed—to their outraged critics—some of the disturbing directions the gospel might be taken.

Understanding their duty, political authorities who adopted the Reformation kept order by deciding which form of Protestantism could take root within their borders. To protect their sovereignty, they policed and suppressed dissent, whether from recalcitrant Catholics or disobedient evangelicals; they decided which freedom of which Christians was acceptable. Princes and magistrates who sided with the Reformation created the distinction between Protestants who were politically protected and those who were persecuted, or magisterial and radical Protestants, respectively. Such protection gave Lutherans and Reformed Protestants an enormous advantage in promulgating their versions of the gospel.

By the early 1530s, both the Holy Roman Empire and the Swiss Confederation were divided between Protestants and Catholics as well as among different groups of Protestants. The consequences of these divisions are essential to understanding the Reformation and why it still matters today. But they wouldn't have mattered nearly as much if the Reformation had remained just a "German problem," as some other rulers in Europe initially called it.

Just as the Reformation began with Luther but sparked a powerful movement in the Holy Roman Empire and Swiss Confederation, the movement spread throughout Europe, defining an era and fundamentally changing the course of Western history. In different ways, the Reformation inspired both followers and opponents, forcing decisions and prompting new initiatives by political rulers and intellectuals, well-to-do merchants and urban artisans, members of the nobility and ordinary folk throughout Europe.

In the Reformation era, from 1520 until 1650, Lutheran and Reformed Protestantism shaped millions of lives alongside and in competition with a revivified Roman Catholicism. Disagreements about doctrine that arose in the 1520s did not disappear but rather grew both more diversified and more entrenched. The conflicts of the early Reformation turned out to presage more of the same, only on a much bigger scale and with many more casualties.

CHAPTER 3

A TROUBLED ERA

I N THE EARLY 1520S, as the Reformation proliferated in the Holy Roman Empire and Swiss Confederation, sympathetic clergy and humanists, merchants and travelers spread the movement much more widely. Publications in German and Latin were translated into Dutch, French, and English. Luther's ideas started to make institutional headway with rulers in Sweden and Denmark, and small circles of evangelicals began forming outside German-speaking lands. When the Reformation spread and solidified throughout Europe, it became not simply a German phenomenon but the defining development of an entire historical era.

In every territory and kingdom in Europe, political authorities had to decide for or against the Reformation—including in overwhelmingly Catholic regions such as Spain, where the Reformation was harshly, and violently, suppressed. Differing decisions about the Reformation led to political divisions, reflected disagreements, and contributed to conflicts whose consequences still influence us today. A full understanding of the Reformation and its long-term impact requires understanding the Reformation *era*—the different Protestant traditions that form as well as the relationships *between* Protestants and Catholics and *among* Protestants themselves.

Beginning in the 1530s, city magistrates in Geneva work with the refugee reformer John Calvin to make their French-speaking Swiss city a stronghold for his version of Reformed Protestantism. Their decision has a major impact on France, England, Scotland, and the Low Countries, as well as on parts of Germany and other regions of central Europe. Outside of Lutheranism and Reformed Protestantism, other expressions of the Reformation—those of the different Anabaptist groups, spiritualists, and other radical Protestants—are usually outlawed, depending on time and place. Mostly these Christians want just to be left alone, at least before the 1640s in England.

At the same time, Catholic rulers such as Charles V who decide to *oppose* the Reformation help foster a reenergizing of Catholicism in the sixteenth century, a phenomenon usually referred to as the Catholic Reformation or Counter-Reformation. Reform efforts that were under way in Christendom before 1517 are extended and expanded, while new ones are also taken up. The Council of Trent, a major meeting of Catholic Church leaders, convenes three times between 1545 and 1563. The Reformation era is thus marked as much by the renewal of Roman Catholicism as by the creation of magisterial and radical Protestant traditions.

Despite their competition and mutual hostility, magisterial Protestants and Catholics undertake some initiatives in parallel with each other from the early sixteenth into the eighteenth centuries. Political authorities and clergy, whether Lutheran, Reformed Protestant, or Catholic, all seek to channel their constructive, creative religious commitment into action. Well-trained clergy preach sermons and teach catechisms, reconcile feuds and encourage devotion, console the grieving and comfort the dying, praise piety and excoriate sin. They're all trying to create well-informed communities of dedicated and law-abiding laity.

The process is not smooth or uniform, and it doesn't succeed nearly as well as many political leaders and clergy would like. Yet the net result in the early modern period is that European countries forge the dominant, state-supported religious identities of their subjects and carry them into the modern world: Lutheranism in Denmark, Sweden, and much of Germany; Reformed Protestantism in Scotland, England (in some respects), the Netherlands, and parts of Germany and Switzerland; and Catholicism in Spain, Portugal, Italy, France, Austria, Bohemia, Poland, Ireland, Belgium, and the remaining parts of Germany and Switzerland.

Not all the laity appreciate these efforts. Some reluctantly comply but resent conscientious clergy as obnoxious and intrusive. Other laypeople drag their feet, doing as little as they can get away with, ignoring sermons or resisting catechetical efforts. Still others dissent and pursue radical Protestant alternatives, a by-product of the sometimes heavy-handed methods clergy use to try to control lay behavior. This resentment will have repercussions, eventually inspiring in alienated men and women desires for a liberation very different from that advocated by Luther or other early evangelicals.

At the same time, these parallel efforts to create communities of well-informed Christians coexist with disagreements about God's truth and ongoing hostilities between rival Christian regimes. The Reformation transforms the religion at the heart of medieval Christendom into a divisive problem.

Beginning with Luther's initial criticisms of Catholic teaching, controversies over Christian doctrine soon rip apart the early evangelical movement. As the sixteenth century unfolds, these controversies continue and become institutionalized. Doctrinal conflict turns into a permanent feature of the period. The leading protagonists of these disputes are mostly university-trained theologians. But their views are also expressed in polemical propaganda—pamphlets, sermons, songs—that denounce either papists or heretics, depending on the author's position. By the 1650s, theological experts have come no closer to reconciling their disagreements than they were in the 1520s, despite their sometimes formidable learning. (Or rather partly because of their learning.) Neither have lay Catholics and Protestants—though in many parts of Europe, they're grudgingly forging ways of coexisting day to day.

Not wanting to give ground is understandable: disagreements about doctrine are deepened by the so-called Wars of Religion, which are really wars of *more*-than-religion, because religion encompasses so much more than religion as we usually think of it. These religiopolitical conflicts bring death, disease, and dislocation. They create religious refugees; they cause suffering and bitterness.

The Reformation era, then, is both constructive and destructive. Distinct, socially exclusive churches, religious traditions, and Christian identities—among Lutherans, Reformed Protestants, radical Protestants, and Catholics—are created and continue into the modern era. Those confessional identities are protected and promoted by political regimes whose conflicts play out most destructively when rulers decide for or against the Reformation in the Holy Roman Empire, France, England, and the Low Countries.

Lutheranism Beyond Luther

Most rulers in Latin Christendom do not accept Martin Luther's ideas about the gospel. Those who do, however, decide on Lutheranism as the public form of Protestantism in much of central Europe and all of Scandinavia. In doing so, they make possible a new form of Christianity. Lutheranism brings into being a different institutional relationship between church and state and a new way of being Christian understood as divinely willed expressions of lay life. After Luther's death in 1546, Lutheranism itself will undergo its own self-inflicted, more-than-religious divisions.

The city magistrates and territorial princes who adopt Luther's ideas ensure the success of his version of the Reformation. In the wake of the Peasants' War and the Anabaptist Kingdom of Münster, they are well aware that the gospel requires political oversight and surveillance lest rebellious radicalism rear its head again. Receiving protection from the Schmalkaldic League permits additional free imperial cities to opt for Lutheranism in the 1530s. In principle and in many respects in practice, this political patronage is a good thing for the new Lutheran churches. Political protection for Lutheranism takes shape in the Holy Roman Empire as well as in the kingdoms of Denmark (which includes modern-day Norway) and Sweden (which includes Finland), whose rulers also embrace the Reformation in stages in the 1520s and 1530s.[1] Political protection provides the stability necessary for Lutheran Protestantism to grow and survive. Lutheran churches, schools, and universities will in turn strengthen the hand of the political regimes that feed them.

But as time wears on, Lutheran territorial princes—who become the main political bulwark of Lutheranism against Emperor Charles V and his successors in the Holy Roman Empire—start to limit the independence of the free imperial cities, taking full advantage of the semi-autonomous political self-determination afforded by the empire's patchwork arrangement of territories and cities.[2]

As in medieval Christendom, Luther envisions political and ecclesiastical authorities cooperating rather than competing with each other.[3] But he wants them to do a much better job than their medieval forebears. In parallel with Luther's distinction between the "outer" and "inner" human being, political and ecclesiastical authorities are supposed to tend to their respective responsibilities, which are divided between external affairs and the inner domain of faith. This is intended to eliminate the conflicts that arose repeatedly in the Middle Ages between political authorities and the Church. In the new arrangement, political authorities will exercise all public power and political sovereignty while the Church will exercise none.

Ideally, rulers will keep public order and maintain peace. They will support the revamped churches, where God is worshipped rightly and where clergy teach the restored gospel to households of well-informed, law-abiding subjects. These subjects in turn will listen to their pastors and support political authorities, who, as Luther emphatically insists, echoing the apostle Paul, have been "instituted by God" and are "not a terror to good conduct, but to bad" (Romans 13:1–3). Good government and good Christians go hand in hand.

Beginning in the 1520s, Christianity in Lutheran lands looks very different from what prevailed before the Reformation. The religious orders central to Christendom before the Reformation are gone, their vast properties seized by princes or magistrates.[4] Gone too are the abundant lay confraternities, processions and pilgrimages, shrines and chapels. Public religious life now focuses resolutely on the local parish community. The saying of endowed masses ends. Side altars, which once ringed church interiors, are removed, and pulpits—for publicly proclaiming God's Word to an assembled congregation—assume a new prominence. Though not eliminated, religious images in churches become much less profuse, supplemented by biblical verses prominently painted on church walls.[5] Saints are no longer invoked as intercessors, or at least are not supposed to be. There are many fewer clergy and many fewer church feast days to celebrate. Religious life is simplified and streamlined, with less of it left to individual choice than in the late Middle Ages. Wherever the Reformation is established, the range of permissible religious options contracts in people's day-to-day lives.

In the first years of the Reformation, nearly all Lutheran clergy are either members of Catholic religious orders or parish priests. In subsequent generations, Lutheran clergy train to become pastors by studying scripture and theology at Lutheran universities; Wittenberg will remain preeminent among these institutions into the seventeenth century. Like Luther, pastors marry and become husbands and fathers and heads of households, just like other laymen. It is a dramatic social expression of Luther's "priesthood of all believers," a visible statement that the clergy are not spiritually superior to the laity. All occupations are equally holy, valuable, and legitimate in God's eyes. Lutheranism validates ordinary work in the world, sanctifying lay life in robust ways. Although Lutheran clergy are not set apart by ascetic commitments, they begin to constitute something of a multigenerational caste: pastors' sons often follow their fathers into the clergy, and pastors' daughters often marry husbands who become clergymen.

Lutheran laity also differ from their medieval forebears, their less varied religious lives more directly connected to the Bible. They're generally more literate, the result of education which occupies a newly important niche in Christian life. As humanists had already stressed before the Reformation, education is the gateway to grasping basic Christian teachings, a view taken up in Lutheranism and put to constructive use. In Sweden, where political authorities oversee an especially close relationship between the church and schooling, literacy rates by the late seventeenth century are the highest anywhere in Europe.[6]

Households too are newly charged with religious significance: they are where fathers and mothers live out their divinely ordained vocations. Parents raise sons and daughters in markedly patriarchal families with sharply demarcated gender norms. A strong emphasis on the fourth commandment in the Old Testament ("Honor your father and your mother") reinforces lines of deference and obedience so that children in relation to parents and wives in relation to husbands mirror the proper relationship between subjects and political rulers. A thriving literature for married lay householders prescribes strongly gendered duties of husbands and wives, fathers and mothers.

Lutheran clergy and laity are bound together by worship and instruction, preaching and pastoral advice, scripture and singing. Sermons expounding scripture become much more central to worship, a regular centerpiece rather than a special bonus in the seasons of Lent or Advent. And worship takes place in the people's language. A vernacular liturgy (whether in German, Danish, or Swedish) becomes the norm starting in the 1520s, although Latin hymns continue to be valued in Lutheran worship, just as Latin remains the principal language of instruction in all advanced education.

Lutherans sing like the members of no other Christian tradition in the period. They collectively embrace Luther's own love of music and hymn writing. Of the nearly two thousand editions of German hymnals printed between 1520 and 1600, at least three-quarters are Lutheran. Most of them are small, compact editions intended for domestic use rather than public worship. Regular singing around the family table after meals or in the evening helps to form pious households.[7]

Another hallmark of Lutheran Protestantism is religious instruction, which takes place hand in hand with education. In order to know what faith is and to experience justification by faith through grace, Lutherans first have to know the law and gospel, as well as the story of humanity's original fall from grace and redemption through Christ.

Following inspections of parishes throughout the Saxon countryside in the late 1520s, when Luther, Melanchthon, and their colleagues discover what they consider lay superstition and ignorance instead of sound religious practices, Luther writes his *Small Catechism* and *Large Catechism,* intended for beginners and more advanced learners, respectively. These books become bestsellers: by 1600, the shorter work is published in over 150 editions and the longer in more than 50.[8] The *Small Catechism* also becomes a common textbook in schools. The basic goal of catechesis and education, as of preaching and singing, is to form educated lay Christians—children and teenagers, men and women who know what they believe and why as well as how to live in gratitude for the gift of salvation.

The goal, unsurprisingly, is not always achieved—whether because the clergy are overbearing or uninspiring, the laypeople are indifferent or lazy, or the means of instruction involve memorizing through repetition, repetition, and more repetition.[9] Neither does the hoped-for cooperation between the distinct spheres of rulers and clergy always work out in practice: the clergy, who depend on the princes for political support, are also their subjects, required to submit to their political control.

In Lutheran territories as elsewhere, what is idealized as a *partnership* between church and state plays out as a *subordination* of church to state. However free the "inner man" might be in conscience and faith, the embodied person is subject to political control. And in society, rulers not clergy call the shots. In a different form of lay triumph, the state exercises power over the church.

Nor does everything work out smoothly in terms of Lutheran doctrine. After Luther's death in 1546 and the defeat of the Schmalkaldic League by Charles V's armies in 1547, German Lutheranism is torn apart by a series of theological disagreements with social and political consequences. As in the early Reformation of the 1520s, Protestants' commitment to scripture alone sets them against each other, this time within established Lutheran institutions. In the end, the central issue is the fundamental one of what scripture says and whose interpretation of it is correct.

A rift opens between Philippists, named after their leader, Philip Melanchthon (1497–1560), and the self-described Genuine Lutherans, led by Matthias Flacius Illyricus (1520–1575) and centered on the city of Magdeburg.[10] The Genuine Lutherans think Melanchthon and the Philippists are betraying Luther's views with mistaken interpretations of scripture on a whole range of doctrines concerning faith, grace, and works, among other issues. A practical consequence is that the Philippists are less adamantly opposed to Catholics and Reformed Protestants, which enrages the Genuine

Lutherans, who accuse the Philippists of selling out. This bitter dispute inspires hundreds of Lutheran-versus-Lutheran polemical treatises for the next thirty years, from the late 1540s to the 1570s, as well as social divisions between Lutheran congregations until the Formula of Concord in 1577. Ratified and published in 1580, the formula reconciles about three-fourths of these congregations along largely Genuine Lutheran lines while providing a doctrinal foundation for the future for most German Lutherans.

The years 1546 and 1547, with the death of Luther, the defeat of the Schmalkaldic League, and the beginning of decades of conflict between Philippists and Genuine Lutherans, prove to be watershed years for Lutheranism. By this point too, Lutheranism has been established in Denmark and Sweden. But nowhere else in Europe does it become the state-supported form of the Reformation. There are pockets of Lutherans in the Low Countries, Latvia, and Estonia, and larger numbers in Hungary. But after the late 1540s, rulers who reject Catholicism for the Reformation do not choose Lutheranism. Those who've already done so focus on consolidation within their own kingdoms or territories rather than on evangelizing outside of them.

Reformed Protestantism, however, the other politically supported expression of Protestantism in the era, develops differently. Beginning in the 1540s, Reformed Protestantism becomes the more influential and internationally significant of the two traditions and remains so throughout the period.

Calvin, Geneva, and
Reformed Protestantism

So great is John Calvin's influence on Reformed Protestantism that it is sometimes simply called "Calvinism." No reformer other than Luther makes such a major impact on the Protestant Reformation as a whole. With Calvin, the center of Reformed Protestantism shifts from German-speaking Zürich to French-speaking Geneva, which becomes the single most important Protestant city of the sixteenth century. Calvin's Geneva takes in thousands of refugees and trains hundreds of ministers. The city becomes a leading center for Protestant printing and new Protestant institutions. Visitors who admire its rigorous religious ethos take this ethos with them when they leave, seeking to transplant it in far-flung countries such as Scotland, France, the Low Countries, and Poland-Lithuania. In so doing, they help to create conditions for religiopolitical conflicts across a continent.

Calvin was born in 1509 in the small town of Noyon, not far from Paris in northern France.[11] In the 1520s he was a brilliant student in the French capital city, deeply influenced by humanism. Calvin's father wanted him to become a lawyer, and unlike Luther, he dutifully obeyed. Studying law at Orléans and Bourges influenced his theology, including his legalistic use of texts as evidence and his precision in his arguments. He regarded scripture as a divine last will and testament notarized by the Holy Spirit, and he appreciated God's law as a positive guide for public Christian life.

Sometime in late 1533 or early 1534, Calvin has a conversion experience. In late 1533 he leaves Paris, to which he had briefly returned, then flees the country altogether and becomes a religious refugee a year later, in late 1534. While Luther remains deeply rooted in Saxony, Calvin remains a refugee for the rest of his life, which also influences his theology, though his thoughts never stray far from concern for the land of his birth.

Not long after his conversion Calvin weds his humanistic learning, legal training, and knowledge of scripture into a synthetic statement of Reformed Protestant doctrine: *The Institutes of the Christian Religion,* published in early 1536 when Calvin is all of twenty-seven years old. Written in Latin, with a preface addressed to King Francis I of France, the *Institutes* embodies Calvin's single-minded concern for true doctrine and pure worship. Immediately it establishes his reputation as a lucid, rhetorically powerful theologian and will become the single most influential treatise of Protestant theology in the Reformation era. Like Luther, Calvin is a superhumanly productive writer of treatises, biblical commentaries, and correspondence throughout his career, but the *Institutes* is his masterwork. He continues to revise and expand it, in both French and Latin, until the final Latin version in 1559, which is four times longer than the original.

Soon after the *Institutes* is published in 1536, Calvin heads for Strasbourg, but military unrest forces him to detour to Geneva. There he meets Guillaume Farel, the zealous French evangelical leader. Farel urges Calvin to ignore ivory-tower scholarship and concentrate instead on the practical demands of reform. Geneva, Farel convinces Calvin, needs him in the trenches. Recently liberated from Rome's dominion, the city is still in thrall to the residue of Catholicism: idolatry, immorality, and liturgical ignorance. But in their attempts to institute sweeping changes in Geneva's church order, Calvin and Farel try to do too much too quickly. In 1537, they present the city council with a series of inflexible ecclesiastical ordinances. The council resists, and tensions escalate through the spring of 1538, when Calvin and Farel are exiled from Geneva.

The outcasts go to Strasbourg, where Calvin learns firsthand from Martin Bucer how to enact city reformation. Among the most important lessons Bucer teaches Calvin is how to deal with political authorities. During this second exile, in Strasbourg, the French-speaking Calvin ministers to French refugees in the German-speaking city. He gains invaluable practical experience as well as a keen sense of what the Reformation looks like across linguistic lines and political boundaries, which prove important when city council members in Geneva ironically call Calvin back to the city in 1541 following troubles with religious reform there.

Calvin's apprenticeship in Strasbourg pays off. The Genevan city council accepts his revised ecclesiastical ordinances, which become the basis for a working relationship between magistrates and ministers. Together, ecclesiastical and political authorities endeavor to make Geneva a concrete urban expression of the gospel as Calvin understands it, embodied in the city's institutions, worship, behavior, and ethos. Crucial to this enterprise are laws, institutions, and discipline, which provide a stable framework for the pure worship, right preaching, and godly living that mark Calvin's vision of a truly Christian city, an anti-Münster.

In Geneva and beyond, Calvin stipulates four ministries in the church, all of which are derived from his interpretation of Paul's writings in the New Testament. Responsible for preaching the Word of God and for instructing and admonishing lay Christians, *pastors* also administer baptism and the Lord's Supper. *Doctors* are learned teachers (*doctor* comes from the Latin *docere,* "to teach") responsible for preserving and imparting true doctrine to insure a supply of able pastors. *Elders* are laymen chosen by the magistrates, who work together with pastors to supervise the morals and behavior of everyone in the city in a new disciplinary institution called the consistory. This body meets weekly, punishing infractions for everything from falling asleep during sermons to participating in forbidden Catholic religious practices to drunkenness, swearing, dancing, and adultery. The final group of ministers are the *deacons.* Like the elders, deacons are laymen, and they are responsible for administering poor relief, a significant concern in a city where thousands of newcomers include many men and women who are struggling financially. The Genevan Academy, established in 1559, becomes important for training pastors, many of whom set off as missionaries and serve communities of Reformed Protestants in France and elsewhere in Europe.

Calvin fundamentally agrees with Luther that justification by faith alone is Christianity's cornerstone doctrine, but for each of them it functions rather differently. For Luther, justification by faith alone is your point of arrival: your soothing solace and comfort after interior torment and spiritual anxiety, like a storm-tossed ship finally arriving in safe harbor. It brings tranquility and a sense of relief. For Calvin, justification by faith alone is your point of departure: buoyed by grace and energized with gratitude, you load your cargo and ready your ship for a lifetime of courageous voyaging in God's service, whatever the weather. Justification by faith alone imparts zeal and a sense of duty. Overwhelmed by God's providence, you have to venture all for his sake, come what may, because nothing can repay God's gift of electing you for eternal salvation among the (real) saints. So no sacrifice can be too great for God's elect.

As a result, committed Calvinists are self-conscious Christian activists. Being grateful for God's unmerited gift of salvation requires an unceasing commitment to build his kingdom. As in Lutheranism, this obligation is fulfilled through family and work. But more than Lutherans, Reformed Protestants sanctify ordinary lay life by laboring to make it better. Reformed Protestants want to sanctify lay life so that it sanctifies them. Similarly, Reformed Protestants extend Lutheran expectations of political authorities. Political regimes exist not just to preserve the public peace, which allows the church to do its thing, but to create and sustain a godly public social and political order. To build a godly order, it may become necessary, as some Calvinists start to advocate in the 1550s, to disturb the peace and actively oppose Catholic rulers who are suppressing the gospel. Maintaining godly order depends on receiving political support for the purifying of worship, the same sort of support Zwingli received in Zürich in the 1520s. In Geneva too, the mass is condemned as a horrifying idolatry, and city authorities completely reject it along with the Catholic priesthood. The four hundred or so clergy in Geneva before the Reformation are summarily replaced by only ten Calvinist pastors.[12]

Wherever Calvinism spreads, iconoclasm accompanies it. Ridding cities and churches of religious images is godly and right. A proper church interior is bare and spare, not a riot of brightly colored sculptures and evocative paintings. God's Word must remain the focus of worship, proclaimed and preached in sermons. Reformed Protestant services include nothing like the Lutheran effusion of music; the only worship music Calvin approves for Geneva are the Psalms, which are translated into a metrical French.

Beyond replacing the Catholic parish clergy and religious orders with Calvinism's four new church ministries, the Reformation deeply affects the city of Geneva in other ways as well. Between 1530 and 1560, Geneva's population more than doubles, to some twenty-one thousand, mostly due to the immigration of religious refugees. Among them are printers, who help to make the city a thriving center of Reformed Protestant publishing, pouring out hundreds of editions of religious works from the city's presses starting in the 1540s.[13]

While refugees continue to find their way to Geneva, publications and missionaries continue to flow out. Despite its modest size, Geneva becomes important in the 1540s because of Calvinism's influence beyond its walls. In a very real sense, Calvin is less the reformer *of* Geneva than the reformer *out of* Geneva: from the city as a hub, spokes radiate outward, spreading Reformed Protestantism in all directions by every means possible.

In the British Isles, during the short reign of Edward VI (1547–1553), Reformed Protestantism exercises a decisive influence in England. Its impact continues in more complex ways during the long reign of Elizabeth I (1558–1603), most conspicuously through those English Calvinists better known as Puritans, who seek to complete the renewal of a church (as they see it) "but halfly reformed." In the seventeenth century, some Puritans will carry their faith, families, and future across the Atlantic to New England. Reformed

Protestantism comes forcefully to Scotland in the person of John Knox, who as a refugee in Geneva rhapsodizes about the city before returning to Scotland, where he leads a successful Reformation in 1559–1560 inspired by Geneva's example.

Reformed Protestantism makes deep inroads on the European continent as well. A shared language gives Geneva an added connection to Calvin's native France, where the number of Reformed Protestant communities of Huguenots (as French Calvinists are known) explodes during the late 1550s despite harsh suppression. In the Low Countries too, following a similar pattern with a few years' lag, the number of Calvinists grows by leaps and bounds. By the 1580s Reformed Protestantism is supported as the public church of a new country, the Dutch Republic. Calvinism also spreads to the Holy Roman Empire, where starting in the 1560s more than a dozen German territorial princes abandon Lutheranism for Reformed Protestantism's more ambitious conception of godly rule. Farther east, Calvinism becomes especially influential in Bohemia and Hungary.

Reformed Protestantism thus becomes an international movement in ways that Lutheranism never does: it is activist and ambitious, dynamic and disruptive from the mid-sixteenth to the mid-seventeenth centuries. But everywhere its most committed protagonists are frustrated in one way or another. Calvin cannot realize his vision to his satisfaction even in Geneva, confronted as he is with political opponents, eye rollers, and foot draggers. Yet despite this resistance, seeking to reshape a few thousand lives within the densely populated confines of a walled city is far easier than seeking to reshape a few million lives in large kingdoms with open borders.

Moreover, the political resistance Calvin faces in Geneva is nothing compared to what Reformed Protestants experience from Catholic authorities in France or the Low Countries, where tensions erupt in violence that lasts for decades. And living under Calvinism is one thing when people who consider themselves among God's elect embrace it willingly; it's another thing to endure Calvinist rule if you regard the "godly" as insufferably self-righteous oppressors worse than lackadaisical papists ever were. Though Calvinism disrupts and divides, it rarely conquers, at least not in any widespread way.

For all of Calvin's intellectual rigor and clarity, Reformed Protestantism proves no more immune from problems related to the foundational appeal to "scripture alone" than is Lutheranism. The Lutheran antagonism between Philippists and Genuine Lutherans is paralleled by conflict between Arminians and Calvinists, which becomes the most divisive rift within Reformed Protestantism in the Reformation era. At the heart of this conflict are theological disagreements about human nature, will, sin, and grace derived from differing interpretations of scripture. Jacob Arminius (1560–1609), a theology professor at the Dutch Republic's new University of Leiden, arrives at conclusions about core Protestant doctrines that are at odds with those of Calvin (and Luther). According to Arminius, original sin does not completely corrupt human nature; human beings do have some free will and so can cooperate with God's grace in salvation. To card-carrying Calvinists, this is crypto-Catholic backsliding, like taking Erasmus's position against Luther in their debate about free will and salvation.

In the early seventeenth century, this theological disagreement explodes in public controversy in the Dutch Republic and is divisive in England as well. During a meeting among the Dutch adversaries at the Synod of Dort (Dordrecht) in 1618–1619, Calvinists eventually get their way, but this only drives the Arminians off into their own congregations and churches in the cities of Holland. Like the disagreement between German Philippists and Genuine Lutherans, the Calvinist-Arminian controversy shows yet again that the principle on which the Reformation rests—"scripture alone"—is powerful enough to generate rival assertions about what the Bible actually says and therefore rival views about how it is to be applied.

The Radical Reformation After Münster

One of the great paradoxes of the Reformation era is that even though the vast majority of Protestants in the period are either Lutherans or Reformed Protestants, the vast majority of Protestant *interpretations* of God's Word belong to neither group. The Christians who espouse them are politically suppressed rather than protected. So persecution keeps their numbers comparatively small, even though the ways they understand scripture flower profusely in number and variety.[14]

Throughout Europe, authorities mindful of the German Peasants' War and the Anabaptist Kingdom of Münster remain vigilant well into the seventeenth century. They fail to keep religious radicalism in check only when their political control of religion in general breaks down, as we'll soon see happens during the English Revolution (1640–1660). Unshackled from the fetters of political authorities during these decades, Luther's revolutionary principle of "scripture alone" resurfaces again with more open-ended vitality than at any time since the early 1520s in the Holy Roman Empire.

Crucial aspects of the Protestant Reformation have long been misunderstood, largely because its two politically supported expressions—Lutheranism and Reformed Protestantism—are regarded as the normal or mainstream expressions of the Reformation. All other expressions have been marginalized as deviations or oddities, in much the same way that most other Christians viewed them at the time. But the fact is that *most* Protestant groups at the time (though not the majority of individual Protestants) reject *both* Catholicism *and* magisterial Protestantism. Lutheranism and Reformed Protestantism exert much more influence in the Reformation era because, like Catholicism in the regions where it is supported, they enjoy sustained political backing. But in this respect *they* are the Reformation's great exceptions.[15]

In its open-ended variety, the radical Reformation simply reflects the Reformation, period. It shows what "scripture *alone*" led to when political authorities did not enforce the biblical interpretations of reformers such as Luther, Zwingli, or Calvin. It reveals what the freedom of Christians looked like when you actually left people free to believe what *they* believed was true. It's not easy to see that this was the nature of the Reformation all along. After Münster and before the English Revolution, political authorities were quite successful in holding radical Protestantism in check. Paradoxically, it is only in the modern era, when religion has been redefined and Protestant dissenters are no longer persecuted, that we can look back and understand the essence of the Reformation from its very beginning. We can recognize in retrospect that magisterial Protestantism cannot be equated with the Reformation or with Protestantism.

The most striking thing about the radical Reformation in the sixteenth and seventeenth centuries, and therefore about the Protestant Reformation as a whole, is its sheer variety. From militant apocalypticism to pacifist withdrawal, conflicting assertions about the meaning of God's Word and God's will continue to emerge, encompassing virtually every imaginable assertion about the Bible. Radical Protestantism in the period includes all the expressions of Western Christianity that are not magisterial Protestantism or Roman Catholicism. Because persecution keeps their numbers small, no radical Protestant group exerts much influence on wider cultural trends. None develops institutions of higher education, such as Lutheran or Reformed Protestant universities, until after the Reformation era, and none shapes the beliefs and practices of entire populations.

That said, the experiences of radical Protestants are linked to the political decisions of ruling authorities no less than those of magisterial Protestants, although in vastly different ways. Like magisterial Protestants, radical Protestants can prosper and their numbers can grow when authorities leave them alone or even on occasion protect them. When they are persecuted, the opposite is true.

Many different Anabaptist groups, for instance, persist after 1535 or emerge in the shadow of the Münsterites, most of them in the Holy Roman Empire or Low Countries. At times, they are severely persecuted; in the sixteenth century many more Anabaptists than magisterial Protestants or Catholics are executed for their religion. Both German- and Dutch-speaking Anabaptists enthusiastically celebrate their martyrs, writing and singing literally hundreds of songs preserving their memory and encouraging fellow believers to persevere in faith despite the threat of death. Not until the 1560s do some of these sources about martyrs really begin to be published, partly because Anabaptists do not have the ready access to printers enjoyed by Lutherans or Reformed Protestants.[16]

When they're at least tolerated, though, some Anabaptist groups attract more members and flourish. This happens in the late sixteenth and seventeenth centuries in the Dutch Republic among the Mennonites, who take their name from Menno Simons (1496–1561), another former priest who left the Catholic Church to become an evangelical reformer committed to believers' baptism. Although linked by their opposition to infant baptism, Dutch Mennonites also divide among themselves, as did Philippists and Genuine Lutherans or Arminians and Calvinists, in their case into antagonistic groups disagreeing about how biblically based group discipline should be applied. Be too strict, and you risk shrinking your flock of pure Christians too much to sustain the group. But leave things too lax, and you threaten to dilute the identity you're trying to maintain and for which hundreds of your brothers and sisters have been put to death.

The Hutterites, followers of the martyred Jacob Hutter, are another group of Anabaptists who prosper when they receive political protection. For several decades, from the 1540s until the early 1620s, they practice a biblically rooted communitarian life-style as farmers and craftspeople on the estates of some sympathetic Moravian nobles, in the eastern stretches of the Holy Roman Empire. They reject private property—a practice made notorious by its association with Münster despite the biblical example of the earliest Christians—which sets them at odds with the Mennonites. It also separates them from the Swiss Brethren, another strand of Anabaptism, one that traces its lineage to the earliest days of the movement in Zürich during the 1520s.

Some groups of Anabaptists overlap with other radical Protestants who in one way or another downplay "externals" in Christian life. Collectively known as "spiritualists," even though they aren't a cohesive group in terms of their particular beliefs or practices, some of them take disdain for the external practice of the faith so far as to dispense altogether with the sacraments, even baptism and the Lord's Supper. Instead, as Caspar Schwenckfeld did in the 1520s, they emphasize the inner life of faith and sometimes the direct inspiration of the Holy Spirit or new revelation from God. If God revealed himself in ancient times, why not also in the present—especially if the end of the world is near? Surely God has the power to do so if he wishes?

Most Christians in the sixteenth century think it an insult to Christ to disguise your faith to avoid persecution, not to mention that it also blatantly rejects his warning, "Whoever denies me before others, I also will deny before my Father in heaven" (Matthew 10:33). Calvin and others repeatedly condemn this practice in strident terms. But some radical Protestants have no problem with it. Hendrik Niclaes, for example, from the Low Countries, the charismatic leader of a spiritualist Protestant group called the Family of Love (or Familists), thinks it's fine to pretend to be Catholic or Calvinist—whatever the local political authorities are imposing. Dissembling to avoid tyranny is no sin, and God knows what you really believe. Familist groups pursue their camouflaged religious lives in the Low Countries and also gain a following in Elizabethan England.

Radical Protestants live in other areas of Europe as well and are distinctive in ways besides insisting on believers' baptism or emphasizing the interiority of faith to the exclusion of "externals." Some reject the central doctrine of the Trinity, the early Christian teaching that God is mysteriously one God in three persons—Father, Son, and Holy Spirit—a doctrine linked to regarding Jesus Christ as truly both God and man. An important early anti-Trinitarian is the Spaniard Michael Servetus, who bases his rejection of the Trinity on a philosophically and philologically sophisticated interpretation of scripture. With Calvin's enthusiastic approval, Servetus is burned in Geneva in 1553. Influenced by Servetus, anti-Trinitarians, the predecessors of modern Unitarians, surface in Italy in the later sixteenth century. From then into the seventeenth century, anti-Trinitarian communities are able to lead relatively unmolested lives in Poland and Transylvania. Like Lutheranism and Reformed Protestantism, the radical Protestantism that began in the 1520s in the Holy Roman Empire and Swiss Confederation spreads throughout Europe.

The Reformation era ends as it began, with an explosion of politically ambitious and socially subversive claims about the Word of God. Rather than Germany in the 1520s, the time and place is England in the 1640s. Already in the early decades of the seventeenth century, different sorts of radical Protestants reject the Church of England. Although the English Church is officially Reformed Protestant in its teachings, many ardent Puritans are not satisfied with how those teachings are being practiced (or not practiced). This is even before Charles I starts making things worse, once he becomes king in 1625, by acting in ways that look not just insufficiently Protestant but downright Catholic.

Anyone who belongs to the established Church of England in the early seventeenth century is potentially a radical Protestant. All you have to do is reject it based on your own views about scripture and doctrine, like Luther rejected the Roman Catholic Church at the start of the Reformation. Around 1610, for example, English Baptists begin refusing infant baptism. And like the schisms among Dutch Mennonites, by the 1630s English Baptists are divided among themselves over Arminian versus Calvinist views about divine grace and free will.

The crisis of religion and politics in England brought on by Charles I in 1640 leads first to political polarization between supporters and opponents of the king, then to two civil wars and the breakdown of effective political control over the Church. As a result, a wide variety of different Protestant groups emerges very quickly, just as it did in the early German Reformation. No longer is a central political authority enforcing a prescribed set of doctrines and practices, as in Lutheran Saxony or Calvinist Geneva, so people can more freely interpret the Bible as they wish. In other parallels to the early German Reformation, the collapse of censorship permits a flood of printed propaganda, and apocalyptic expectations run rampant.

Radical Protestants in the English Revolution really come into their own after the execution of Charles I and the proclamation of the Republic in 1649.[17] Gerrard Winstanley and his Diggers champion a biblical vision similar to the Hutterites: an agrarian, communitarian Christian commonwealth without private property. The radically different George Fox and other early Quakers are spiritualists who claim illumination by the same "inner light" that they believe inspired Jesus's first apostles. Utterly different again are the Fifth Monarchists: their Christian duty, as they understand it, is to take up arms against Oliver Cromwell's regime in their own country, hastening the Second Coming of Christ. Seventh-Day

Baptists depart from the already existing General (Arminian) and Particular (Calvinist) Baptists by insisting, as do some other groups, that the Sabbath be celebrated on Saturday rather than Sunday. And Ranters, like Ebiezer Copp, allegedly take Christian freedom and rejection of the Old Testament law to mean complete sexual permissiveness—for, as scripture says, "To the pure all things are pure" (Titus 1:15). If you don't think something is sinful, it's not sinful for you.

If this all sounds confusing and complicated, that's because it was—much more chaotic and complex than any brief account can convey. Like the early German Reformation, the English Revolution shows that scripture interpreted through the Spirit, as Luther emphasized, could come to mean almost anything. This of course was true for the entire Reformation era, but it is often overlooked because only two forms of Protestantism received ongoing political support while other expressions were routinely suppressed.

When political authorities did not enforce a particular interpretation of scripture, people could take "scripture alone" in virtually any direction they wished. And people did, and they still do. As we'll see in chapter 4, this freedom that emerged in Germany in the 1520s and was so evident in England in the 1640s and 1650s is also obvious in modern liberal democracies, especially the United States.

Roman Catholicism Renewed

If everyone who agreed with Luther had also agreed about *how* to reject Rome, the Reformation would have looked completely different. At the same time, the Reformation *era* would have looked totally different if everyone had thought Luther was right to begin with. But they didn't, and this fact critically shapes the Reformation era as it unfolds.

As we've seen, Pope Leo X solemnly condemns Luther as a heretic in 1521. But later in the sixteenth century, at the Council of Trent, the Roman Catholic Church more deliberately condemns Luther's key teachings and those of many other Protestant reformers. In the sixteenth and seventeenth centuries, hundreds of Catholic theologians write literally thousands of treatises against the most basic Protestant convictions regarding scripture, grace, salvation, ministry, the Church, and more. They denounce Protestant doctrines as deadly errors, heresies that threaten millions of souls with eternal damnation. Theologians also serve in the Roman Inquisition and compile the Indexes of Prohibited Books, both of which come into their own in the 1540s to protect those same souls from these heresies.

But the Roman Catholic Church doesn't simply oppose Protestantism. For Catholic clergy and laity, the sixteenth century is not just an anti-Protestant "Counter-Reformation." It's also the period of a positive, rejuvenating "Catholic Reformation." Just like Protestant reformers, Catholic clerical leaders exhibit remarkable energy and constructive creativity. They renew traditional religious practices and institutions and devise new ones, affirming traditional doctrines and defining others explicitly for the first time.[18]

The Catholic Church influences large populations in entire countries because some rulers decide to remain Catholic or in some cases become Catholic after having been Protestant. They protect and promote Catholic teachings and practices in their lands, just as their Lutheran and Reformed Protestant counterparts are doing with their own teachings and practices. What's more, the Reformation era sees a huge geographical expansion of Catholicism to the Americas and Asia as the religion accompanies Portuguese merchants and Spanish colonizers. In the sixteenth century, Roman Catholicism becomes the world's first global religion as missionaries spread its practices and institutions everywhere from New France (in what is now Canada) and Peru in the New World to the Philippines and Japan in Asia.

In many respects the creative dynamism of the Catholic Reformation simply continues the reform and renewal that preceded the Protestant Reformation. We saw in chapter 1 that before Luther appears on the scene, various forms of renewal are thriving, such as Christian humanism, the reforms of religious orders, reflective lay piety, and an emphasis on charitable practices. After 1520, the challenge of the Reformation infuses all these Catholic developments with fresh urgency.

Catholic leaders reject the most basic premise of the Protestant reformers, that the Church's root problem is false doctrines. According to many Catholic authorities, there are plenty of problems in Christendom, to be sure, but they derive from sinful abuses and a lack of holiness among clergy and laity—a view that many medieval reformers had shared. In the eyes of sixteenth-century Catholic leaders, Protestant reformers starting with Luther veer disastrously off course by rejecting the Church's authority and thinking that scripture alone is the solution to the "problem" of false doctrines. Protestants are actually the ones with the false teachings, and sacred duty demands they be condemned in order to protect the faithful, just as the Church's leaders had condemned other heresies for over a thousand years. When Catholic bishops meet at the Council of Trent, their twin emphases are "the extirpation of heresies and the reform of morals."[19] In other words, the council encourages both Counter-Reformation and Catholic Reformation, opposing false teachings and fostering holiness.

For years before the Council of Trent finally gets under way in late 1545, Pope Paul III and Charles V bicker over where it should be held and what its order of deliberations should be.[20] The delays enable the Reformation to spread in the Holy Roman Empire under the protection of the Schmalkaldic League after the Diet of

Augsburg in 1530. Once the council finally does convene in Trent, a culturally Italian town situated at the extreme southern edge of the Holy Roman Empire, deliberations are interrupted in early 1547 by concerns about a possible local epidemic. The council temporarily shifts to Bologna, where it founders on tensions between pope and emperor. It does not reconvene until 1551, when the bishops and other invitees meet again for the better part of a year. Interrupted again in the spring of 1552 because of military conflicts in the region, the council leaves unfinished business that is not taken up again until nearly a decade later, when following the hardline pontificate of Paul IV (1555–1559), it reassembles for the final time from early 1562 to late 1563. Altogether, the Council of Trent renders formal decisions on matters of doctrine and discipline that are more extensive than those of any other such council in the history of the Catholic Church, which will remain true until the Second Vatican Council in the 1960s.

With "the extirpation of heresies," the Council of Trent condemns cornerstone teachings of the Protestant reformers and reaffirms Catholic doctrines. Pushed by Protestant developments, it also articulates certain doctrines for the first time, such as an explicit Catholic doctrine of justification. Spelling it out wasn't needed before, because it was taken for granted that you made some contribution, however small, to your salvation, cooperating through your actions with divine grace. Erasmus had argued this in his debate with Luther, and the Council of Trent states it explicitly.

What the Reformation condemns, Trent reasserts. The council upholds the mass as a re-presentation of Christ's once-for-all sacrifice; it confirms transubstantiation; and it defends a biblical basis for all seven sacraments. It insists that the Church's sacred tradition is essential for interpreting scripture correctly, and it reaffirms the Church's authoritative role as the arbiter of doctrine—a bulwark against the whims of individual interpreters.

Similarly, what Protestant reformers such as Luther and Calvin assert, Trent condemns. It rejects justification by faith alone as well as Protestant claims about the total sinfulness of human nature and complete lack of free will after the Fall. The council also denies that it is impossible to fulfill God's commands and that your actions contribute nothing to your salvation.

As for "the reform of morals," the Council of Trent addresses the long-standing calls for reforms in the Church. The aim is to clean the house, not to tear it down. In most instances the council wants to reform existing institutions and practices rather than abolish them. Thus Trent affirms practices such as praying to the saints, venerating their relics, and retaining sacred images in churches and elsewhere so long as everything is done reverently. The problem is the abuse of such practices, not their existence. Trent's answer to anticlericalism is not to get rid of religious orders and establish a married clergy but rather to educate them to become dedicated, devout, and actually celibate priests. For the effective theological and pastoral formation of parish priests, Trent calls for every diocese to establish a seminary. According to Matthew's Gospel, Jesus told his disciples that some "have made themselves eunuchs for the sake of the kingdom of heaven. Let anyone accept this who can" (Matthew 19:12). Catholics who accepted it were those, male or female, who willingly took solemn vows of celibacy. Trent reaffirms sexual asceticism as integral to the highest imitation of Christ and greatest Christian self-sacrifice, a tradition stretching back more than a thousand years through the Middle Ages to the early church.

Clergy are the key figures in the Church's renewal, imparting and supervising, preaching and teaching, consoling and cajoling the laity in their care. Quality pastoral care of the laity is central to Trent's aspirations. For this reason, bishops are to reside in their dioceses and priests in their parishes, putting an end to clerical absenteeism. The answer to the Reformation's splintering of Christianity is a resounding affirmation of the Church's hierarchical nature under the authority of the pope as the rightful successor to St. Peter and the Vicar of Christ. Under the pope, bishops are regarded as the rightful successors to Christ's apostles, and ordained clergy are the bishops' deputies on the ground, saying masses, administering the sacraments, supervising piety, and encouraging lay holiness in parishes throughout Catholic Europe.

The Council of Trent, then, is both a point of arrival and a point of departure. It shapes both Roman Catholicism and the Reformation era. Trent addresses ideas and issues that were coursing through Christendom long before 1517 and that the pressure of the Reformation had made more urgent. With official solemnity and the full weight of the Roman Church, the council condemns many central Protestant doctrines, thus sealing with institutional gravity the religious divisions opened by the Reformation. Trent reinvigorates Catholicism, with a renewed city of Rome and a reenergized papacy at its center. A new-model clergy will seek to mold a new-model laity in a new-model Roman Catholicism.

At the same time, Trent doesn't seek to answer every theological question raised by the Reformation, nor does it end debate within the Catholic Church. Questions about grace and free will that vex Protestant theologians also trouble their Catholic counterparts. In the seventeenth century, especially in France, Jansenists, named for the Netherlandish theologian Cornelius Jansen (1585–1638), will espouse a radically Augustinian view of human sinfulness, God's grace, and human will that looks a lot like Calvinism. A series of papal decisions will condemn Jansenism between the 1650s and the early eighteenth century, yet in France, Italy, and the southern Netherlands, its political and cultural influence will prove tenacious. Nevertheless, the Catholic Church, because of its hierarchy and centralized authority, possesses ways to address heterodoxy that the Protestant Reformation lacks.

The members of male and female religious orders are key participants in the process of forging a new-model Catholicism, though their commitment and zeal owe little to the Council of Trent in a direct way.[21] In Catholic Europe and overseas where Catholicism spreads, the period from the late sixteenth into the early eighteenth centuries is another golden age for both women and men in religious orders. Existing orders are renewed and new ones thrive. Among the latter are the Ursulines, a female order that begins in Italy in the 1530s at the initiative of Angela Merici (1474–1540) and comes to focus on the education of girls. Decades before the Council of Trent, the Capuchins, a male order, originate in Italy in the 1520s as an ascetic reform of the Franciscans; they grow to encompass thousands of friars in Catholic countries. Another reformed religious order is the male and female Discalced ("shoeless") Carmelites, whose members include the important Spanish mystics and spiritual writers Teresa of Ávila (1515–1582) and John of the Cross (1542–1591), both of whom will later be canonized as saints in the Catholic Church.

The most influential new religious order is the Society of Jesus, or Jesuits, founded by the Spaniard Ignatius Loyola (1491–1556), whose zealous eccentricities led him to be suspected of heresy. The Jesuits receive formal papal approval in 1540 and engage in a wide variety of ministries "to help souls," as they put it, with a zeal no less than that of committed Calvinist ministers. Ignatius wants them to "set the world on fire" with their ardor, and by 1550 they are concentrating especially on education.[22] A century later more than 15,000 Jesuits will serve around the world, staffing more than 550 colleges and teaching more than 150,000 students.[23] They became the Reformation era's most influential Catholic educators and most important Catholic intellectuals, as well as leading opponents of the Jansenists. Jesuits are renowned as theologians, philosophers, and biblical scholars as well as historians, archaeologists, astronomers, political theorists, and playwrights, authoring literally thousands of plays intended to teach moral and religious lessons.[24] In all of their endeavors, Jesuits seek to move the heart as well as the head.

The art of the Catholic Reformation grows alongside its newly energized theology. In stark contrast to the austere worship spaces of Reformed Protestantism, cleared of all distractions so that the faithful might focus on the unadorned Word of God, Catholic members of orders and new-model parish priests lead worship in richly ornate aesthetic surroundings. Baroque architecture and art of the later sixteenth and seventeenth centuries express the exuberant confidence of the Catholic Reformation, with cascades of gilt angels, sculptures of inspired saints, and visions of the triumph of God's true Church proclaiming a faith tried and tested by heresy but thereby strengthened rather than vanquished.

Like their Protestant counterparts, Catholic leaders before, during, and after the Council of Trent take up the humanist idea of employing education to serve lay religious formation. They also hope, once the Reformation gets under way, that these efforts will help inoculate Catholic laity against Protestant propaganda. Beginning especially in Italy and Spain, then gaining traction elsewhere in Catholic Europe, the Catholic Reformation eventually succeeds quite well in creating a new-model laity. By around 1650, many more lay Catholics are literate and catechized in their faith than had been the case in 1520. This is truer among the well-off than among the poor, in cities more than in rural areas, and among men than among women. Catholic devotional books, pamphlets, and engravings pour off presses as aids to religious life. In Paris in the early 1640s, for example, 48 percent of all books published deal with the Catholic faith.[25] Educated lay Catholics have been formed in their faith and have acquired religious identities parallel to those of their Lutheran and Reformed Protestant contemporaries.

But the identities Catholics acquire are different in important respects. They obviously believe different things—about the pope, Church, sacraments, and so forth—but they also engage in different practices and develop different sensibilities related to those beliefs. In fact, in their devotion Catholics often deliberately emphasize what Protestants reject. As a member of the Catholic laity in the early seventeenth century, you might spend time in individual meditation before the consecrated Eucharistic host displayed in a monstrance, an ornate gilt stand custom-made to hold the body of Christ, or participate in an elaborate community procession where the monstrance is reverently carried aloft. Or you might make a special pilgrimage to a holy site such as Altötting in Bavaria, Germany's most resolutely Catholic region, or Scherpenheuvel in Brabant, part of modern-day Belgium.[26] You might spend time in the prayers and charitable works undertaken by one of thousands of lay confraternities (or sodalities) dedicated to the saint of saints, the Virgin Mary.[27] Or you might say the Hail Marys and Our Fathers of the rosary, which becomes an even more popular devotion than it had already been in the late Middle Ages. Or you might do all of the above and also ask a Jesuit to guide you through some form of Ignatius Loyola's *Spiritual Exercises*.

As before the Reformation, a different sort of Christian freedom pervades Reformation-era Catholicism in its cornucopia of devotional options. Even with Trent's aspirations to uniformity, the religious menu of lay Catholics offers more choices than the menus of their Lutheran or Reformed Protestant counterparts. Which is in Protestants' view part of what remains wrong with the Catholic menu, aside from the chefs still cooking up so many spiritually poisonous dishes in the first place.

There's no doubt about the creative, constructive character of Christianity in the Reformation era. In different yet parallel ways, all its expressions provide their respective adherents with answers about what is true and how to live, creating identities and communities through which to live out these answers. Lutherans, Reformed Protestants, and Catholics alike benefit from the protection of political authorities who share their respective views. Political protection sustains institutions and initiatives that shape the religious identities of large numbers of people over generations. Politically suppressed radical Protestants, far fewer in number but espousing a wider variety of views about true Christianity, get by as best they can. They all carry their beliefs and commitments, practices and sensibilities, experiences and institutions beyond the Reformation era and into the modern period.

At the same time, all these Christians—their clergy, communities, and claims—remain rivals. What started as a reform of one Church produces an open-ended array of competing churches, which virtually no one at the time considers as a good thing. Throughout the era, European Christians inhabit the milieu of more-than-religious conflict that follows in the Reformation's wake. They wage fierce intellectual battles over doctrines and violent military conflicts over territories, creating serious problems that endure together with the expressions of Christianity that gave rise to them.

Beginning in the seventeenth century, how people respond to these problems starts to usher in a modern world that will become an unintended successor to the Reformation era. That's the subject of chapter 4. To understand these later responses, though, we need to understand what they were responses *to*. And that means seeing how political decisions and religiopolitical conflicts between 1520 and 1650 created the problems in question.

War to War in the Holy Roman Empire

The religiopolitical conflicts of the Reformation era appear most obvious in the countries or regions where they were most intense, which certainly includes the Holy Roman Empire, the birthplace of the Reformation. In the century after the Anabaptist Kingdom of Münster, Catholic and Protestant political authorities manage to contain radical Protestants, but not the belligerence of magisterial Protestants and Catholics toward each other.[28]

The Schmalkaldic League provides a framework within which Lutheranism can grow during the 1530s and 1540s. But Charles V hasn't given up on the Edict of Worms; he is simply preoccupied with other concerns, such as warring against Francis I of France. The emperor does not accept the league's defiance of his authority or its embrace of the Augsburg Confession in 1530. Catholic and Lutheran theologians alike have not given up on reconciliation. More than once they meet in the 1530s and early 1540s, seeking to overcome their disagreements.

In 1541, Melanchthon and the Italian cardinal Gasparo Contarini lead delegations in a theological colloquy in the German city of Regensburg.[29] By calling on all their resources of humanist rhetoric and theological subtlety in pursuit of reconciliation, they hammer out a tortuously worded doctrine of justification, a core doctrine of the Reformation dividing magisterial Protestants and Catholics. Yet they can't agree on much else. It's the reverse of the Marburg Colloquy in 1529, when Luther and Zwingli agreed on everything *except* the Eucharist. But the results are similar: doctrinally and socially divided Christians in mutually exclusive churches. The Regensburg Colloquy in 1541 is the last major attempt Lutherans and Catholics make toward doctrinal reconciliation in the Reformation era. After this attempt fails, war looms in the empire.

The Schmalkaldic War begins in 1546 between the armies of Charles V and armies of the Schmalkaldic League led by Philip of Hesse. After years of his subjects' disobedience, Charles V can no longer stand their disregard for his imperial law. At the Battle of

Mühlberg in 1547, Charles V wins a decisive victory, a triumph that the Italian artist Titian later immortalizes in a monumental painting of the emperor on horseback. In the following year, Charles V imposes the Augsburg Interim, a temporary solution to the religious situation until the Council of Trent, at that moment trying to shift its venue to Bologna, can meet again to finish its work. The Augsburg Interim makes certain concessions, such as accepting already-married Lutheran clergy, but it amounts to forcing Catholicism back onto Protestant cities and territories, and the leaders of these cities and territories are understandably none too pleased. Yet some are willing to compromise: how they react to the new law divides the more compliant Philippists from the more defiant Genuine Lutherans. Some Protestant leaders choose exile rather than accept the terms of the Augsburg Interim. Martin Bucer, for example, moves to England, leaving Strasbourg, where he had served as a pastor for over twenty years.[30]

While Charles V can defeat a Protestant coalition in battle, he can't reimpose Catholicism in the far-flung empire, with its myriad principalities and cities. The conflicts continue until the Peace of Augsburg in 1555 undoes the Augsburg Interim and establishes something unprecedented: a Holy Roman Empire with two religions, Lutheran and Catholic.

Far from a declaration of individual religious freedom, however, the Peace of Augsburg is a legal and political attempt to negotiate the religious disagreements that solidified after 1520. Augsburg is intended to last only until a religious reconciliation is reached. In the meantime, individual princes continue to choose either Roman Catholicism or Lutheranism as the religion of their territories. With few exceptions, their subjects are obliged to conform or move away as religious refugees. A later Latin catchphrase describes this arrangement: *cuius regio, eius religio*—"whose jurisdiction, his religion." While the Peace of Augsburg gives a robust, either-or religious choice to territorial rulers, it does not grant such freedom to the vast majority of Christians in the empire.

The Peace of Augsburg also conspicuously excludes mission-minded Reformed Protestantism, which creates a new problem when Frederick III of the Palatinate illegally converts to Reformed Protestantism, adopting it for his territory in 1562 during what is sometimes called Germany's Second Reformation.[31]

This development irks Lutherans for several reasons. Reformed Protestantism is spreading, and in subsequent decades it will win over the rulers of more than a dozen imperial territories. In every instance, those princes were originally Lutheran. Because none of them converts from Catholicism, every princely Calvinist gain comes at Lutheran expense. When they make their legal case for the switch to Reformed Protestantism, German Calvinist princes and theologians claim they're just following the Augsburg Confession. But this claim enrages the Genuine Lutherans, particularly because the Philippists are more sympathetic to the Calvinists and vice versa. Small wonder, then, that the Lutheran Formula of Concord in 1577, an ambitious resolution born of meetings spearheaded by the Genuine Lutherans with the goal of reconciling their division with the Philippists, is markedly anti-Calvinist.

Rising tensions between Lutherans and Calvinists accompany the advance of German Calvinism. That said, both groups tend to shelve their differences when faced with the common threat of German Catholicism. The short-lived political success of the Augsburg Interim camouflages the low ebb of Catholic religious practices and institutions in Germany. Renewal starts slowly in the 1550s, helped in part by direct influence from Rome and the Jesuits. Led by the Dukes of Bavaria in southern Germany, the Catholic resurgence picks up considerably in the 1570s and 1580s, after the conclusion of the Council of Trent.

This renewed Catholicism is militantly confident and aggressively assertive, buoyed by the decrees of the Council of Trent. Its clergy work to forge alliances between the Church and committed political authorities. This new-order Catholicism stands in marked contrast to the Church that was blindsided by the early German Reformation in the 1520s. And the stronger and more forceful it grows, the more ominous it looks to Lutherans and Reformed Protestants. When push comes to shove, they fear it more than they hate each other.

In the face of a rejuvenated Catholicism, a number of Lutheran and Reformed Protestant princes establish a Protestant Union in 1608 under the leadership of Frederick IV of the Palatinate.[32] In response, Duke Maximilian of Bavaria forms a Catholic League in 1609, escalating tensions further. The lack of strong imperial political leadership doesn't help during the long reign of Emperor Rudolph II (1576–1612) or that of his successor, Matthias (1612–1619).

In some respects, it's impressive that relatively peaceful coexistence works as well as it does in the decades after the Peace of Augsburg. But war breaks out again, this time with much greater geographical scope, endurance, and destructiveness than in the Schmalkaldic War during the late 1540s. That conflict and its aftershocks played out within the borders of the empire. But this time the Thirty Years' War ensnares all of Europe.

In May 1618 Calvinist nobles in Bohemia object to their new ardently Catholic king, the Habsburg Archduke Ferdinand. Ferdinand won't recognize the nobles' existing religious privileges, and he aspires to make Bohemia as thoroughly Catholic as Bavaria, the territory of his older cousin, Duke Maximilian. The Calvinist nobles convey their objections by throwing two imperial representatives out of the window of Prague Castle in the famous "defenestration of Prague."

After Emperor Matthias dies in 1619, Ferdinand succeeds him as Emperor Ferdinand II. Together, Ferdinand and Maximilian of

Bavaria constitute a formidable combination, a united front of *militant* Catholicism in both senses of the word. Protestant nobles depose Ferdinand as king of Bohemia and in his place elect Frederick V of the Palatinate. International military alliances quickly coalesce, followed soon thereafter by conflicts.

The first decade of the Thirty Years' War is marked by Counter-Reformation military success and Protestant retreats and defeats. Near Prague in late 1620, the army of Catholic commander Johann Tilly routs Frederick V's forces in the Battle of the White Mountain. Frederick is deposed as king of Bohemia, he loses the Palatinate, and he is driven into exile. Supported by Maximilian of Bavaria and Philip III of Spain, Ferdinand seeks to recover the entire empire for Catholicism—to achieve what Charles V sought in vain to accomplish during the Augsburg Interim seventy years before.

On the Protestant side, Christian IV of Denmark, allied with James I of England and the Dutch Republic, attacks Catholic armies in Germany. Again Tilly thoroughly defeats the Protestants, this time with the help of Albrecht von Wallenstein, another accomplished and ruthless field commander, who by 1628 has a force of 110,000 soldiers under his command. The Catholic advantage on the battlefield yields the Edict of Restitution, which mandates the return of multiple bishoprics and more than a hundred monasteries that Protestants had taken since 1552. Following the edict—the military and political apex for Ferdinand II in the Thirty Years' War—it looks as though he might remake the Holy Roman Empire in the image of an aggressive new-model Catholicism.

But a year later, in 1630, the tide suddenly and dramatically turns. King Gustavus Adolphus of Sweden, "the Lion of the North," has already proven his military mettle against Russia and Poland, essentially turning the Baltic Sea into a Swedish lake. Now aided by Dutch money, the Lutheran Adolphus enters the conflict in Germany. In 1631 Gustavus crushes Tilly's army in the Battle of Breitenfeld, not far from Leipzig. Breitenfeld ends Ferdinand II's advance, and Gustavus's troops plunder previously untouched Catholic regions of central Europe, including Bavaria. Though the Swedish king is killed in battle in 1632, less than two years after he entered the war, his influence is decisive. Before his death, he neutralizes the imperial Counter-Reformation juggernaut, and a chastened Ferdinand II backs away from his earlier ambitions. The Peace of Prague of 1635 is a compromise, very different in tone from the Edict of Restitution, which it suspends, seeking to return the situation in Germany to what it had been before the invasion by Gustavus Adolphus.

If other European leaders had decided to leave the Holy Roman Empire alone, the Thirty Years' War might have ended then. But they didn't. Cardinal Richelieu, Catholic France's chief minister under Louis XIII, recognizes an opportunity to strike against the Habsburgs and a weakened Holy Roman Emperor, who despite their shared Catholic faith is the French king's major traditional rival. This drags the conflicts on for another decade. Large swaths of central Europe suffer immensely from the war, which kills not only combatants but also large numbers of civilians. Shockingly, in the siege of Magdeburg in 1631, well over 90 percent of the city's population perishes.[33] Armies live off the land, their soldiers plundering, raping, and killing. When they aren't paid on time, soldiers mutiny or desert. Wherever they go, armies and their many suppliers and followers spread disease, which ultimately kills more people than three decades of military conflict. Men and women in many parts of Germany suffered all this for years before the Peace of Prague in 1635, but after that date, too weak to resist, they have to endure years more. Negotiations to end this war of all wars begin in 1643 and in a fittingly grim way grind on for five years.

The Thirty Years' War finally ends in 1648 with the Peace of Westphalia, which creates a framework for Protestants and Catholics to coexist in a multiethnic empire. Few consider the

agreement ideal, but nearly everyone thinks it better than the horrors that central Europeans have lived through during the previous
thirty years. The Peace of Westphalia establishes the basic religiopolitical arrangements of Europe that will persist into the nineteenth
century.

The more-than-religious wars of the Reformation era in the
Holy Roman Empire do not produce a winner. Instead, they inflict
punishing losses all around. By 1650, it looks as though all the political leaders who were confident God was on their side were wrong.
Perhaps God had never been on anyone's side.

France and the Wars of
More-than-Religion

The Reformation in France unfolds differently from the Reformation
in the Holy Roman Empire. There's no widespread movement in
the 1520s inspired by Luther or any other reformer. Beginning in
the early 1540s, Protestantism arrives and endures in the form of
Calvinism, and the number of Huguenots grows by leaps and bounds
in the late 1550s, just when the Peace of Augsburg enables the start
of decades of relatively calm religious coexistence in the empire.
Starting in 1562, militant Calvinism meets militant Catholicism in
a series of eight bloody civil wars of more-than-religion. All told,
from start to finish, these eight civil wars last longer than the Thirty
Years' War, and they end in 1598 with the Edict of Nantes, after
which the Huguenots are grudgingly tolerated until Louis XIV
revokes the edict in 1685.

The Reformation unfolds differently also because France is a
single kingdom, not a conglomerate of semi-independent cities and
territories, as is the Holy Roman Empire. France in the sixteenth
century encompasses a much larger political territory than any

single territory within the Holy Roman Empire, and in this united territory Catholic rulers are determined to oppose the Reformation. The French king (by French law always a king, never a queen) is an absolute monarch bound by a sacred coronation oath to protect the Catholic Church in his kingdom. He exerts control over this "Gallican" Church by nominating bishops for papal approval. In the later Middle Ages, increasing royal oversight of the Church is a common pattern in the stronger European monarchies such as France. At issue is jurisdictional control, not a rejection of papal authority.

Precisely that rejection is central to the Reformation. But it comes later to France than to the Holy Roman Empire. In the 1520s and 1530s France sees nothing like the explosiveness of the early German Reformation, although Christian humanists advocate for reforms, as do a few evangelicals inspired by Luther or other early Protestant reformers. But for the most part, the realm is deeply resistant to the Reformation from the start. The faculty of theology at the University of Paris remains the most prestigious in Europe, and shortly before the Edict of Worms, it condemns Luther in early 1521.[34]

More important than the judgment of the Paris theologians is the will of the French king, Francis I. The chief political rival of Charles V, he is also a cultured patron of learning and the arts, a monarch whose patronage lured the aged Leonardo da Vinci from Italy to France, where he died in 1519.[35] Francis approves of Erasmus's vision to reform Christianity through erudition and education, supporting to this end the efforts of a reforming bishop, Guillaume Briçonnet. In the early 1520s, in the diocese of Meaux, just east of Paris, Briçonnet is trying to implement an Erasmian vision of reform that includes the participation of France's leading biblical scholar, the elderly Jacques Lefèvre d'Étaples (ca. 1460–1536).[36] But Briçonnet's initiative also attracts to this same reforming circle in Meaux preachers with overt evangelical sympathies, including the fiery Guillaume Farel, the same man who in the following decade persuades Calvin to stay in Geneva. The mother of Francis I, Louise of Savoy, is more suspicious of the Meaux circle than is her son. When the king is taken prisoner by Charles V in 1525 following the Battle of Pavia in northern Italy, a crucial conflict in the ongoing wars between France and the empire, Louise of Savoy has the Meaux circle broken up, and many of its members flee France. After his release Francis protects those who remain, but the circle never regains its former vitality.

In the 1520s, Francis wants to believe that the Reformation is a German problem, that he can embrace Erasmian reform without becoming a monarch of heretics. When the Peasants' War spills over into francophone regions in 1525 it is troubling, but it doesn't endure. Essentially the king is willing to countenance cultured, courtly reform that steers clear of heresy and avoids public disturbance or iconoclasm.

"Public disturbance" hardly does justice to what happens on the night of October 17, 1534.[37] In multiple cities throughout the French kingdom—including on the door of the king's own bedchamber in his chateau at Amboise—are posted copies of *True Articles on the Horrible, Enormous, and Unbearable Abuse of the Papal Mass,* a shocking broadsheet. This is a carefully coordinated Reformed Protestant attack on the heart of Catholic belief and practice, and it reflects the clandestine growth of evangelical support in Paris and other cities, including even at the royal court. The king and the Parlement of Paris (the kingdom's chief royal judicial court) respond with force. Throughout the rest of October, they conduct investigations and trials and execute those convicted of heresy. The Reformation has become a French problem too.

What makes the Reformation a big deal in France is Calvinism. Calvin flees his native France as a refugee right after the Affair of the Placards. In the preface of his *Institutes of the Christian Religion*

(1536), he insists to Francis I that evangelicals are politically obedient subjects, unlike the anarchic Anabaptists in Münster. But that's
a difficult case to make to a king who is bound by a sacred oath to
politically promote and defend Catholicism. The first French translation of Calvin's *Institutes* appears in 1541, which Calvin soon
follows with other vernacular treatises denouncing Catholic superstition and idolatry.

Along with other publications, many of them published in
Geneva and smuggled into France, these writings contribute to the
spread of Calvinism, which in turn is harshly suppressed. An attempt
to establish a Calvinist congregation at Meaux in 1546 is met by
multiple executions. Francis I's son and successor, Henry II, establishes a special court in Paris in 1547 for trying cases of suspected
heresy; it is called the "burning chamber" (*chambre ardente*).[38]

Yet as late as 1554 there are still no established, organized
Calvinist churches in France despite the steady increase in the number of underground followers. By 1562, just eight years later, perhaps eight hundred such churches exist, with more in the making.
Most are in the south, far from Paris, the kingdom's political, commercial, and cultural capital. Another group of churches clusters
west of the city in Normandy, and others are scattered throughout
the realm. What's more, the rapidly growing number of churches
emboldens Huguenots to become more publicly assertive and
aggressively antagonistic. In multiple cities they destroy church art,
deface altars, demonstrate in public, and harass clergy.

Converts to Calvinism are disproportionately urban and literate. At their peak in the 1560s, the Huguenots probably make up
about 10 percent of France's twenty million inhabitants, but they
constitute a much higher percentage of the nobility. This matters
because no sixteenth-century ruler, however theoretically absolute,
can govern without noble support. A divided nobility makes for a
divided country.

In 1559 King Henry II dies from wounds suffered in a jousting accident, plunging the monarchy into a political crisis, one compounded by the alarming growth and assertiveness of the Calvinists. Francis II, Henry's inexperienced teenage son, becomes king at a moment when experience is most needed. Things go from bad to worse when Francis dies from an infection in late 1560, leaving Catherine de Medici, the widow of Henry II, as the regent for the boy-king Charles IX. Catherine's immediate goal is to defuse the growing religious hostilities. In the fall of 1561, she calls together a dozen Calvinist theologians to meet with Catholic bishops at Poissy. The meeting is an utter failure, starkly revealing just how far apart the two sides have grown.[39] Calvinists regard the consecrated Eucharist, the very thing Catholics revere as the body and blood of Christ, as an appalling idol, a "god of paste." Just as the failure of the Regensburg Colloquy between Lutheran and Catholic theologians in 1541 is followed by the Schmalkaldic War, so the failure of the Colloquy of Poissy will be followed by the first of the French wars of more-than-religion.

These French civil wars involve three powerful, extended families with three different views about religion and politics. The Valois, the reigning royal family, generally pursue a policy of moderate Catholic conciliation, seeking to negotiate with the Huguenots in order to avoid or at least ameliorate destructive conflicts wherever possible. Catherine de Medici, the queen of compromise, leads the family at the outset of the wars. Two of her sons, as they grow older, reign in succession as king: Charles IX (who rules from 1563–1574) and Henry III (who rules from 1574–1589). Many members of another leading noble family, the Bourbons, convert to Calvinism. They want at least religious toleration, though their ultimate dream is to shepherd in a Calvinist France, similar to the religious regime change John Knox has just managed to establish in Scotland in 1559–1560. Finally, the Guises champion an uncompromising,

militant Catholicism. They condemn the Huguenots as dreaded heretics. They scorn the Valois as a weak ruling family willing to sacrifice God's cause for political expediency.

It's a volatile combination when you consider that by the early
1560s, virtually every other noble family in France is aligned with
one of these three families through ties of marriage and patronage.
And it's made more combustible because these three French families
forge alliances with foreign rulers during the wars. The Bourbons
receive support from German Calvinist princes, for example, and
the arch-Catholic Guises from Philip II of arch-Catholic Spain.

Such is the situation at the beginning of 1562. Pressured by the
Protestants, Catherine seeks other means to diminish animosities
after the failed Colloquy of Poissy. In January she issues an edict of
toleration, but neither the Huguenots nor the Guises get what they
want, and both disdain its compromises. The energized Calvinists
ramp up their protests and iconoclasm.

In March 1562, members of the Duke of Guise's retinue kill
dozens of Huguenots at worship in Vassy, a small town in north-
eastern France. Both sides mobilize for military conflict, which
begins in July and lasts until March 1563. The ensuing pacification
is again a compromise that satisfies neither side, temporarily stall-
ing rather than ending the hostilities. This pattern is repeated again
when subsequent wars erupt in 1567 and 1568, leading in each case
to unstable truces that pacify neither side.

The first major watershed during the French wars of
more-than-religion comes in 1572 with the St. Bartholomew's Day
Massacre, the most famous—and infamous—of all such incidents
in the Reformation era.[40] Seeking to mitigate the hostilities through
an alliance across the religious divide, a match is arranged between
Catherine de Medici's daughter Marguerite and Henry of Navarre,
a key Huguenot leader. Virtually all the leading French Calvinists
come to Paris for their wedding in August 1572, and they linger

afterward, as is customary for such affairs in the sixteenth century.

Four days after the wedding, Gaspard de Coligny, the leading Huguenot military commander, is shot in an assassination attempt. Fearing reprisal, Charles IX orders a preemptive strike against him and all other Huguenot leaders in the city. This triggers an unplanned massacre of some two thousand Huguenots in Paris, as Catholics at large vent their rage against the heretics. As word of the Parisian massacre spreads throughout France, so does the violence. All told, in cities including Rouen, Toulouse, Lyon, and Bordeaux, several thousand more Huguenots are killed.

The St. Bartholomew's Day Massacres are devastating for the Huguenots. How can this have been an expression of divine providence, they wonder, a sign of God's loving care for his elect? Thousands renounce their faith and return to Catholicism while others flee to England or the Low Countries. Those who remain steadfast, however, are steeled in their resolve, hating murderous Catholics more than ever and determined to weather the Lord's trial. The massacres of 1572 inspire a raft of political treatises that justify rebellion against a tyrannical ruler—such as Charles IX or his brother Henry III, who succeeds him as king in 1574.

The next major turning point in the wars comes in 1584. Henry III leaves no children, so after his final living brother dies, there are no Valois heirs to the throne—and the next in the line of succession is the Huguenot Henry of Navarre. This galvanizes the Guises more than ever. Under the leadership of Henry, Duke of Guise, they reinvigorate the Catholic League, a radically anti-Protestant organization. For the Guises and members of the league, a Protestant king of France is a contradiction in terms, an impossibility. The Guises oppose the notion so strongly that they make an alliance with Philip II, king of Spain, France's political enemy.

Relations between Henry III and the Catholic League sour and harden during the later 1580s. The members of the league mercilessly criticize the Valois king for being weak on the Huguenots, while Henry III is appalled that a French political rival is in cahoots with the Spanish king. By mid-1588 the tension reaches the breaking point, and the league in Paris grows strong enough to force the king out of the city. In response, the humiliated Henry III takes the drastic step of having both the Duke and Cardinal of Guise assassinated, cementing his own alliance with the Protestant Henry of Navarre against the Catholic League.

The Catholic militants take their revenge in August 1589. A Dominican lay brother, Jacques Clement, assassinates Henry III in retaliation for the murder of the Guises. Yet this brings the members of the league face-to-face with their worst nightmare, a Protestant heir to the throne. Still, the league controls Paris, and it prevents Henry of Navarre from entering the city and assuming the crown. Henry of Navarre decides to convert to Catholicism, reportedly saying, "Paris is worth a mass." Conspicuously public, Henry's formal conversion ceremony in 1593 is carefully orchestrated for maximum political effect. With his conversion helping to stabilize the country and pointing the way toward some measure of recovery, Parisians welcome him as Henry IV into the city in the spring of 1594.

The Edict of Nantes ends the wars four years later, in 1598, and creates restricted space for a Huguenot minority within Catholic France. Unlike the Peace of Augsburg in 1555, which provided religious parity in the Holy Roman Empire between Catholics and Lutherans, the Edict of Nantes does not recognize equal treatment of the religions. However, the Huguenots do receive freedom of worship in the approximately two hundred towns they control, including on the estates of Protestant nobles, and they gain access to education, to positions at court, and to royal offices as well as permission to keep armed troops protecting fifty or so of their towns. In the end, they are not afforded a degree of lasting toleration because the Edict of Nantes is never intended as such; rather, it's a temporary provision for a wounded, shattered kingdom, a provision widely regarded at the time as preferable to continued bloodshed.

Ultimately, the Edict of Nantes is an expression of Henry IV's will, and the seventeenth century shows just how provisional a monarch's will can be. Military conflicts continue to flare up in southwest France in the 1620s. In 1629, the Atlantic-coast city of La Rochelle, the last remaining fortified Huguenot city, falls under royal control, marking the definitive end to the French wars of more-than-religion. Left without military protection, the Huguenots are vulnerable to the erosion of the privileges granted by the Edict of Nantes.[41] From the 1660s on, King Louis XIV enacts numerous royal initiatives that undermine Protestant resolve. Catholic converts are prohibited from returning to Protestantism. Huguenot churches are shut, while occupations in the law and royal bureaucracy previously open to Calvinists are closed off, and soldiers are forcibly billeted in Huguenot homes. In the early 1680s, conversions to Protestantism are outlawed until Louis XIV finally revokes the Edict of Nantes altogether in 1685, reflecting the still-powerful desire for a religiously uniform France. Over the next five years, more than two hundred thousand Huguenots flee France as religious refugees, immigrating to England, the Dutch Republic, Calvinist territories in the Holy Roman Empire, and the Carolina coast of North America.

England, Kingdom of Religious Division

Let's say you're born in England around 1517. By the time you're in your mid-forties, you have every reason to be confused about religion. No other major kingdom in Europe has been religiously whipsawed like England during these decades, beginning with the reign of Henry VIII. For all anyone knows, your new queen, Elizabeth I, might die after a short reign like her two half-siblings before her, Edward VI and Mary I. Between the early 1530s and the early 1560s, religion and politics in England might have seemed like a soap opera if everything hadn't been so disorienting, disruptive, divisive, and violent.[42]

How different things were when you were a child! Then, like everyone else in your village, you participated in parish life in traditional ways, following in the footsteps of your parents and their parents before them. Like you, they were taught to pray for the pope. Like you, they made pilgrimages to St. Thomas's shrine in Canterbury and St. Cuthbert's in Durham in a country covered with sacred sites and dotted with centuries-old monasteries and friaries. When word of the German heretic Luther reached England's shores, your own king, Henry VIII, led the attacks against him, as well as against the handful of evangelical sympathizers in London and the university towns of Cambridge and Oxford.

In 1521, with the help of some theological advisers, Henry VIII personally authored a Latin *Defense of the Seven Sacraments* against Luther's *Babylonian Captivity,* partly because he coveted and duly received the accolade "defender of the faith" from Pope Leo X, to whom he had dedicated the work. But in the following decade, the same king who so stoutly defended papal authority just as thoroughly denounced it, declaring the "Bishop of Rome" a usurper in his kingdom.[43] Pressuring Parliament, Henry severed all ties with the papacy and, despite being a layman, declared himself the head of the Church in England. And in 1535 he started severing the heads of those who wouldn't take an oath acknowledging his new status, including John Fisher, the aged Bishop of Rochester, and Thomas More, previously Henry's trusted adviser and lord chancellor, the kingdom's highest civil officer.

Henry VIII destroyed the shrines to St. Thomas, St. Cuthbert, and other Catholic saints. Within a few years, he gutted all the friaries and monasteries, seizing for himself their lands and possessions and wealth, more than tripling the crown's property. To finance his war with France, Henry sold off much of it within a decade and leased the rest. And he did all this without becoming a Protestant.

Henry's Reformation wasn't about scripture alone or justification by faith alone. It wasn't even about Roman Catholicism or Protestantism. Henry's Reformation grew out of two interrelated desires, both aimed toward controlling the Church in England by his authority alone. First, Henry wanted a son as his heir. His daughter Mary was born in 1516, but she didn't suffice, though in England, unlike France, a woman could rule in her own right as queen. Second, Henry desired an attractive young woman who lived at his court, Anne Boleyn. He could fulfill both desires if he could marry Anne and she bore him a son.

Unfortunately for Henry, he was already married to Catherine of Aragon, his wife of seventeen years. To annul his marriage with Catherine and wed Anne, Henry needed a papal dispensation. Doubly unfortunately for Henry, Catherine of Aragon's nephew was the Holy Roman Emperor Charles V, whose armies sacked Rome in 1527 and who therefore had Pope Clement VII in an impossible bind. Henry wasn't going to get from the pope a dispensation insulting the emperor's aunt. So the king dispensed with the pope and received his dispensation instead from the royally appointed Archbishop of Canterbury, Thomas Cranmer, England's new top churchman.

Henry's Reformation was not carried out as steps known in advance from a master plan. It proceeded in piecemeal fashion, growing together with his ambitions. It started with pressure on the English clergy in 1529, continued by subjugating them in 1531, and culminated in the Acts of Succession and Supremacy in 1534, which made Henry the head of the Church of England and required subjects to take an oath of allegiance that acknowledged the king's newly asserted authority.

Yet the Reformation under Henry was more complicated. Although the king opposed Protestantism, those in high places took advantage of the new royal supremacy over the Church to advance the gospel whenever possible. Some were Protestants themselves, including the new queen, as was Thomas Cromwell, Henry's new chief adviser. Evangelicals were enthusiastic about William Tyndale's translation of the New Testament in English, published in Germany by this religious exile and smuggled back into England starting in 1526. Indeed, the king himself was persuaded to sanction an official edition of the whole English Bible in 1538.

But as happened so often with Henry, he suddenly changed his mind. Henry's Reformation was both anti-Roman and anti-Protestant. It followed his will alone. From 1539 to his death in 1547, Henry punished whoever challenged his authority. On June 30, 1540, two days after he ordered the execution of Thomas Cromwell, he burned three Protestants for heresy and ordered three Roman Catholics hanged, drawn, and quartered as traitors for denying the royal supremacy.

When Henry died in 1547, everything changed. Reformed Protestantism arrived in England with a vengeance.[44] The first protector and overseer of the new king, nine-year-old Edward VI— Henry's son by Jane Seymour, the third of Henry's six wives—was Edward's uncle, the Duke of Somerset, who initiated the process of Protestantizing in cooperation with Archbishop Cranmer. Beginning in 1549, Cranmer along with the Duke of Northumberland, Somerset's successor as Edward's protector and chief adviser, endeavored still more aggressively to turn England into a Reformed Protestant kingdom. They repealed the anti-Protestant legislation of Henry's late reign. They allowed clergy to marry, and laypeople received wine in the Lord's Supper for the first time. They abolished the idolatrous mass, tore down the idolatrous altars, and purified the churches of their idolatrous paintings and sculptures. They stopped the saying of masses for the dead, which countless thousands of medieval Catholics had paid for. They seized gold and silver chalices, candlesticks, and other objects used for worship from parish churches, just as Henry had done with the monasteries. Defining the key doctrines of the Church of England in the *Forty-Two Articles,* Cranmer created a new liturgy in English around the *Book of Common Prayer.* In place of altars at the east end of churches, communion tables were set up in the middle of the congregation.

The religious changes of the early 1550s were the most obvious and radical in parishes since Henry VIII seized control of the English Church. A minority of enthusiasts cheered the changes, but many others resisted, and in some places they even rose in rebellion against them. Regardless of their own views, most people just conformed—the most common response to politically imposed religious changes everywhere in the sixteenth century, the easiest way to stay out of trouble. But England's Reformed Protestant revolution had little chance to take root because Edward VI died in 1553 when he was only sixteen.

Another monarch, another dramatic change in religion—this time an about-face return to Roman Catholicism.[45] Edward was succeeded by Mary I, Henry's daughter by Catherine of Aragon, his first wife. Like her mother, Mary had remained a devout Roman Catholic, despite the intimidation that led her to acknowledge her father as the head of the English Church in 1536. When she got her chance, she reversed everything her half-brother and his cadre of Protestant advisers had done and returned England to union with Roman Catholicism. From Rome, Mary recalled Cardinal Reginald Pole, who had fled to Italy to avoid Henry's Reformation, to serve as her Archbishop of Canterbury. Under Mary's authority,

Pole reestablished throughout England the Catholic mass, religious orders, and other Catholic practices. He also restored religious sculptures, paintings, and stained glass, some of which had been hidden by parishioners and priests from the Edwardian iconoclasts.

Mary also revived laws against heresy, and she and Pole approved trials and executions for heresy. Around three hundred were carried out during her reign, which lasted less than five years, from 1553 through 1558; hence the nickname "Bloody Mary." The flow of Protestant refugees now surged in the opposite direction. Several hundred Protestants with sufficient means and connections fled abroad, many of them to strongly Reformed Protestant cities such as Geneva or Basel.

But then Mary and Cardinal Pole died on the same day in late 1558. Her marriage to Philip II of Spain had produced no children, so the crown passed to Henry and Anne Boleyn's daughter, Elizabeth I. Like her younger half-brother, Edward, Elizabeth was a Protestant though, unlike Edward, not of an uncompromising Calvinist stripe. She undid everything her half-sister Mary had done to undo Edward's legacy, ending once again England's connection with Rome, in this respect following in the footsteps of her father, Henry VIII.

At the end of the 1550s, Elizabeth inherits a religiously divided and disquieted kingdom, and the last thing she wants is a religious settlement that itself is unsettling. She dearly wishes to avoid the fate of France, which at the start of Elizabeth's reign is sliding toward its civil wars of more-than-religion. The *Thirty-Nine Articles* of her religious settlement in 1563 remain very close to the Reformed Protestantism of the Edwardian *Forty-Two Articles*. And she brings back a slightly modified version of the *Book of Common Prayer* (1559), though with deliberately more leeway for individual interpretations of the Eucharist, seeking to avoid the disputes that are causing so much rancor in the era. But she simultaneously keeps bishops, medieval canon law, and clerical vestments that look a lot more Catholic than Calvinist.

Elizabeth's Reformation is not Anglicanism—some just-right Goldilocks mix of Protestant and Catholic elements in a sensible church that expresses the supposedly moderate character of the pragmatic English people. It is Reformed Protestantism without Calvin's emphasis on transformative activism, social discipline, or pure worship. And it is overlaid awkwardly on what survives of late medieval and Marian Catholicism plus the influence of Henry's and Edward's very different Reformations.

That's why Elizabeth's religious settlement frustrates the most committed members of the Elizabethan Church, including exiles from Mary's reign who return from the continent to assume positions as bishops, university theologians, and diocesan administrators. During their time abroad they've seen what real Reformed Protestantism looks like, which inspires their religious ideal for England. Unfortunately for them, Elizabeth doesn't share their enthusiasm. They call themselves "the godly," but they're more popularly known as "Puritans," originally a term of derision.[46] In different ways and at different times, these Puritans are set on edge by most people's—including the queen's—contentment with an undemanding religious conformity. But even by the last decade of Elizabeth's reign, in the 1590s, only small numbers of the godly grow so discontented that they leave the established church as dissenting radical Protestants. It will be a different story with their religious heirs a half century later.

The others who remain disgruntled and marginalized by the Elizabethan settlement are the Catholics. They include two main groups: leftovers from Mary's reign and before, and gung-ho new-model missionary clergy trained on the continent along with the well-instructed laity in England to whom they minister. The missionary priests start arriving in the 1570s, including the Jesuits in

1580, once their hopes for England's return (again) to Rome continue to be delayed. Unfortunately for committed Catholics, though Elizabeth falls gravely ill in 1562, she doesn't follow the early-death-in-reign script. Her strongest suit is her longevity: she rules from 1558 to 1603, forty-five years, even longer than her father, Henry VIII. It's enough time to stabilize institutions and create continuity, even if godly Puritans, committed Catholics, and Protestant dissenters remain discontented.

The Elizabethan intertwining of religion and politics makes life difficult and dangerous for English Catholics. Multiple plots are foiled and attempted invasions repulsed, most famously the naval battle against the Spanish Armada in 1588. And through it all the violence continues, only with different targets: Catholic priests are defined as traitors, and more than a hundred, in addition to dozens of laity who aided them, are executed during Elizabeth's reign.[47] In 1587, Elizabeth approves the execution of her Catholic cousin Mary, Queen of Scots, whom many think is next in line to succeed Elizabeth.

Elizabeth accomplishes the goal of avoiding overt wars of more-than-religion, but she certainly doesn't avoid religiopolitical violence. The seesaw swings of the three decades preceding her reign, plus her unsettling religious settlement, mean that religion remains a constant source of division and disruption. The "Virgin Queen" (from which Virginia in England's North American colonies takes its name) never marries and thus leaves no heirs. The Tudor dynasty ends with her death in 1603.

The new king is James I—already James VI of Scotland—the son of the beheaded Mary, Queen of Scots. Unlike his Catholic mother, James is a committed Reformed Protestant. He takes a serious interest in theology and gives sustained royal support to a new translation of scripture that bears his name: the *King James Bible* (1611), which adopts from Tyndale's translation the large majority of the New Testament.[48] Despite the continuing discontent of Puritans and radical Protestants, James's experience as King of Scotland cements his view that the established church and its institutions are a cornerstone of social and political order. "No bishop, no king," James says. Puritans are none too pleased when, late in his life, he grows cooler toward Calvinist views about grace and predestination, instead tolerating and even promoting rival Arminian bishops and other clergy prior to the end of his reign in 1625.

To the godly, however, far more disturbing than James is his son, Charles I, who looks for all the world as though he's leading England back toward Catholicism. He marries a French Catholic princess and openly tolerates at his court Catholics and, more troublingly, the mass itself. In the 1630s, in an act that enrages Puritans, he appoints William Laud as his Archbishop of Canterbury, who begins to overhaul church architecture, decoration, and worship to express what Laud calls "the beauty of holiness." Laud's initiative emphasizes Catholic-style spectacle and downplays preaching. Puritans are so offended that hundreds start emigrating across the Atlantic to Massachusetts, where they try to create the Puritan paradise denied them in England.

When Charles I tries to impose a Laudian-inspired prayer book on Calvinist Scotland in 1637, all hell breaks loose.[49] The resulting protests and rebellion do not sit well with the king, who decides to raise an army to enforce his will. The sums of money he needs require approval by Parliament. But Charles hasn't called a Parliament since 1629. When he finally does so in the spring of 1640, after years of contentious religious measures and unpopular political policies, the members of Parliament are seething. With disdainful arrogance Charles at first dismisses them after just three weeks, but when a Scottish army invades northern England in the fall, he's forced to summon Parliament again.

To secure Parliament's support this time, Charles is forced to accept the impeachment of Archbishop Laud. But Parliament's religious discontent is itself fractured and unstable, and it can't be contained. Divisions that open in 1641 lead to civil war between those who oppose the king, the monarchy, and the established church with its bishops, on one side, and those who despite their misgivings continue to support Charles. England's civil wars of more-than-religion arrive, though in a different form from what Elizabeth feared in the late sixteenth century. In league with the Scots, the Parliamentary army routs the royalist forces in 1646. That same year, the Puritan-controlled Parliament issues the *Westminster Confession of Faith,* which establishes a Presbyterian (Calvinist) church order in place of the recently abolished bishops. But the political situation is too unstable for either to take hold.

The late 1640s are particularly tumultuous, culminating in Parliament's execution of Charles I as a traitor in 1649, the abolition of the monarchy, and the proclamation of England as a republic. The Reformation in all its true variety is most visible in England during the English Republic, which lasts four years, from 1649 to 1653, and in subsequent years, when Oliver Cromwell, the former Parliamentary army leader, is named England's "Lord Protector" (1653–1658). Not since the 1520s in Germany has the Reformation in its open-ended breadth been so visible, with competing claims apparent among groups such as the Diggers, Quakers, Ranters, Baptists, Muggletonians, and Fifth Monarchists in addition to Presbyterians and Episcopalians, plus other sorts of Protestants, confused and exhausted, who long for the return of something resembling stability.[50]

Stability returns after Charles II is restored to the throne in 1660. The Restoration brings back the monarchy and the bishops, the *King James Bible, Book of Common Prayer,* and some room for theological views outside Reformed Protestantism within the medieval institutional structure of dioceses and parishes—in what we can start to call Anglicanism. Over the previous twenty years, England has endured a wringer of religious and political upheaval, which produces an understandable reaction against political radicalism and suspicion of religious "enthusiasm," as it is dismissively called by its opponents. As a result, in the early years of the Restoration, radical Protestants such as Quakers, Baptists, and dissenting Puritans are persecuted.

By comparison to the 1640s and 1650s, the kingdom is calmer, though that isn't saying much. England is still religiously divided as a result of its back-and-forth Reformation. Its conspicuous lack of a shared religious culture is a dramatic contrast to what existed before Henry VIII began to fancy Anne Boleyn. Religion remains a problem. Dissenters such as radical Protestants or Roman Catholics will still have to be managed. As in the rest of Europe, religion will have to be contained.

Violence, Revolt, and Breakup in the Low Countries

The Reformation also brings disruption, division, and violence to the Low Countries, the region covered by modern-day Belgium and the Netherlands. The Reformation era unfolds differently in the Low Countries than in the Holy Roman Empire, France, or England: while the northern provinces assert their independence from Spain and become a new country, the southern provinces remain tied to the Spanish crown. By the early seventeenth century, these distinct religious cultures are a study in contrasts. The Spanish Netherlands becomes almost exclusively Catholic whereas the Dutch Republic supports a Reformed Protestant "public church" with pragmatic innovations that prove influential throughout the century and long beyond.

In many ways, the Low Countries in the early sixteenth century looks much like other regions in central Europe where the Reformation takes off early.[51] It includes many prosperous towns located relatively close to one another. More of its urban inhabitants are literate than in most other regions of Europe. Cities such as Louvain and Antwerp enjoy a strong humanist tradition, one that extends beyond Erasmus, who for all his cosmopolitanism is a Dutchman by birth and upbringing. Several towns include communities of Observant Augustinians, Luther's religious order, some of whose members even spend time in Wittenberg between 1516 and 1520. Because the Dutch language is fairly close to German, more of Luther's works are soon translated into Dutch than into other languages. Yet despite all these similarities, no strong evangelical movement emerges in the Low Countries in the 1520s.

The main reason is repression by political authorities. Although the Low Countries belong to the Holy Roman Empire, they're subject to more direct control by the Habsburgs than are the free imperial cities or most German territories. The emperor, Charles V, was born in Ghent, a leading city in Flanders, and he is especially concerned about preventing heresy in his native region, though he often ends up playing political tug-of-war over heresy with local urban magistrates. Still, in the early 1520s the Flemish emperor, city magistrates, and clergy work more or less together to successfully stifle evangelical ideas.

In 1522, Antwerp's Observant Augustinian friary is shut down as a hotbed of Lutheran heresy. After two of its members refuse to recant, despite pressure from Charles V's inquisitors, they are burned as heretics on the main city square in Brussels in July 1523, celebrated by sympathizers as the first Reformation martyrs. There will be more executions for heresy in the Low Countries than anywhere else during the Reformation era—more than 1,300 by the pivotal year of 1566.[52]

Despite Charles V's resolve, the Anabaptist Münsterites successfully recruit followers among the Dutch, which contributes to
the many executions for heresy. After their kingdom is subdued
in Münster in 1535, dozens of beleaguered Anabaptists are put to
death in the Low Countries, a pattern that persists into the 1560s.[53]
Most of them, including the followers of Menno Simons, who begin
fissuring among themselves in the 1550s, denounce sedition and
violence, although their rhetoric against Catholic authorities is as
fierce as possible. The "baptism-minded" (*doopsgezinde*), as they're
known in the Low Countries, will remain part of the region's religious landscape throughout the Reformation era and throughout
the modern period. Yet after the Münster debacle they cease to have
much influence on the main course of the Dutch Reformation.

Instead, that role is taken up by Reformed Protestants. Just as
in France, Reformed Protestants are the Reformation's difference-
makers in the Low Countries,[54] though their growth and impact
lag a few years behind those of the Huguenots in France in the late
1550s. Yet both groups share a similar pattern.[55] Direct Calvinist
influence in the Low Countries tends to follow boundaries of language: it is most marked in Wallonia, the French-speaking southern
half of modern-day Belgium. There, Reformed missionary efforts
in the mid-1540s are violently suppressed by the local inquisition,
which Charles V reorganizes in 1546. More successful are the efforts
to establish Dutch-speaking Protestant communities a decade later
in Antwerp, right around the time Calvinists start organizing their
first church in Paris.[56]

Starting in the early 1560s, the number of Dutch Reformed
Protestants begins to climb. So too do acts of iconoclasm and public
Protestant preaching, as they had in France a few years earlier. The
Dutch converts receive international support from their Reformed
counterparts in London, where Elizabeth I has undone the
Catholicism previously reestablished by Mary I. Help also arrives

from Emden, just over the border in northern Germany, which for years served as an important haven for refugees and a center of Reformed Protestant printing.[57] Dutch Reformed Protestants also benefit from those who bristle at the region's severe antiheresy measures. Those policies are ratcheted up after Charles V steps down and cedes control of the Low Countries to his son, Philip II, the king of Spain. Not all Netherlanders who resent their new sovereign's heavy hand against heresy become Reformed Protestants, but by the mid-1560s converts are growing more plentiful.

The years 1565 and 1566 in the Low Countries look a lot like 1561 and 1562 in France: Reformed Protestants grow numerous and politically influential enough to force changes that they want. In late 1564, Dutch nobles petition Margaret of Parma, Philip II's regent in Brussels, to soften the antiheresy laws. Informed of this request, their Spanish-to-the-core king sharply rebuffs them in absentia, saying by letter that he'd rather lose all his lands and die a hundred deaths than be the sovereign of heretics.[58]

In April 1566, the resistance turns less polite: more than three hundred armed nobles ride into Brussels and present Margaret of Parma with the Compromise of the Nobility, a petition with hundreds of signatures demanding that the antiheresy laws be relaxed. With little recourse, the embattled Margaret relents. It's rather like the French edict of toleration that Catherine de Medici issues in January 1562 in response to Huguenot pressure.

In the Netherlands, 1566 is known as "the Wonder Year," *het wonderjaar.* The Compromise of the Nobility is like a spark to dry tinder: in the late spring and summer of 1566 Calvinism explodes in the Low Countries. Open-air preaching draws crowds of thousands in Ghent and Antwerp, while exiles pour back into the region from London, Emden, and other Reformed Protestant cities. Denunciations of Catholic idolatry and Spanish tyranny boil over on August 10 at Steenvorde in West Flanders, now just over the

Belgian border in France. Stirred by incendiary preaching, a bois-
terous crowd descends on a nearby monastery, sacks it, smashes
its statues and stained glass, and destroys its paintings, kicking off
the Iconoclastic Fury and, with it, the Dutch Revolt, the start of
what the Dutch call the Eighty Years' War. The initial incident at
Steenvorde sets off a chain reaction of destruction, which in the
ensuing months sweeps through Flanders, Brabant, and other provinces, including Holland to the north. In Flanders alone more than
four hundred churches are ransacked, looted, and vandalized.[59]

When Philip II receives word of the destruction taking place
in his lands a thousand miles to the northeast from Madrid, he
resolves to punish the sacrilegious rebels with a retaliation that will
make them yearn for the suspended antiheresy measures instead.
The enraged Philip sends the Duke of Alva, a distinguished and
severe military commander, to the Low Countries at the head of an
army of more than 10,000 men. To punish the perpetrators of the
Iconoclastic Fury and its associated rebels, Alva sets up a special
tribunal in 1567 called the Council of Troubles. Between 1567 and
1573 it tries more than 12,000 people, deprives more than 9,000
of some or all of their property, and executes more than 1,000.[60]
Small wonder the Council of Troubles is nicknamed the "Council of
Blood" by its critics. At the same time, several new taxes imposed at
Philip II's behest provoke ire among Calvinists and Catholics alike,
creating an opportunity for the emergence of a more ambitious
Dutch resistance.

Seizing the opportunity, the nobleman William of Orange tries
to keep religious antagonism separate from opposition to Spain in
order to unite Dutch Catholics and Calvinists against the Duke of
Alva and Philip II. Twice, in 1568 and again in 1571, he tries to
invade the Low Countries, but both times the Spanish army turns
him back. The following year, however, is a watershed year in the
Low Countries. Bands of Dutch Calvinist pirates, calling themselves

the "Sea Beggars," start recapturing towns in Holland. Joined by William of Orange's troops, they retake all the major cities in the province except Amsterdam by mid-1573. As they drive out Catholic magistrates and clergy, they seize church valuables, just as Henry VIII and Edward VI had done in England, and take over the looted churches in the name of Calvinism. Yet the Sea Beggars' murderous anti-Catholicism—they kill dozens of priests in 1572 and around 130 altogether[61]—threatens William's goal to keep Catholics and Calvinists together in a united front against the Spanish. His own religious views tend more toward pragmatic toleration. He acknowledges his debt to the Sea Beggars by joining a Reformed Protestant congregation in Delft in 1573, but he keeps quiet about his personal religious views, which earns him the nickname "William the Silent."

The 1570s are a decade of fierce fighting and much bloodshed. Philip II can't afford the massive outlay he needs to sustain large armies in both the Low Countries and the Mediterranean, where he's battling the Ottoman Turks, winning a huge victory against them at Lepanto in 1571. His troops in the Low Countries go unpaid, and as a result they mutiny repeatedly after 1572. These outbursts culminate in the sack of Antwerp, northern Europe's richest city, by frustrated troops during the Spanish Fury of November 1576. Although less famous than France's St. Bartholomew's Day Massacre, more than four times as many people (over 8,000) are killed, with more than 1,000 houses and other buildings also laid waste.[62] Again there's a brief opportunity to keep anti-Spanish resistance united across religious lines, but again Reformed Protestant militancy subverts any such hope, as Dutch Calvinists violently take over leading cities, including Ghent in 1577 and Amsterdam in 1578, which turns many Catholics against Dutch Calvinists and dilutes hostility toward the Spanish.

Over the next few years, the Dutch political coalition against Spain splits along religious lines, fracturing the Low Countries right along with it. Before his assassination in 1584 by a militant Catholic named Baltasar Gerard, William of Orange sees his dream of a united Netherlands free of Spanish control come to a dramatic end. In 1579, the provinces of Holland and Zeeland lead the way in forging the Union of Utrecht among the seven northern provinces. Their status as a new nation, the United Provinces of the Netherlands, or Dutch Republic, is formalized in 1581 when provincial representatives declare their independence from Philip II. No one at the time can possibly imagine how important these events will be or how influential the Dutch Republic will become in the seventeenth century, in ways that will eventually transform the Western world as a whole.

The southern provinces (essentially modern-day Belgium) move in the other direction. Starting in the late 1570s, Philip II can once again pay his troops. His brilliant new military commander, Alessandro Farnese, first galvanizes the Wallonians in the Union of Arras (1579) and then leads his troops to a series of triumphs over the Reformed Protestant urban regimes, including Antwerp. In the judgment of some, Catholicism under Spanish control is better than the violent aggression wrought by militant Calvinists. In 1585, Philip II installs Farnese as governor-general in Brussels, and Farnese begins stabilizing the southern provinces for Catholicism and a continuing Spanish presence in the Low Countries.

Yet the war doesn't end. The conflicts between the Dutch Republic and the Spanish Netherlands continue off and on all the way until 1648, when their resolution is folded into the Peace of Westphalia that concludes the Thirty Years' War. But, as the Reformation in the Low Countries plays out through the first two decades of the Dutch Revolt, the basic realignment of religion and politics in the north and south are essentially in place by the late 1580s.

After 1585, the Spanish Netherlands becomes a northern

European bastion of the Council of Trent's self-conscious, assertive Catholicism, with governing archdukes installed by the Spanish
king.[63] The archdukes become powerful patrons of the Catholic
Church and promoters of Catholic religious practices, much like the
dukes of Bavaria in southern Germany. The Spanish Netherlands
resembles France after Louis XIV revokes the Edict of Nantes: a
thoroughly Catholic state with robust antiheresy laws. After Farnese
reconquers the southern provinces in the 1580s, Protestants of all
sorts flee. Most head north, to the Dutch Republic, while others
become refugees to England or Protestant territories in the Holy
Roman Empire.

At first glance the Dutch Republic resembles a mirror image
of the Spanish Netherlands. To the south the archdukes sustain
the Catholic Church in the Spanish Netherlands, while the Dutch
Republic in the north supports a Reformed Protestant "public
church," paying its ministers' salaries. Only Calvinists are free to
worship in public and permitted to use the churches, almost all of
which had already been built and were Catholic churches before the
Dutch Revolt.

But upon closer inspection, the Dutch Republic is vastly different
from the Spanish Netherlands, specifically concerning the relationship between religion and politics. In fact, that relationship in the
Dutch Republic is unique in Western Europe. In the Dutch Republic
there is no *state* church, as there are in France, Spain, England, German Lutheran territories, Scandinavian countries, or the Reformed
Protestant territories of the Holy Roman Empire. People in the Dutch
Republic do not have to belong to a particular religion. Well into the
seventeenth century, the dominant, state-supported, public church in
the Dutch Republic includes only a small minority of the population.
Equally unique is the fact that, from its establishment, the Dutch
Republic remains a haven for religious groups of all sorts. Especially
in Amsterdam political authorities are relatively tolerant, allowing

almost anyone to believe and worship together however they wish, provided they worship behind the closed doors of "hidden churches" and remain politically obedient. As a result, large numbers of Catholics remain in the Dutch Republic, where they coexist with Lutherans, a wide variety of Mennonites and other radical Protestants, and even Sephardic Jews.

The Dutch hit on something important: they learn by experience that this sort of religious toleration, based on distinctions between public and private space, state support and individual preference, is good for business. And the most politically influential Dutch citizens are Holland's urban merchants. The wave of the future is Amsterdam, where merchants prioritize profits over piety. Within a few years, Amsterdam takes Antwerp's place as northern Europe's leading commercial city, which will prove crucial for the future— for the Dutch Republic and many other countries.

Religion as More-than-Religion: Creativity, Conflicts, and Impasses

As the Reformation spread from the Holy Roman Empire throughout Europe in the sixteenth century, political authorities had to confront it. They were forced to make hard choices—for or against it. What followed were equally hard decisions about how to implement the Reformation or how to resist it in practice in the local, face-to-face interactions where human life is lived.

Their decisions sometimes did not last long. Rulers could change their minds, leading to territorial changes of religion, as happened in the late sixteenth century when some German princes left Lutheranism for Calvinism. Or matters might get messier when a sovereign reversed a predecessor's religious decisions, as happened repeatedly in England between the 1530s and 1560.

Regardless of the form it took, political power was central to the Reformation era. Religion in the period can't be understood apart from politics, and neither can politics be understood apart from religion. Without the support of political authorities, no form of Christianity could shape the hearts and minds and practices of large numbers of men and women in a sustained way. In kingdoms or territories where Lutherans, Reformed Protestants, or Catholics lived as persecuted minorities, their experiences were less like those of their politically protected fellow believers and more like the experiences of beleaguered radical Protestants.

Magisterial Protestants, radical Protestants, and Catholics all showed constructive creativity, commitment, and courage during the Reformation era. Clerical leaders in all these traditions sought to instill in lay believers the teachings, sensibilities, and practices they thought God required of them. To this end, extraordinary efforts were made to instruct, educate, catechize, exhort, encourage, advise, admonish, and console. Thousands of religious publications were printed, with millions of copies sold, purchased, distributed, read, and reflected upon throughout Europe. Schools aimed to form educated Christians at every level, from teaching basic literacy to young children through offering rigorous university instruction in Latin.

In Protestant traditions, distinctive readings of the Bible inspired divergent ways of worshipping and praying, and new grooves of religious experience were worn into the channels cut by new doctrines about Christian faith and life. Among Catholics, traditional ways of worshipping and praying were infused with new energy, augmented by new devotions and boosted through lay instruction on a scale unknown in the Middle Ages. Depending on the place and time, Catholics, magisterial Protestants, and Anabaptists alike all demonstrated their willingness to endure hardship, persecution, and even death for their religious commitments.

The Reformation era was a period of extraordinary religious vitality. It extended and deepened the long-standing medieval assumption that Christianity *should* influence and infuse all areas of human life because it came from God and expressed God's will for all human beings. Nothing lay outside God's creation. So of course, religion *should* be about more than just beliefs, worship, and devotion; it *should* also inform the exercise of power, shape social relationships, constrain economic transactions, and mold higher education. And in order to do this, religion had to be shared; it had to be collective, not merely individual.

Yet this widely shared assumption was precisely what made Christianity such a profound problem in the Reformation era. The most fundamental and influential fact about the Reformation era is its sustained disagreement. The particular forms of trouble varied, as historical realities always do, influenced by a thousand and one contingencies; France's civil wars differed from the Thirty Years' War, and the Dutch Revolt and Eighty Years' War looked different than the English Revolution. But all these conflicts shared serious, more-than-religious problems that could not be separated from the religious disagreements that began roiling Europe in the 1520s.

We would like to look back and see that by 1650, Christian theologians had been substantially changed by more than a century of conflicts and controversies. It would be heartening if we could see that by the mid-seventeenth century they were making steady (or even any) progress toward resolving their differences about scripture, authority, ministry, the sacraments, or the nature of the Church.

But they weren't. Conflicting claims about Christian truth were no more settled by 1648 than they had been in the 1520s.

When theologians and clerical leaders during this era mustered up toleration, it was usually—at best—grudging. They reluctantly accepted coexistence as a lesser of two evils; it was preferred over more rounds of war. They'd seen too much of battles and killing and sieges and suffering born of mutual distrust and hatred. The Reformation era did not inspire much warm-hearted ecumenism.

The very foundation of Christendom turned into its central problem, so it fractured violently. Both the disruptiveness of the Reformation and rulers' determined resistance to it appeared already in the early 1520s and remained throughout the period. In many different, often prolonged, and frequently convoluted ways, both Reformation and resistance played out across the European continent for over a century. In this process the Reformation's leaders and opponents turned Christianity itself into an unprecedented problem throughout Europe. By the mid-seventeenth century, a new sort of creativity was needed if an exhausted continent was to avoid destroying itself.

The responses that some people began to express in the seventeenth century still live with us today. The modern Western world, in its basic ideas, institutions, and assumptions, is in large measure the product of the interrelated responses that arose to address problems inherited from the Reformation era. Of course, that's not obvious at first sight. Technologically and economically, our world in the early twenty-first century differs dramatically from the predominantly agrarian, rural world of preindustrial Europe and North America. But in the seventeenth century, intellectual, institutional, and economic innovations began to address the problems left in the wake of the Reformation. The developments since then have been transformed in many ways, but they extend seventeenth-century responses that remain continuous with the dominant institutions, ideas, and practices of the early twenty-first century.

At the heart of these innovations lies a rethinking and repositioning of religion. Because religion as more-than-religion proved to be so problematic in the Reformation era, religion thereafter will begin to be circumscribed and restricted. It will begin to be separated from the many domains of human life it had previously informed, demoted to being just another part of life. Besides being redefined and narrowed in scope, religion will be refashioned as a matter of individual choice—another major modern innovation. The freedom of a Christian will come to include the freedom *not* to be a Christian—or a Jew or Muslim or member of any other religious tradition. Freedom *of* religion will imply the potential for freedom *from* religion.

The long-term outcome of the Reformation era—and its ultimate irony—has been the gradual, unintended secularization of modern Western society. That process still goes on today, which is why the early twenty-first century can't be understood apart from the Reformation, whether we like it or not.

CHAPTER 4

A NEW WORLD

THE REFORMATION is a paradox: a religious revolution that led to the secularization of society.

In the later seventeenth century and well into the eighteenth, most European rulers continued to regard religious uniformity as the ideal for a well-regulated state, even after the Thirty Years' War and the English Revolution. Seeing the devastation wrought by such disruptions convinced them more than ever that religious division was dangerous. Sharing a common faith would support the obedience that rulers wanted in both the Protestant and Catholic regimes of Western Europe. And so political authorities continued to pursue religious uniformity, as did Charles II in 1660 when he reconstituted the Church of England or as Louis XIV did when he took measures against the Huguenots in France that culminated in the revocation of the Edict of Nantes in 1685. For most political authorities, nonconformist religious minorities remained a problem.

New ways of trying to deal with the difficulties of the Reformation era did not emerge all at once. No European rulers, reeling from the Thirty Years' War, made a beeline for modern liberal democracy or toleration or pluralism or capitalism. Not at all. In retrospect, we can see that scattered practices pointing in these directions started as early as the sixteenth century in local settings where Christians from different traditions rubbed shoulders. Encounters between Catholics and Protestants did not automatically lead to violence; Christians sometimes began hammering out face-to-face ways of putting up with heretics or papists they may have disdained or even despised. Their pragmatism in trying to work out day-to-day accommodations implies that they considered grudging coexistence better than disruptive hostility, let alone war.[1]

In subsequent decades and indeed centuries, the ideas, behaviors, and institutions that contributed to secularization spread across Europe, unplanned and uncoordinated. They coalesced out of the countless human desires, decisions, and actions taken at the local level, which taken together contributed to uneven and piecemeal long-term developments. Often it's harder to discern history's gradual processes than its discrete events. In order to see them, we have to stand back and cast a wide gaze on changes across centuries. This is true as well of the unintended processes of secularization that followed the Reformation era; they did not emerge quickly or win the day suddenly in the seventeenth century or even the nineteenth.

Without a doubt, though, these secularizing trends, which developed over centuries, have dramatically transformed the Western world. Today in Europe and North America, no religion has anywhere near the public presence in or the influence upon society that Christianity exerted on European life during the Reformation era and, before that, the Middle Ages. A profound transformation has occurred. Because over the long term it resulted in vastly reducing religion's influence in public life, the Reformation has had the overriding *eventual* outcome of bringing about secularization in Western society. It is a secularization that would have dismayed and confounded sixteenth-century Protestant reformers and their Catholic rivals alike, all of whom wanted to make their society and culture *more* thoroughly Christian, not less. But the conflicts that derived from their attempts to do so prompted decisions and actions that, despite their intentions, have made religion much less prominent in public life in the early twenty-first century. Ironically, their actions led to the reactions that have in turn led to this result.

This paradoxical, long-term process of secularization is the broadest and most far-reaching outcome of the Reformation era. Yet there have been other unintended consequences. Two of them we've already seen, both of which have endured since the seventeenth century and have been transformed along the way. The first concerns Protestantism, while the second involves the relationship between magisterial Protestantism and Roman Catholicism.

The first unintended consequence of the Reformation itself was the proliferation of so many rival versions of Protestantism. Luther proclaimed the gospel as he understood it based on what he took to be the Bible's clear, correct meaning. He did not set out to start his own church or to initiate a movement whose outcome would be the construction of separate Protestant churches at odds with each other. Neither did he want to open a Pandora's box of competing interpretations about the meaning of God's Word. But those are the things that happened right from the start of the Reformation in the 1520s as a result of his own emphasis on *sola scriptura*. The very same principle on which he based his rejection of the papacy and the Roman Catholic Church also inspired competing and contentious claims about the Word of God. Separate Protestant churches and rival readings of the Bible have persisted for five hundred years, all the way up to the present.

Between the end of the Anabaptist Kingdom of Münster in 1535 and the beginning of the English Revolution in 1640, persecution and the marginalizing of radical Protestants put a brake on the open-ended pluralism of Protestantism. But that open-endedness is obvious in how diverse Protestant churches and religious groups have proliferated under the political conditions of modern liberal democracies. Nowhere has this been more evident than in the United States since its founding in the late eighteenth century. This proliferation would have horrified Luther and Calvin, who were appalled already by the much smaller numbers of Protestants who disagreed with them in the sixteenth century.

A second major unintended consequence of the Reformation era came out of the relationship between magisterial Protestantism and Catholicism. Just as the reformers never intended to pave the way for any and all interpretations of God's Word, so they never intended to facilitate endless doctrinal controversy or recurrent violence, let alone to divide Christendom itself. Neither Protestant nor Catholic leaders wanted this to be the outcome of the Reformation *era*. Catholic clerical and political leaders wanted the Catholic reforms that were already underway prior to 1517 to continue. They wanted as well a Counter-Reformation that would successfully suppress the Reformation, as medieval heresies had been suppressed, or would at least contain and control the new sixteenth-century heretics. And those Protestant reformers and political leaders who didn't think the apocalypse was nigh wanted the Roman Church to collapse and their own version of the restored gospel to triumph, whichever version theirs happened to be.

Neither happened. From the Catholic perspective, heresy was institutionalized in multiple forms. As far as Protestants were concerned, the Antichrist got a major second wind. The Reformation did not overcome or abolish Roman Catholicism; rather, it actually contributed directly if unintentionally to rejuvenating the Roman Church. While Protestants were rejecting Rome, missionaries from Catholic religious orders, at first Franciscans and then especially Jesuits, were spreading Catholicism more widely around the world than it had ever been spread before. Catholicism in its global diversity remains as much a part of the modern Western world as is Protestant pluralism. It would have chagrined both Catholic and

Protestant leaders in the Reformation era to see how entrenched this unintended Christian split has remained. And Western Christianity remains divided today despite the many ecumenical efforts and achievements of the past half century.[2]

Throughout the modern era to the present, religion has remained a constant presence in Europe and North America. Here, then, *secularization* does not mean the disappearance or elimination of religion. It doesn't mean merely a decline in the number of people who attend worship services or pray or say they believe in God. Instead, it refers specifically to the declining influence of religion in public life—all those areas of human life that in the Middle Ages and the Reformation era Christianity was supposed to inform: politics, law, economics, education, social relationships, family life, morality, and the culture at large.

Indeed, the story of how the modern era took shape in the Western world is fundamentally about how countless human decisions and actions contributed to secularization. This story has everything to do with managing and controlling religion precisely because in the Reformation era Christianity itself became such a wide-ranging problem. Disagreements about Christian doctrine and practice mattered so much because religion was about so much *more* than religion during this life, not to mention its implications for eternity. So when the disagreements gained social and political traction—as they did in the Holy Roman Empire, France, England, and the Low Countries—the results were cataclysmic.

The basic solution to the problem, then, required finding ways to make religion's disruptive and divisive elements matter *less* in public life. For centuries, Christianity had been embedded in all areas of human life and had been intended to influence everything. So moving toward a solution meant that its problematic elements or features would have to be *dis*embedded from everything. What would that look like?

To separate religion from public life first required people to start *conceiving* of religion as something that could be separated from politics, economics, and social relationships. At the same time, they also had to conceive of politics, economics, and social relationships as things that could and should operate apart from religion. In short, religion itself had to be redefined and its scope drastically curtailed. This new way of thinking relegated religion to a combination of one's interior beliefs, preferred practices of worship, and individually chosen devotional practices. These were fine, because they didn't aspire to influence anything that was supposed to apply to everyone. They are essentially what we usually mean by *religion* today.

This redefining of religion went hand in hand with making religion an individual choice: individual religious freedom became possible because religion's scope was greatly restricted. In the Reformation era individuals disagreed about religion, sometimes even within the same families, which meant that religious freedom would have to be protected at the individual level. This too represented a dramatic change from adhering to religious beliefs and practices that were meant to apply to everyone.

Religion, regardless of its content, could be tolerated so long as all who benefited from individual religious freedom agreed on its newly limited scope and agreed as well to obey the political authorities who extended and protected that freedom. Making religion a personal choice and restricting its scope made religious freedom as well as religious toleration *possible*. It also led to separating out many other areas of life from religion. Because restricting religion meant viewing it as separable from the rest of life, those who imagined restrictions on religion also came to imagine the rest of life as separable from religion. Restricting and redefining religion opened the way to secularization through separation, though in practice that detachment remains a complicated process that has been unfolding over centuries.

As an ongoing, long-term process, secularization also has an intellectual dimension. During the Middle Ages, Christian ideas about reality, human nature, and human life provided the intellectual backbone for Latin Christendom. The Reformation turned that backbone into a bone of contention. Theological controversies that opened in the 1520s remained unresolved in the 1650s, after the Thirty Years' War and the English Revolution. How could entrenched religious opponents agree about human nature, morality, the nature of government, and other issues at once fundamental and divisive? They would have to agree to disagree; they would have to set aside their contentious religious views when they embarked on common endeavors. As a religious intellectual endeavor, theology would have to be separated from philosophy and the investigation of the natural world, neither of which could depend on anything divisively religious if either wanted to enlist Christian adversaries in a common enterprise.

It's no accident that modern philosophy and the Enlightenment emerged in the seventeenth century as intellectual reactions to the problems of the Reformation era. Neither is it an accident that two major thinkers whose ideas have deeply influenced the modern world were themselves directly and adversely affected by the wars of more-than-religion: René Descartes (1596–1650), who was a soldier during the early phase of the Thirty Years' War, and Thomas Hobbes (1591–1679), who took refuge in Paris during the tumult of the English Revolution.[3]

Seeking to avoid the theological controversies that followed in the wake of the Reformation, Hobbes, Descartes, and other influential thinkers turned to reason in order to ground morality, justify political authority, and conceptualize society. If descriptions of human beings and prescriptions for human life hoped to persuade people who disagreed about religion, these descriptions would have to avoid contentious references to religion. If you didn't want just to keep preaching to the choir, you had to learn to sing a different song. In principle, secular philosophy would depend on reason and reason alone. While people held different religious beliefs, they all shared the ability to reason, which would allow secular philosophy to avoid the theological controversies that had roiled Europe for more than a century. Or at least that was the plan.

This incremental—and largely piecemeal—process of secularization is the subject of this chapter. The aim is to trace how ideas, practices, and institutions central to modern liberal democracies are interrelated aspects of the ways that the modern Western world addressed problems inherited from the Reformation era. These intertwined ideas, practices, and institutions include individual freedom and autonomy, freedom of religion, religious toleration, the separation of church and state, secular public discourse, and the pursuit of human fulfillment through material well-being, none of which characterized the Reformation era.

Tracing the course of this historical trajectory will show why understanding that alien world from five centuries ago is crucial for understanding our world today. It will thus show why, regardless of your own beliefs and whether or not you're a religious person, the Reformation remains relevant in the early twenty-first century.

Going Dutch: Restricting Religion and Unleashing Commerce

The process of managing religion in order to address the problems of the Reformation era begins in an unlikely place: in a strange little republic at war with Europe's most powerful monarchy, from which it has just declared its independence.

At a time when European monarchs are trying to consolidate and centralize their power, the Dutch Republic emphasizes local

privileges and provinces. The new country has only around a million inhabitants and few natural resources. Large stretches of its
territory are under water or subject to flooding. It has just rebelled
against Spain, with whom it remains at war. Furthermore, it is
home to multiple religious groups at a time when the Reformation
has made religion an unprecedented problem.[4] This isn't the sort of
place that looks poised to change Western history. Yet that's what
happens.

Religious freedom is an issue from the very beginning of the
United Provinces of the Netherlands. According to the Union of
Utrecht (1579), the Dutch Republic's most important founding document, each province is allowed to address religion as it sees fit,
without interference from the other provinces, "so long as each person shall be permitted to remain free in his religion and that no one
shall be permitted to be investigated or persecuted for reason of
religion."[5]

The Union of Utrecht contrasts sharply with the Union of Arras,
which mandates Catholicism as the established religion of the southern provinces in the Low Countries.[6] The only exception to the religious policy proclaimed by the Union of Utrecht is that it prohibits
the reestablishment or restoration of Catholicism by force. Shortly
thereafter, in 1581, amid the ongoing strife of the war with Spain,
Holland officially outlaws Catholic worship altogether.

Because the Unions of Arras and Utrecht diverge so sharply, more
than a hundred thousand Protestant religious refugees—pushed by
fear of persecution and lured by the prospect of religious freedom—
move from the southern to the northern provinces in the years that
follow. Immigrants come from elsewhere in Europe too, including
many Lutherans from northern Germany and Scandinavia.

The economic impact on the cities in Holland, the leading province in the Dutch Republic, is immediate and dramatic.[7] By the
1590s, Leiden, where the republic's first university was established

in 1575, becomes one of the leading centers for textile production in all of Europe. In the seventeenth century, Holland's cities, newly teeming with immigrants, establish niches to capitalize on the suddenly booming Dutch economy. One such city, Gouda, produces huge quantities of cheap clay pipes for smoking tobacco, a New World import cultivated intensively in Gelderland, east of Holland. Delft becomes known for its ceramics, especially the signature blue-on-white designs inspired by Chinese pottery that Dutch merchants bring back to Europe.

Holland's biggest urban economic success story is Amsterdam. In the mid-1580s, as part of the back-and-forth conflicts of the ongoing war, the city benefits from the naval blockade of Antwerp, many of whose merchants relocate to Amsterdam. Within a decade, Amsterdam is on its way to replacing Antwerp as northern Europe's leading center of commerce. Merchants develop and expand an already extensive shipping fleet long used to import grain, and in the seventeenth century the city becomes the maritime hub of the Dutch Republic's fishing, whaling, shipbuilding, construction, and sugar-refining industries, among others. Amsterdam is transformed into the center of the world's first genuinely global commercial empire. Its traders turn Holland's lack of natural resources and coastal location into an advantage by looking outward.

Already in the 1590s, merchants are venturing across the Atlantic to the Caribbean and around the southern coast of Africa to Asia. Established in 1602, the Dutch East India Company, Europe's first joint-stock enterprise, encourages investment and proves enormously profitable by pooling the resources of investors and limiting their individual risks in trade with Asia. Within the next decade, the Amsterdam Exchange Bank and Stock Exchange are set up, and the Dutch West India Company follows in 1621, sparking spectacular economic as well as demographic growth. In less than twenty-five years, the city's inhabitants more than double, growing from 30,000 in 1585 to 70,000 in 1609. By 1622, just thirteen years later, Amsterdam tops 100,000, and by the 1680s its population more than doubles again to 220,000.[8] In less than a century, the city grows seven times larger.

The Dutch economic miracle wouldn't be happening if its most influential magistrates had tried to make Reformed Protestantism into the mandatory religion of the United Provinces, the way magistrates in the southern Netherlands are imposing and maintaining Catholicism. Throughout the cities in Holland, political influence, trade, and wealth all go together. Between 1600 and 1625, three-quarters of the forty-one men appointed to Amsterdam's city government are involved in commerce.[9] And Dutch trade is open to merchants and investors, buyers and sellers, from different religious backgrounds, for much is literally to be gained by this sort of religious toleration. Among the wealthy entrepreneurs are Calvinists, Arminians, Lutherans, Mennonites, Catholics, and even Jews.

Amsterdam's powerful mercantile class buys into a solution to the defining problem of the Reformation era, a solution that facilitates profitmaking and includes religious toleration in exchange for a narrowed view of religion and restrictions on how it can be practiced. This directly concerns what the Union of Utrecht is interpreted to mean by being "free in your religion." Soaring economic prosperity, coupled with permission to believe and worship in private as one wishes, appeals to beleaguered religious minorities; they understandably prefer it to banishment, imprisonment, or worse. By and large, non-Calvinist Christians are grateful.[10] They have it a lot better than do the groups that are considered beyond the pale even in Amsterdam and are officially prohibited. These include Socinians (the predecessors of modern Unitarians, who deny the Trinity and the divinity of Christ) and atheists (an accusation leveled against the Jewish philosopher Spinoza).

By comparison, the situation is better for Amsterdam's Catholics, although not as good as it is for Lutherans or Mennonites. By the second half of the seventeenth century, there are more than twenty partly clandestine Catholic churches in the metropolis, with masses being celebrated behind multistory brick facades that from the street look just like other canal houses. (One of them has been preserved and restored and can be visited today as a museum, called *Ons' Lieve Heer op Solder*—"Our Dear Lord in the Attic.")[11] In other cities the situation is often more difficult. Sometimes local officials accept "recognition money"—in effect, regularly paid bribes—to allow priests to say mass and administer the sacraments. On other occasions, they raid Catholics gathered for worship, arrest priests, and exact fines.[12]

In Amsterdam too, Catholics have to pay off officials, but there you can be a prosperous Catholic, believing and practicing your faith behind closed doors. So long as you don't dream of your religion influencing politics or economic policies or fantasize about staging a public procession on a feast day or organize a pilgrimage to a saint's shrine, you probably won't get into trouble. Sharing their religion with Spain, with whom their own country is at war until 1648, Catholics remain the most problematic of the tolerated religious minorities in the Dutch Republic. Lutherans and Jews, by contrast, receive permission to construct public places of worship in Amsterdam.[13] Small wonder that Holland becomes renowned as a haven for religious refugees from elsewhere in Europe. It isn't perfect if you aren't a Calvinist, but by comparison there is no comparison.

The restrictions on religion affect the state-supported Reformed Protestant Church in a different way.[14] It is the politically backed "public church," yet the ruling magistrates in Holland's cities and above all in Amsterdam don't allow it to dictate the tenor of public life. Political authorities pay the salaries of Calvinist ministers, who have a monopoly on both public worship and the use of church buildings, which gives them a public presence and a source of support enjoyed by no other religious groups. But in contrast to almost everywhere else in Western Europe, you don't face persecution or explicit penalties if you don't belong to the public church. And most people choose not to belong, though the number who do grows during the seventeenth century. Consequently, during the new nation's Golden Age, Calvinists are a paradoxical, politically privileged, state-supported religious minority in the Dutch Republic. Belonging to a church community no longer coincides with belonging to a civic community or being a political subject. Public social and political life are being separated from religious life as part of the secularizing process.

At the same time, this separation is made easier because Christians continue to share so much in common despite their particular religious differences. They're divided over the interpretation of scripture, grace and salvation, the sacraments, the nature of the Church, and other contentious issues. But the vast majority of Christians still share the same fundamental ideas about marriage, family relationships, responsibilities to others, civic duties, and morality in promotion of a shared urban life and its day-to-day interactions. Some Protestants even make explicit appeals to basic Christian doctrines and piety to foster concord and coexistence.[15]

But even in Amsterdam there remains no shortage of hard-core Calvinists who reject such appeals as a dilution of true Christianity. Similar to their English Puritan contemporaries, they dream of a city more in line with Calvin's Geneva. But even while they try to attract more non-Calvinists into the Reformed public church, they don't get their way. Amsterdam's wealthy and powerful magistrates, related by intermarriage and commercial ventures, call the shots. And this mercantile oligarchy creates the most unusual urban experiment in Europe for addressing the problem of religion that follows in the wake of the Reformation. It marries a limited religious toleration and religious freedom with a restricted public church and a dynamic economy. Hundreds of men from dozens of families make spectacular fortunes through global trade in spices or luxury goods, armaments or slaves. Multiple generations of the Trip family, for instance, derive the core of their fortune from iron and armaments and later branch into commercial ventures and banking services. Two of the Trip brothers build a spectacular house on Amsterdam's Kloverniersburgwal in the early 1660s, like other wealthy men who build along Amsterdam's canals beautiful homes that four centuries later continue to project power and prosperity.[16] But these families are just the most conspicuous tip of the iceberg.

What really makes Holland's economic miracle miraculous—and its innovative solution to the problem of religion so eventually influential—is how many thousands of people literally profit from it. In Amsterdam and other cities in Holland, artisans, shopkeepers, lawyers, teachers, ministers, and merchants' employees all get richer. With their money they pursue and buy more possessions. Thousands of them can even afford original paintings, such as the portraits and landscapes and still lifes that make Golden-Age Dutch art famous. It is an unprecedented display of more widely distributed social commercial power, and it contrasts sharply with the few wealthy patrons in the fifteenth century who commissioned Italian Renaissance art. Urban manual laborers in the Dutch Republic benefit also, enjoying increases in real wages of some 20 to 40 percent from the 1580s until around 1640.[17]

Seventeenth-century visitors to Holland often comment on both its prosperity and its distinctive approach to religious pluralism. In a book-length description of the republic in 1673, William Temple, England's ambassador to the United Provinces, writes that "as in other places, 'tis in every man's choice, with whom he will eat or lodge, with whom go to market, or to court; so it seems to be here, with whom he will pray or go to church, or associate in the service or worship of God; nor is any more notice taken, of what everyone chooses in these cases, than in the other." Like eating or shopping, religion has become an everyday matter of individual choice. Temple states that its power "lies in every man's heart" and that through it "everyone falls most into the company or conversation of those whose customs and humors, whose talk and disposition they like best."[18] In Temple's estimate, religion in the Dutch Republic has become a matter dependent on your likes and dislikes.

At the same time, Temple makes clear that political authorities are anything but indifferent to religion. Knowing that religion can cause trouble—just as it had during the early German Reformation, among the Anabaptists at Münster, during the English Revolution, in the Dutch Revolt, and in the conflict between Dutch Calvinists and Arminians in the 1610s—magistrates keep watch on the gatherings of religious groups, alert to "anything that passes there to the prejudice of the state, in which case the laws and executions are as severe as against any civil crimes."[19] In other words, the authorities determine whether and when religion becomes objectionably political, and they take action if it does. They oversee religion and control it.

The urban magistrates of Holland, no less than Louis XIV in France or Charles II in England, are seeking to control religion. But they're doing it very differently: through a public church that is not a state religion, combined with a redefinition of religion that restricts it to individually chosen beliefs, worship, and devotional practices distinct from politics, economic transactions, and social life at large. Religion is being separated from domains of human life in ways it had not been before. Compared to the coercion, persecution, and violence taking place elsewhere during the Reformation era, the Dutch stick isn't too menacing and its carrot is appetizing: you get to worship in private with your fellow believers with less harassment, and there's the prospect of payoffs regardless of your religious views in the booming Golden-Age economy.

The Dutch innovation provides not only different sorts of Christians but also Jews the opportunity to devote themselves to something besides religion. It turns out that regardless of their religion, almost everyone likes more and better material things. More and better possessions make their lives more comfortable as they pursue them according to their own preferred beliefs and priorities. Religion can no longer hold society together. That has become painfully obvious since the outset of the Reformation, despite repeated, determined attempts to make it work through political coercion and military force. But maybe a new vision of the good life as the goods life can substitute for religion, if everyone buys into it.

The Dutch turn conventional wisdom inside out. Tolerating false religion is supposed to provoke God's wrath while fostering true religion is supposed to elicit divine approval, and the presence of multiple religious groups is supposed to be a recipe for conflict. The Dutch show instead that toleration of restricted religion combined with political obedience is a promising formula for peace and prosperity. No wonder their experiment appeals to religiously divided men and women! Whatever its shortcomings, it looks a lot better than the prospect of additional more-than-religious hostilities.

The widespread desire to gain more possessions, which fuels the embrace of economic ambition, departs in a striking way from the views of the major Protestant reformers as well as their Catholic counterparts and medieval predecessors. Luther was even more hostile to usury—the charging of interest on loans—than were medieval Catholic scholastic authors or their intellectual heirs in the sixteenth century. Calvin railed against showy dress, and in 1557, Geneva had approved loans at between 6 and 7 percent to restrain greed not stimulate it.[20]

In medieval Christianity, greed, or avarice, was one of the seven deadly sins. Jesus warned about it in the Gospels: "Be on your guard against all kinds of greed; for one's life does not consist in the abundance of possessions" (Luke 12:15). Greed is denounced repeatedly throughout the Bible. When Dutch Calvinists, Catholics, Lutherans, and Mennonites start down the Golden-Age path to riches as the solution to the Reformation era's problems of religion, they're walking away from what scripture and more than fifteen hundred years of Christian tradition warned about: avarice, wealth, and the pursuit of possessions endanger Christian faith. As it turns out, down the road this aspect of secularization will continue to sell very well.

Not everyone is content among the seventeenth-century Dutch or thinks affluence comes without costs. Some Mennonites bemoan that their congregations are being *harmed* by toleration and the wealth that accompanies it. Through the hardships of persecution and martyrdom in the sixteenth century, Anabaptist communities retained a clear sense of community and a strong sense of identity, but over time toleration and assimilation risk sapping them of their spiritual strength. The most famous Mennonite martyrologist, Thieleman Jans van Braght, writes that life is *more* dangerous for their communities at the height of the Dutch Golden Age than it was in the sixteenth century. At that time Satan attacked them openly, but now he seduces them with the money and possessions that are pouring into Holland's port cities from around the world.

Enlightenment, Enrichment, and a New Empire

In the early seventeenth century the Dutch also are observing the natural world and using it in new ways—which is not surprising since these endeavors are closely connected to commerce and moneymaking. If you understand what plants, animals, and minerals are made of, you can figure out what they're useful for and how to turn

them into a profit.[21] Observing and describing nature is available
to Lutherans, Catholics, Calvinists, Arminians, Jews, and everyone
else in equal measure. The same is true for charting the courses of
the stars or figuring out the motions of the planets or determining
that the physical forces involved with moving objects on earth can
be represented with mathematical formulas.

Discussing such things in the early seventeenth century doesn't
involve broaching the interpretation of scripture or the nature of
the Church; these things can be set aside. Investigating the natural world in pursuit of knowledge and truth can be bracketed from
divisive doctrinal disagreements. Similarly separable from religion
is technology. That is, rival interpretations of Christian doctrines
matter little for how the new knowledge of the natural world can be
applied to serve human desires—including desires for more possessions, comfort, and enjoyment. Not only in the Dutch Republic but
just about everywhere else in Europe, people are keen on acquiring
material things to make their lives more pleasant.

Across the channel from the Dutch Republic in England, Francis
Bacon (1561–1626) thinks human beings should not just observe
nature but actively intervene in it—experiment on it—in order to
develop new ways to alleviate suffering and promote enjoyment.
In France, René Descartes, who fought in the Thirty Years' War,
holds a similar view, as do many other Enlightenment thinkers in
the seventeenth and eighteenth centuries. Descartes conceives of the
natural world as a vast mechanism of interconnected causes and
effects. The better they're understood, the better they can be turned
to human advantage.

Whereas theology relies on divine revelation, philosophy and
natural philosophy rely on human observation and reason alone,
apart from revelation, which has divided Christians since the 1520s.
Unlike theology, which shows no signs of resolving the controversies
of the Reformation era, natural philosophy can actually be applied

to get the things people want. Within modern philosophy and the Enlightenment lies a strong impulse to turn away from theology and toward the investigation of nature, to cordon off references to anything supernatural. Or at least to bracket the contentious aspects of theology, such as interpretation of the Bible, and issues that depend on particular interpretations of scripture, such as sin, grace, salvation, sacraments, ministry, and authority. This endeavor is called "natural theology"—talking about God on the basis of reason alone, without reference to revelation or scripture. Natural theology contributes to secularization by relegating more explicit, robust Christian theology to the sidelines, away from public life.

The mid-seventeenth century is a watershed not only in ideas but also in the principal motivations for war among European nations. In 1648 the Peace of Westphalia ends the Thirty Years' War, which started in central Europe in the midst of fierce, more-than-religious tensions in the late 1610s. Between 1652 and 1674, however, the Dutch and English fight a series of three naval wars. Trade and money, not religion, animate these conflicts between northern Europe's two leading Protestant powers.

These naval wars plus a costly land war, restrictions on trade, high wages, and other developments mark the 1670s as the decade when the Dutch magic begins to fade.[22] Weak central institutions earlier served the United Provinces well, but now their absence has become a liability. Meanwhile, the English are headed in the opposite direction, despite their crisis of the 1680s, when James II, a Catholic, ascends the throne in 1685 and provokes considerable anti-Catholic consternation. Leading English Protestants invite William III of Orange and his wife, Mary, from the Dutch Republic to oust the papist king in the "Glorious Revolution" of 1688, which they do. (Five years later the first college established in England's North American colony of Virginia will be named William and Mary in their honor.)

After English-Dutch conflicts in the previous decades, England's relationship with the Dutch Republic becomes less belligerent but more controlling.[23] In addition to gaining experience through their own maritime endeavors, the English have been trading with and learning from the Dutch for a century. Now they watch Dutch military and economic clout wane, and London replaces Amsterdam as Europe's leading commercial city. The English wed the know-how they've acquired to a stronger and more ambitious empire of their own, one with many colonies abroad. It includes their colonies on the east coast of North America, before and after the union of England with Scotland creates Great Britain in 1707.

From the Dutch, the English also learn something about commercial ruthlessness and limited religious toleration, which they meld with their own fraught history of Christian conflicts since the days of Henry VIII. After 1660, measures against dissenters at first are harsh, with the memory of more-than-religious "enthusiasm" still fresh from the 1640s and 1650s. Then these measures are softened to accommodate nonconformists who embody and exemplify the unsought Protestant pluralism of the Reformation. New theories of religious toleration are articulated as Enlightenment ideas. In 1689 John Locke publishes *A Letter Concerning Toleration,* which is based on a sharp separation between states and churches, politics and religion, external and interior things, bodies and souls.[24] In the same year, a Toleration Act is passed by Parliament that permits anyone who wants to remain outside of the Anglican Church to do so, ending a process that originally sought to include as many Protestant dissenters as possible within that Church.[25] A smaller fraction of English subjects belong to the state church than at any time since its creation by Henry VIII.

Protestant pluralism in England continues to increase. As the political control of Protestantism in England diminishes, the open-endedness of the Reformation itself becomes more obvious.

Isaac Newton's scientific breakthroughs inspire new varieties of Protestantism with minimal connections to the Bible. This is ironic, since the majority of Newton's own writings concern biblical prophecy and apocalypticism, but they remain unpublished at the time and therefore unknown until much later. Newton's published views, by contrast, overlap with natural theology and inspire deism. Deists believe in a God who created the universe and kick-started its vast cause-and-effect mechanism but then stepped aside and does not interact at all with the world, including with human beings. Scripture matters little to deists, except perhaps as a way of reinforcing moral views they believe can be independently derived from reason alone. Just the opposite is true of John Wesley and his followers, called Methodists, starting in the 1730s, with their emphases on the Bible and individual religious experience.[26]

This English and Scottish Protestant pluralism travels with colonists to the east coast of North America beginning in the early seventeenth century. In 1614 the Dutch start colonizing what will become the British middle colonies, between New England and the Chesapeake Bay, with New Amsterdam becoming New York in 1664 and reminders of its Dutch past lingering in names such as Harlem, Brooklyn, and Wall Street, the place where Dutch colonists built a wall to shield themselves from Indians.[27] Only in Virginia is the Church of England the established church. Puritans who hate Archbishop Laud's "beauty of holiness," his Catholic-looking aesthetic and liturgical changes in the Church of England, leave for Massachusetts beginning in 1630—and within a decade they encounter the same problems of dissent and separatism that marked Reformed Protestantism in England. One of those separatist dissenters, Roger Williams, heads south and establishes a haven of religious toleration in Rhode Island. Starting in the 1670s, William Penn and thousands of Quakers emigrate to Pennsylvania and New Jersey, only recently switched from Dutch to British political control. After

Louis XIV revokes the Edict of Nantes in 1685, Huguenot refugees settle along the Carolina coast. And all of them, like the Catholics who emigrate to Maryland beginning in the 1630s, participate in the increasing commerce and consumption that characterized the Dutch and then the English.

The city of Boston illustrates how the relationship between religion and commerce changes in England's North American colonies between the 1630s and the 1750s.[28] The earliest New England Puritans rail against greed and endeavor to punish it in ways that would have made Calvin proud. By the late seventeenth century, however, with several different sorts of Puritan churches, plus Anglicans, Huguenots, Quakers, and other Protestants living in Boston, many Puritans have undone the position of their predecessors. They now interpret material prosperity, including the highly profitable participation in the Atlantic slave trade, as part of God's benevolent plan for the chosen people of England, his elect imperial nation. In a dramatic reversal, the pursuit of profit is being *aligned* with religion, not regarded as a deadly sin or a grave danger to your soul or the common good. By 1750, it's becoming difficult if not impossible to tell a revivalist fan of the famous preacher and theologian Jonathan Edwards from a Quaker from a Newtonian deist in terms of their economic practices. They're all buying and selling and acquiring and aspiring in similar ways, as participants in the same market-driven economy. Their shared practices and those of everyone else doing likewise are helping to hold the colonies and the expanding British Empire together.

Religion is no longer restraining economic behavior. In fact, if anything, increasingly it is thought to sanction and even *encourage* the pursuit of money and possessions as part of God's providential plan. More and more, religion is being limited to your personal beliefs, worship, and devotional practices, whatever those happen to be. Economic life and politics will go their own ways no matter what you believe. But economic life and politics are still the product of how you and everyone else lives, the outcome of a vast, unplanned process made up of individual decisions and actions. So, depending on what beliefs people hold, public life can still be informed and influenced by religion, despite the ways that religion is being redefined and restricted to address the problems inherited from the Reformation era.

Founding Secularization: Religious Freedom in the United States

In the early United States, religious freedom belongs to a larger story of secularization. This is a paradox. Usually religious freedom is regarded as the opposite: the foundation for why the United States has been so religious throughout its history, in contrast to modern European countries with their state churches. American religious freedom is often viewed as a story of how individual freedom of conscience, belief, and worship are enshrined in the country's founding documents and how this politically protected freedom then inspires similar protections in other countries.[29] That story is true, *and* it's exactly what makes it part of the story of secularization. The guiding ideas and founding documents of the United States construe religion narrowly, as an individual matter of what you believe and of how, where, and with whom you worship. The ideas within the documents themselves imply that religion is something separable from the rest of life.

Right in the founding documents of the United States, the freedom *of* religion contained within itself the possibility of freedom *from* religion. In this new country you will have the right to believe whatever you want, including the right to believe that nothing religious is true or that all religion is harmful, dangerous, and worthy of criticism. And everyone else will have these same rights. How American society and culture develop will depend crucially on how individuals exercise their politically protected right to freedom of religion and how their actions and the new American laws and institutions inform collective public life. And as it happens, the ways in which American religious freedom has been exercised have changed dramatically over the course of the country's history.

The United States of America follows the United Provinces of the Netherlands in declaring its independence from a powerful empire, in its case separating from the British rather than the Spanish. Unlike the Dutch, the Americans break new ground in declining to support a public church. In the First Amendment of the U.S. Constitution, church and state are separated in support of individual religious freedom.

Things are more complicated, though. It turns out that the individual *states* aren't necessarily separated from churches, even though the *federal government* doesn't establish any church or favor one church over another. But some of the most influential American thinkers in the 1770s and 1780s share the winnowed view of what religion had become for the Dutch in the seventeenth century: a matter of individually chosen beliefs and worship practices, separable and increasingly separated from public life. The public arena of this new country fosters commerce, and Americans in their slave-holding republic are devoting themselves eagerly to pursuing money and material possessions. Like their colonial predecessors earlier in the eighteenth century, they engage in acquisitive pursuits no matter what their religious beliefs happen to be, now acting on their protected rights to "life, liberty, and the pursuit of happiness."

And yet, for the fledgling United States, problems inherited from the Reformation era have not been left behind in Europe. Questions persist about how to manage the religious pluralism exported from Britain and elsewhere in relation to politics and the rest of public life. In the later 1770s and 1780s, individual states face the question of whether to support an established church. If so, which one, and what form should it take? What would the consequences be? Throughout the colonial period, Virginia supported the Anglican (or Episcopalian) Church, a position that in the early 1780s continues to have its defenders.

James Madison disagrees. He takes notes on this issue during a meeting among Virginia's delegates in late December 1784. Madison's remarks show how the same contentious doctrines that had divided European Christians since the 1520s remain alive and well in the young United States. Here's what Madison writes:

> What is Christianity? Courts of law to judge.
>
> What edition [of the Bible], Hebrew, Septuagint, or Vulgate? What copy—what translation?
>
> What books canonical, what apocryphal? The papists holding to the former what Protestants the latter, the Lutheran the latter what other Protestants and papists the former.
>
> In what light are they to be viewed, as dictated every letter by inspiration, or the essential parts only? Or the matter in general, not the words?
>
> What sense the true one, for if some doctrines be essential to Christianity, those who reject these, whatever name they take, are no Christian society?
>
> Is it Trinitarianism, Arianism, Socinianism? Is it salvation by faith or works also—by free grace, or free will—etc., etc., etc.[30]

Which edition and translation of the Bible should be used? How should it be interpreted, and by whom? What does the Bible teach, and which of its teachings are essential as opposed to secondary?

How are disagreements about such disputes to be adjudicated? It might as well be the 1580s as the 1780s.

Madison's questions echo more than two and a half centuries of divisive controversies and disagreements. What they produce in the United States is religious pluralism, divergent and separate Christian churches. Is there any reason to think that Madison's questions can find answers in 1784? Every one of them, if answered in a way that supports an official state church, will fail to satisfy the religiously divided citizens. This is exactly the problem with *all* proposals for an established, state-supported church. The unintended Christian pluralism from the Reformation era hasn't been resolved. And now the thirteen individual states have to figure out how they're going to address it.

Madison and his friend Thomas Jefferson devise influential answers to this problem in the 1770s and 1780s. Their solutions follow along lines pioneered by the Dutch. Religion has to be construed as something that will not disrupt public life or divide citizens. That means its scope has to be restricted, and what it applies to has to be limited. If citizens agree to this reduction, then the permissible *content* of religion can be expanded—theoretically to include anything. This move will extend religious freedom beyond what the Dutch Republic had allowed. If you let everyone believe what they want and worship how they please in exchange for political obedience, then you can dispense with a state-supported public church altogether.

Following in this tradition, Madison grounds the "free exercise" of religion in the "individual conscience," conceiving religion as fundamentally an interior and individual matter, crucially restricting the *range* of religion. "The religion then of every man must be left to the conviction and conscience of every man," Madison writes in 1785, "and it is the right of every man to exercise it as these may dictate."[31] Left unsaid, though fully understood, is Madison's belief that the *way* you exercise religion cannot impinge on anyone else or on public life in a way that affects anyone else against their will.

Jefferson thinks it doesn't matter what you believe so long as it isn't publicly disruptive or damaging. "It does me no injury for my neighbor to say there are twenty gods, or no god. It neither picks my pocket nor breaks my leg."[32] Note the sharp difference suggested here between someone's expressed beliefs, which Jefferson implies are not injurious, and bodily actions, which could be. It's this founder's version of "sticks and stones may break my bones, but names will never hurt me."

This view or something close to it has become what most Americans and Europeans today think religion is: your individual beliefs, worship, and practices of devotion, such as prayer. It's a separate area of human life for those who decide to embrace it. What you choose to believe and how you decide to worship are completely up to you. You are your own final, supreme religious authority, with total freedom to change your beliefs and practices at any time and for any reason. And everyone else is their own final, supreme religious authority in just the same way.

At the same time, for you and everyone else, religion is *not* about how political authority is exercised or how the economy is regulated or what laws get made and enforced. Not only state and church but also politics and religion are separate things, and they should remain separate. This idea is partly due to the impact of Jefferson, Madison, and earlier Enlightenment thinkers who influenced them, such as John Locke. It seems obvious in the early twenty-first century to many people that this is the solution to the problem of religion as more-than-religion that we inherited from the Reformation era. It enables people who believe different things about the deepest concerns of human life to coexist in relative tranquility. And in the judgment of many commentators in recent years, it also highlights a basic difference today between Western Christianity and Islam, a tradition in which it remains much more widely thought that religion can *and of course should* influence public political life and shape the wider society and culture.

The modern Western understanding of religion succeeds in the early decades of the United States, but not because Americans are rugged religious individualists, each eager to go her or his own way. It succeeds because most of them are Christians, especially English-speaking white Protestants, who continue to share so much in common despite the disagreements that divide their churches. The federal government *can* dispense with an established church because there are already so many established churches to which Americans belong—and more of them spring up and thrive in the early nineteenth century.

A few Americans exercise their individual religious freedom by starting new religions; Joseph Smith, who founds Mormonism in the 1830s, is the best-known example. But most Americans exercise their religious freedom by belonging to one or another Christian church, the vast majority of which are Protestant of some sort. American Protestant pluralism in the early nineteenth century reflects the Reformation's founding principle of *sola scriptura*. Recall that disagreements about the meaning of God's Word have divided Protestants without interruption since the early 1520s. In the United States, because the range of scriptural interpretations is not restricted by political authorities, as in the magisterial Reformation, the radical Reformation can flower. Or, put another way, in the United States the distinction between the magisterial and radical Reformations disappears. The new religious freedom of an American citizen vastly exceeds Luther's very particular freedom of a Christian. The Reformation looks very different once political authorities stop enforcing some particular version of Protestantism and instead let the Reformation be itself.

Nineteenth-century American Protestants demonstrate abundantly that you can read the Bible in whatever way you want. In the United States, the Reformation is democratized in ways that had not taken place anywhere in Europe, even in the Golden-Age Dutch Republic.[33] Beginning in the 1790s, the Second Great Awakening, a powerful Protestant religious revival, infuses much new energy into this process. The movement emphasizes transformative personal experience and individual conversion. It helps to power the astonishing growth of multiple Protestant denominations whose boundaries it also overspills: the 460 Baptist churches in the United States in 1780 mushroom to 12,000 by 1860, while 14,000 American Methodists in 1784 swell to nearly 20,000 Methodist *churches* by the start of the Civil War.[34]

In principle, the American right to individual religious freedom opens the way to secularization. By construing religion narrowly, it separates religion from the rest of life. Individuals can simply choose not to be religious. For those who are religious, their religion will remain separate provided they stick strictly to their beliefs, worship, and devotions and do not seek to influence public life—to keep their beliefs to themselves and not try to impose them on others, as the saying goes. *In practice,* however, the right to individual religious freedom helps to explain why Protestantism of one sort or another ends up marking American society and culture to the extent that it has in U.S. history. The large majority of Americans for most of the country's history exercise their religious freedom by being Protestants of one denomination or another. And in practice most of them view religion less restrictively than Madison or Jefferson did.

In Madison's phrase, their "conviction and conscience" dictate that they *should* exercise their faith in ways that include concrete, real-life, public actions to influence their neighborhoods and communities and to shape society and culture. In this respect, American Protestants extend a Reformation-era and even medieval tradition but within a very different political and legal context, one that protects individual religious freedom rather than prescribing a particular version of Christianity. And for a big chunk of American history, the available individual choices within Protestantism share enough in common that they help to inform and stabilize society, in a similar way that European regimes of the Reformation era had sought to achieve through mandated religious orthodoxy.

Because Americans continue to hold in common so many religious views, as well as moral convictions derived from them, the American disestablishment of religion in the late eighteenth and early nineteenth centuries works for quite some time. Americans transmit beliefs, values, and virtues that not only sustain their religious communities but also influence their public coexistence as citizens. And those beliefs and values inform politics as well within individual American states, which at the nation's founding are not subject to the federal constitutional restrictions on support for churches. Connecticut, for instance, continues to fund select churches until 1818, while Massachusetts continues the practice until 1832. Virtually all states also pass laws that favor Protestantism, including laws that punish blasphemy and impose religious restrictions on who may hold public office. Many of these laws will remain influential well into the twentieth century.[35]

In the late eighteenth and most of the nineteenth centuries such laws seem normal and natural to most American citizens. Largely drawn from what most Protestants of British background share in common, these commitments make it seem normal and natural, for example, to prescribe Protestant prayers and the reading of the King James Bible in public schools. Registering their dissatisfaction, however, American Catholics exercise their religious freedom by creating a separate system of their own church-supported schools, which eventually grows into the largest such system in any country in the world. Paradoxically, the increasing number of religiously self-aware Catholic and Jewish immigrants who immigrate beginning in the nineteenth century will play a key role in the advance of secularization. Their mere presence demonstrates that there is no natural or necessary connection between American politically protected freedom of belief and Protestantism of any kind.

Suspending Secularization: Tocqueville on Religion in America

One of the most astute observers of the American relationship between religion and politics in the early nineteenth century is the French aristocrat and political thinker Alexis de Tocqueville (1805–1859). He spends several months traveling in the United States in the early 1830s. Tocqueville grew up in a France sharply polarized between harshly antireligious supporters of the legacy of the French Revolution and strongly religious Catholics who favored a privileged relationship between the French state and the Catholic Church. When he arrives in the United States, Tocqueville is astonished by American religious freedom and its relationship to democracy: "The religious atmosphere of the country was the first thing that struck me on arrival in the United States," he writes in his masterpiece published a few years later, *Democracy in America*.[36]

Tocqueville is amazed that religion in the United States, without any mandated state church, is contributing to the country's social cohesion rather than fostering conflicts. Through individual religious freedom, it seems, the country has solved the problem of religion and politics inherited from the Reformation era. Of course, particular doctrinal differences still divide American Christians, just as they have divided European Christians since Luther. Baptists, Methodists, Disciples of Christ, and other Protestant groups augment the already existing Protestant pluralism, which includes Presbyterians, Lutherans, Episcopalians, Congregationalists, and other older groups. Yet beneath these differences, they still share moral assumptions, values, and priorities that taken together inform the wider society and culture. Tocqueville sees that the divisive doctrinal differences of the respective churches are distinct from their shared moral commitments, and that distinction is critical for moving beyond the vexing and destructive problems of the Reformation era.

Well aware of how the Reformation is playing out in American Protestant pluralism, Tocqueville comments, "There is an innumerable multitude of sects in the United States. They are all different in the worship they offer to the Creator." Yet despite the divisions and differences in worship among Americans, Tocqueville adds that "all agree concerning the duties of men to one another" and "all preach the same morality in the name of God."[37] That is, they continue to share more than just beliefs and worship: they embrace public duties and the religiously inflected morality that informs public life in common.

The influence of religion on American public life *remains* social and political, but it's *indirect and uncoerced;* it's the collective outcome of millions of Americans practicing their religion as guaranteed in the new republic under the Constitution. Religion is playing a role in public life, not because political authorities are imposing and policing Reformed Protestantism or Lutheranism or Catholicism, but rather because people of their own free will are exercising their politically protected freedom of religion. "Religion, which never intervenes directly in the government of American society," Tocqueville concludes, "should therefore be considered as the first of their political institutions."[38] He is underlining the political and social significance of religion in the United States, even though the country sponsors no official state religion or federally established church. In this new country, the state doesn't support any church, but the churches support the state and sustain society.

This is astonishing: by *not* having an established church—letting Americans believe what they want and worship as they wish—the society is held together by religion in ways that European nations had sought to achieve through state churches. In Europe, politically backed churches had resulted in the recurring more-than-religious conflicts of the Reformation era; in the nineteenth century, European countries modify this practice in different ways. Most of them decriminalize religious dissent during the course of the century, although religious discrimination remains common, as indeed it does against non-Protestants in the United States. But official, privileged state churches remain the norm in Europe.

Not so in the United States, where there is only a religious *society* with shared morality and mores despite doctrinal disagreements between Protestant churches. Religion, by informing individual consciences, continues to influence people's actions in public life, including in politics. What you believe continues to influence how you live, what you care about, and the sort of person you become. The result is played out in the society and culture as a whole. In Tocqueville's words, "All the sects in the United States belong to the great unity of Christendom, and Christian morality is everywhere the same."[39]

What Tocqueville observes is not the unity of Christendom of the early sixteenth century, before the Reformation. At that time, the religious beliefs and practices and institutions of medieval Catholicism were simply taken for granted; they influenced every area of life. But neither is the United States in the 1830s a nation in which each individual has her or his own religious beliefs and practices, different from those of everyone else. Not even close. What Catholics and many kinds of Protestants and Jews share in common is substantial. Their commonalities inform the political and cultural identity of the young nation.

Paradoxically, a secularizing foundation has made possible this

particular religious outcome in the United States around 1830. At
the same time, the secularizing foundation renders that outcome
contingent and fragile. The founding documents of the United
States did not establish a common culture; they presupposed one.
Jefferson's phrasing in the Declaration of Independence acknowledged that individual rights are divinely endowed by a creator; he
even claimed that his assertions are "self-evident" truths: "We hold
these truths to be self-evident: that all men are created equal; that
they are endowed by their Creator with certain inalienable rights;
that among these are life, liberty, and the pursuit of happiness."[40]
That people are created by God—a fundamental Christian (as well
as Jewish) belief—explains why "all men" are equal and *have* rights
to begin with. In the late eighteenth century this notion is not in
dispute among Protestants or between Protestants and Catholics—
though nearly all of them seem blind to the possibility of applying it
equally to black slaves in the United States and to white women as
well as white men.

Neither the Declaration of Independence nor any other American
founding documents say anything about how you should live, what
it means to exercise your liberty, or what you should do to pursue
happiness. That, of course, is by design; the whole point is to leave
people free to provide their own answers rather than prescribing
answers, as Reformation-era authorities had done. In the early nineteenth century most people *happen* to embrace answers given by
one of Tocqueville's "innumerable multitude of sects." But no one
has to. Legally, you can believe whatever you want, just as Jefferson
implied in his remark about "twenty gods, or no god."

New implications of Luther's stance from the early sixteenth
century have thus begun to emerge in a very different context. In
the mid-1790s, Thomas Paine, the pamphleteer of the American
Revolution, inspired a voluntary—and impressively successful—
effort to promote largely traditional Protestant views of scripture

and morality. At the same time, he wrote, "My own mind is my own church."[41] Both Jefferson and Paine recognized that radical individualism is implied in the Declaration of Independence and First Amendment. In this American form of individualism, Luther's "Here I stand" is applied to everyone, regardless of what they believe.

Tocqueville also comments insightfully about the pursuit of money and material possessions in the United States. This is the other practice that contributes powerfully to the cohesion of American society. He sees that Americans effortlessly marry their passion for acquisition with their religious views. Medieval and Reformation-era Christians, Catholic and Protestant alike, repeatedly were taught the biblical view that the pursuit of money and possessions is closely related to sinful and dangerous avarice. Seeking more than you need when others don't have enough for the basic necessities of life damages both your soul and the common good. Following the Dutch, British, and other northwestern Europeans in the eighteenth century, Americans reject and reverse this assessment.[42] Enlightenment thinkers such as Adam Smith, first and foremost a moral philosopher, tell them that their pursuit of more and better possessions is an expression of natural self-interest, and exercising that self-interest would have no adverse effects on the common good.[43] On the contrary, Smith writes in *The Wealth of Nations*, "the natural effort of every individual to better his own condition," if left unimpeded, "is so powerful a principle" that even without assistance it is "capable of carrying on the society to wealth and prosperity."[44]

Pursuing your own desires for more and better things, in Smith's vision, helps to improve life for everyone. Not ascetic self-restraint but acquisitive self-seeking is the key to improving society. In the late eighteenth and early nineteenth centuries more Christians are coming to believe that the market's "invisible hand"—Smith's image—is the very mechanism through which God exercises divine providence. More of them are coming to think that providence is the same thing as "progress," which becomes one of the central buzz-words of the nineteenth century on both sides of the North Atlantic.

In the United States, Tocqueville writes in *Democracy in America,* "religion is often powerless to restrain men in the midst of innumerable temptations which fortune offers," and it "cannot moderate their eagerness to enrich themselves."[45] In many cases, though, this isn't even an issue. The real point is that so many Americans fail to see any problem in the pursuit of fortune and enrichment *because* of their religion—starkly reversing the teachings of the major Protestant reformers, the Bible, and Christian tradition from the first through the sixteenth centuries. Listening to American preachers, Tocqueville notes, it's often hard to tell "whether the main object of religion is to procure eternal felicity in the next world or prosperity in this." Consequently, "people want to do as well as possible in this world without giving up their chances in the next."[46]

The American "prosperity gospel" has deep historical roots. In 1835, for example, Jonathan Mayhew Wainwright, the Episcopal vicar of Trinity Church, Boston, preaches a sermon defending inequality of wealth as divinely willed for "the political, the intellectual, and the moral and religious improvement of the human race." Indeed, inequality is "essential to producing the greatest amount of knowledge, virtue and happiness."[47] Many Americans enthusiastically embrace this version of the gospel, extending what their colonial predecessors had inherited from Britain. Tocqueville writes that in the United States "love of comfort has become the dominant national taste. The main current of human passions running in that direction sweeps everything along with it."[48]

Americans are hardly alone in their devotion to the goods life as the good life in the late eighteenth and nineteenth centuries.

Their colonial predecessors had acquired their habits of consumption and nourished their taste for commerce by participating in the British Empire's thriving Atlantic trade in slaves as well as in cotton, sugar, tobacco, and other commodities. Nineteenth-century industrialization—beginning in Britain but quickly spreading to North America—is fueled by desires for more and better possessions, more comfort, and more leisure. All of these are widely viewed as contributing to greater contentment and happiness, although the conditions for workers in the factories of newly industrial cities such as Manchester hardly seem conducive to either. Industrialization spreads on the European continent too. In nation after nation, industrial entrepreneurs make fortunes by manufacturing everything from clothing to chemicals to steel for railroads; citizens at every income level buy more manufactured things more cheaply than before; and governments levy taxes to build their bureaucracies and militaries on unprecedented scales.

Higher education begins to play a crucial role in these developments as well. Starting in Germany and then widely imitated in other European countries and the United States, modern research universities are established. The University of Berlin, the first of them, begins with an emphasis on philology and philosophy around 1810, but after midcentury all research universities start to place the natural sciences at their center. Scientists' discoveries are applied in the manufacturing technologies that make businessmen rich and enable factories to supply the things people want to buy. Similarly, in North America, industrial capitalism provides novel opportunities for new objects of desire and new patterns of devotion for many millions of people. It's no accident that modern department stores make their appearance in the late nineteenth century on both sides of the North Atlantic.

By the 1770s and 1780s, Americans take over from the British a belief in themselves as a nation and a people favored by God.

Connected to this belief is economic prosperity and freedom, along with Enlightenment notions of progress. None of it would have been possible without individual religious freedom, the New World solution to the Old World problem of religion, inherited from the Reformation era.

Limiting the scope of religion and turning it into a discrete and separable domain of life—rather than a worldview that informs all of life's domains—makes religious toleration and religious freedom possible. At the same time, these restrictions are essential components for the secularization that will eventually take place in every Western country. Religion is made a politically protected individual choice, separate from direct influences on politics, economic life, law, or education. The character and tenor of public life will remain the collective product of how individual citizens exercise their freedom to believe whatever they want to, and to act accordingly.

Advancing Secularization:
The United States and Europe

The same basic framework that permitted religion to become in the United States, in Tocqueville's words, "the first of their political institutions" has also permitted pervasive American secularization since his time. Values and moral commitments that were then widely shared no longer are. This is the outcome of a long historical process, and it also lies at the root of some widely acknowledged frustrations in American public life and political culture today, difficulties that have never been more apparent than since the election of November 2016.

Major historical developments have contributed to the process of secularization in the United States, stemming in significant measure from the deeper fragmentation of Protestantism itself. The history of the United States has added another, later chapter to the story of this fragmentation that began when the Reformation escaped Luther's control in the early 1520s.

The Bible is a large, complex collection of ancient texts that can be and has been interpreted in many conflicting ways. Because they lack any shared authority outside scripture, Protestants have no one to settle disputes among their competing interpreters and churches. This divisive legacy of the Reformation has characterized Americans throughout their history; it was just as true during the decade of Reagan in the 1980s as it was for Madison and his contemporaries in the 1780s.

The common Protestant ethos, which so impressed Tocqueville, was shattered by regional differences over slavery, race, and the Civil War (1861–1865), as American Protestants simultaneously attacked and defended slavery based on the Bible.[49] In addition, the influence of modern scholarly methods of biblical interpretation, and the view of history they presupposed, which German scholars pioneered, challenged the traditional Protestant view that the biblical text had been straightforwardly received through divine revelation. Charles Darwin's theory of evolution prompted divergent Protestant responses in the late nineteenth century and dealt another major blow to the American relationship among religion, politics, and society that so amazed Tocqueville. Much more than the Scientific Revolution in the seventeenth century, Darwinian evolutionary theory helped to catalyze perceptions that religion and science in and of themselves—not just a certain literalist way of interpreting the Bible, on the one hand, and some particular views of Darwinian theory, on the other—are incompatible.

Protestant groups responded differently to the theory of evolution, and, combined with their differing reactions to modern biblical scholarship, this led to a major split between liberal and fundamentalist Protestants that persists today. In 1925, the Scopes Monkey

Trial in Tennessee focused on whether the theory of evolution could be taught in American public schools, an issue that still arouses opposition from fundamentalist Protestants. Such Protestants tend to believe that the Bible cannot be mistaken about anything, and if the Bible and science appear to conflict, they reject science. They tend to reject the theory of evolution because they think it can't be reconciled with the biblical accounts of creation (there are two of them, one in each of the first two chapters in the book of Genesis).

Liberal Protestants, on the one hand, and fundamentalists and evangelicals on the other, typically hold rival political, social, and moral views—the opposite of what Tocqueville observed. They definitely do not "all agree concerning the duties of men to one another" or "all preach the same morality in the name of God,"[50] as is clear from what are their usually sharp disagreements on abortion, same-sex marriage, gun control, and a host of social justice issues. As a result, Protestantism can no longer inform American society in any coherent way. This has been obvious at least since the upheavals of the 1960s, which divided American Protestants as sharply as did the Civil War in the 1860s.

Influences outside of American Protestantism have also contributed to secularization. Ironically, some derived from the religious commitments of newcomers who were not Protestants, which underscores the challenges associated with religious pluralism. Millions of Catholics and Jews emigrated from Europe to the United States in the late nineteenth and early twentieth centuries. They objected to the Protestant views and values that were woven into laws, schools, and other institutions at the state level, regarding them as sectarian preferences that impinged on Catholics' and Jews' own religious freedom. Legal challenges paved the way for broader federal decisions by the Supreme Court in the 1940s in a series of landmark rulings about the First Amendment and what the separation of church and state means. Chief among these court cases was

Everson v. Board of Education (1947), which nevertheless far from settled the matter.[51]

Separation of church and state remains contentious, especially because it's not identical to the separation of religion and politics. "Church and state" is focused on institutions; religion's influence on politics is more diffuse. But no one can doubt that religion exercises much less influence in American public life today than it has at any point in American history. Certainly it has less influence than in the 1950s, when in the midst of the Cold War "In God We Trust" was first added to American currency, replacing "*E Pluribus Unum*" as the nation's official motto. The 1960s were a major watershed in this as in many other respects, and that decade's influence becomes ever clearer in retrospect.

The sixties were arguably an even bigger watershed for secularization in Europe. In the 1960s Europe experienced a stunning drop-off in the number of Christians who regularly worship and otherwise participate in religious life. This is one of the key differences usually cited to distinguish European secularism from American religiosity in the early twenty-first century. The exclusion of religion from shared public life in both Europe and the United States, though, means the two are more similar than they sometimes seem.

Factors that contributed to secularization in European countries differed from those in the United States.[52] State churches, whether Catholic, Lutheran, or Anglican, endured in modern Europe, and the stronger that European forms of nationalism grew, the more problematic did this legacy of the Reformation era become. State support for churches made it almost impossible for members of the clergy to stand apart from the imperialism and military involvements of their respective countries, which funded and privileged them. In the nineteenth and early twentieth centuries it was hard to be a European Christian and a critic of the nationalism of one's own country. By and large, European church members and preachers defended the colonial activities of their own nations, arguing that they "civilized" indigenous peoples in Africa and South Asia. Indeed, European Christians often openly encouraged such endeavors. Lay Catholics and Protestants were among the politicians and entrepreneurs who fostered "progress" as Europeans divided up Africa and the Middle East for their own competing nationalist ends. When those rival imperialist nations went to war in 1914 in World War I, members of the clergy exhorted the troops on both sides. *Their* cause was noble, just, and right—worth killing and dying for. They transformed the rhetoric of Christian martyrdom and holy war into calls for allegiance to imperialist nation-states. European church leaders and pastors likewise acted on behalf of both fascist and liberal regimes in the 1930s and World War II.

Americans have never experienced anything like what Europeans endured between 1914 and 1945, although many Indian tribes in the United States have suffered longer-lasting barbarities that have devastated their populations. In Europe, the two world wars plus the genocides killed tens of millions, not to mention the untold suffering of the wounded and refugees. (By comparison, probably about 750,000 men died in the American Civil War, which is more than were killed in all other wars in American history combined.)[53] Following World War II, in the period of rapid European decolonization, the truth about European imperialism began to emerge—the truth about what *progress* had meant for the indigenous peoples on other continents whom Europeans had sought to "civilize." It wasn't pretty. And neither, for that matter, were the decades of violent decolonization that followed in many newly independent countries, a fallout from and legacy of European colonialism. After World War II, the horrors of war were followed by revelations that several European states had committed colonial atrocities in many countries, extending back into the nineteenth century. It hardly seems surprising that one way people responded to these shocks in the second half of the twentieth century was to retreat from the churches that had partnered with the states—to leave the churches that together with their nations had legitimated both the wars and the colonial brutalities that had killed so many people.

Separated and Diminished Religion, Secularized and Divided Society

Secularization continues to be paradoxically enabled by the freedom of religion, which itself was conceived as a solution to problems inherited from the Reformation era. What has changed, however, is the range of what people believe and how they exercise their freedom. If we want to understand the kind of society we live in today and where it came from, this range of beliefs and exercise of freedom must be seen in relationship to the ever-expanding opportunities derived from the connections among bureaucratic states, technology, and consumerism.

To judge by most people's actions today, they believe the goods life is the good life, and they devote themselves to this whether or not they also believe in God or engage in worship or prayer. In public culture and society as a whole, in both the United States and Europe, the consumption of goods and pursuit of enjoyment has essentially replaced religion. Whether you happen to be religious has no effect at all on the dominant culture. This would have horrified—if perhaps not surprised—Luther and Calvin and other sixteenth-century Protestant reformers.

At the same time, advanced secularization doesn't mean that religion has disappeared. In the United States, for instance, you have to try hard *not* to see it. But religion doesn't inform public life in anything like the ways that Tocqueville described. Aside from a shared commitment to consumerism, neither Christians nor religious persons in general share moral or political views in common in ways that are capable of informing the wider society. On the contrary, the views of religious women and men *reflect* the divisions that characterize society at large. Like their nonreligious fellow citizens, religious Americans line up as liberals or conservatives, with a smattering of radicals or reactionaries, on opposing sides of divisive political and social issues. When they *do* act according to conscience in the public sphere, they do not change society at large but instead mirror and contribute to already existing rifts and trends.

Advanced secularization means that religion has been separated from politics in the sense that it's incapable of coherently influencing political culture or politics in practice. This could change if, in the future, religious persons came to share the same moral views and acted on them in the public sphere, as American Christians did around 1830. But in recent decades this has not taken place at all—again, aside from a widely shared enthusiasm for the freedom to consume and pursue whatever you happen to want. Apart from this, religious believers share no common values or causes simply by virtue of being religious; they're divided by contentious political and moral issues such as abortion, immigration, national identity, economic inequality, and (in the United States) gun control, just like members of the population in general. Rooted in the upheavals of the 1960s, the American culture wars have demonstrated this since the 1980s, and the election of 2016 provided a startling indication of just how deep the rifts now run.

The law supports this open-ended diversity of beliefs and values. However, today the varieties of "twenty gods, or no god" extend far beyond what American Christians expressed in the nineteenth century. They include rival camps of politically engaged believers who, protected by individual religious freedom, oppose each other fiercely—the unintended consequence of Protestantism's devotion to Luther's principle of *sola scriptura*. Diverging interpretations of God's Word from the early German Reformation established a pattern that never disappeared. In fact, religious freedom in modern nation-states has enabled Protestantism to develop in ways unconstrained by the opinions of reformers or pronouncements of political authorities. You can believe whatever you want, worship as much as you want in whatever ways you want (or none), and do anything else you want as an expression of your beliefs, so long as you obey the laws. It's not surprising, then, that this diversity has resulted in countless claims about what is true, what matters in life, how to live, and what laws and policies countries should adopt. Neither is it surprising that individuals espouse countless rival views on these issues, whether they're religious or nonreligious. This is simply a product and outcome of modern, politically protected individual freedom as an extension of individual freedom of religion.

It's also not remarkable that so many conflicting religious views have contributed to a more familiar meaning of secularization: a decline in the number of persons who profess any religious beliefs or engage in any religious worship or devotion at all (though quite a few people say they are "spiritual not religious" or some variation on that theme; in Europe it is sometimes called "believing without belonging").[54] This has been most conspicuous in Western Europe, where, as noted, regular church attendance plummeted in the 1960s and has remained low ever since. Surrounded by so many incompatible religious views, millions of people seem to have decided not to subscribe to any.

From pluralism, people often infer relativism. The greater the pluralism, the more likely the inference, so it makes sense that relativism's influence on secularization would be greater now than it was in, say, the late nineteenth century. There was contact then, of course, among people with different religious beliefs and from different religious traditions. Indeed, there had already been such contact for centuries. But nineteenth-century means of communication—telegraph and newspaper and travel by steamship—pale by comparison to our instant online communication, constant online news, and unprecedented levels of international air travel. The late nineteenth century was a world of pluralism; ours is a world of hyperpluralism. As a result, more people have become religious relativists. Being exposed to so many different religious claims, enabled by politically protected religious freedom, has itself contributed to secularization.

Tocqueville was struck by the way shared Christian moral views indirectly strengthened American democracy (leaving aside what democracy meant for black slaves, Indians, and women). These moral views have been replaced by an open-ended pluralism of religious and nonreligious beliefs about values, priorities, and politics in a nation that for several decades has been deeply divided. Its raw antagonisms, so visible following Donald Trump's frenzied executive orders and antagonistic tweets beginning in the first days of his presidency in January 2017, led some analysts to start questioning, within weeks of his inauguration, the sustainability of American democracy itself.

Until recently it was common for Europeans to look upon the culture wars of the United States as an American exceptionalism of a sort they had happily managed to avoid. Americans were polarized over moral and political issues, zigzagging back and forth between Republican and Democratic presidents, their Congress mired in partisan gridlock, but sensibly progressive Europeans had evolved beyond such divisions to collaborative cooperation. All the more painfully, then, has the realization dawned among Europeans, especially since 2015, that beneath a veneer of reserved secularity and the umbrella of the European Union, their own countries are similarly divided in ways that make American exceptionalism look less exceptional. The Brexit vote in the United Kingdom in June 2016 and the sharp moral, political, and cultural divisions provoked by the influx of especially Syrian refugees on the European continent has led to considerable anxiety, uncertainty, and hand-wringing. As in the United States, though provoked by different specific influences, there is deep disagreement in many countries, including Germany, France, the Netherlands, Italy, and the United Kingdom, about what should be done and how to proceed. A European commitment to human rights has started to look as though it might be thinner than the commitment of some European countries to their own national sovereignty and desire for self-determination.

The influence of religion on Western societies has declined substantially in the past half century. Nothing has taken its place aside from an ideology of individual choice, asserted with growing militancy. "Do your own thing" has proved to be more than just a passing slogan from the 1960s. To this slogan should be added the crucial corollary of "buy your own things." In the absence of shared norms and values analogous to those once provided by Christianity, what holds our secularized societies together, or at least has held them together in recent decades, is the combination of increasingly assertive individualism, powerful nation-states, and consumerist capitalism.

What the Dutch started four centuries ago, the British extended, and the Americans intensified. Today consumerism has become the taken-for-granted pattern of modern Western human life on both the personal and public levels. In this respect it was only in the twentieth century, and especially after World War II, that Europeans followed the lead of the United States and went all-in for consumerism; shopping malls in Europe were first modeled on American ones.[55] On both sides of the North Atlantic now, it is assumed that whatever else you believe and regardless of your income level, you want more money and better possessions so that you can maximize your choices and enjoy life more. Because the pursuit of money

and possessions is widely regarded as a prerequisite for a fulfilling human life, citizens evaluate their governments based on how
well or poorly they foster this endeavor. Political leaders and parties that can't deliver the goods find themselves voted out of office.
The goods life as the good life is deeply entrenched in the modern
Western world, regardless of your country.

Affluence and consumerism have not only become the substitute for religion, they have also contributed to secularization. Time
that people dedicate to making money so they can buy whatever
they want is time they are not spending in worship, prayer, or service to others. Economists call this "opportunity cost"—what you
give up by making the choices you make. In the contest over what
you should live for, religion has lost out in the dominant culture to
money and material possessions, perhaps even more conspicuously
in the United States than in Europe. The pursuit of more money
and better stuff to serve individual desires is the default objective of
human life in the society as a whole.

It's also the default for the vast majority of those who believe in
God, worship regularly, and pray. And that's because even most religious believers keep their economic and religious lives segregated.
Most people, religious or not, are the heirs of Locke, Madison, and
Jefferson, whether they know it or not. They think of religion as
something personal, individual, and interior rather than something
shared that is meant to inform public life. For individuals who
choose to be religious, religion has become one part of life alongside
others. It does not shape all of human life. It does not inform economic, social, or political life in the public square, and it is variously
forbidden from interfering with it in overt ways.

To grasp the extent of secularization and the pervasiveness of
consumerism as the replacement for religion, ask how much influence those who live deliberately nonconsumerist lives exert on
global capitalism. The answer is none. Constant manufacturing,

advertising, marketing, selling, shopping, and buying churn along regardless, facilitated ever more by technology. Whether or not you choose to live a materially austere life, you can't step outside a global economic system geared toward increasing wealth and consumption. This is true even if you find consumerism objectionable on religious grounds—even if you regard it as fundamentally contrary to what the Bible says about greed and the pursuit of wealth and possessions, as did the sixteenth-century Protestant reformers and their medieval Catholic predecessors.

In modern Western societies, you can believe whatever you want and worship as much as you want and be as devout as you want, thanks to your politically protected right to individual religious freedom. And to be sure, millions of men and women since World War II have been inspired by the example of extraordinary Christian leaders on both sides of the Atlantic, from the German Lutheran theologian Dietrich Bonhoeffer to the lay Catholic activist Dorothy Day, from the evangelical preacher Billy Graham to the tireless champion of the destitute Mother Teresa, from the South African Anglican Archbishop Desmond Tutu to the first-ever celebrity pope, John Paul II. But the impact of this inspiration on global capitalism and consumerism seems negligible at best. Belief, worship, and devotion are unlikely to influence a consumerist culture in which you also have a right to buy as much as you want of whatever you want. You don't have to take account of anyone else as you exercise that right, and everyone else has the same right not to take account of anyone else. This individual, secularized freedom of the early twenty-first century is the long-term, unintended outcome of the Reformation era. Within the laws of the country in which you happen to find yourself, you are your own authority: you can believe whatever you want, live however you wish, buy whatever your means allow, and pursue your self-chosen desires regardless of what they are.

One can hardly imagine a greater contrast to what Luther meant by "the freedom of a Christian": living in paradoxical bondage to selfless, loving service of your neighbors, tirelessly tending to their needs whatever they might be, as a result of gratitude for the unmerited gift of God's saving grace. Freedom as understood by Luther, as well as by the other Protestant and Catholic reformers of the sixteenth century, was based on a radically different understanding of what human beings are, what the point of human life is, and how one ought to live. No wonder it seems so alien today to most Westerners.

In 2017, the five hundredth anniversary of the Reformation, some interpreters are celebrating Martin Luther and the Protestant Reformation as heralding modern individualism and modern freedom. The irony is that Luther would have disdained both and wanted tribute for neither. It is not only misleading but also disingenuous to see the freedom espoused by the Reformation as leading in any direct or substantive way to present-day freedom.

Luther would deride the idea of freedom we know today and disclaim any credit for it. In fact, he would be disgusted by it, because it has nothing to do with what he regarded as the only real freedom, the bound freedom of a Christian.

Neither Luther nor any of the other Protestant reformers sought or envisioned anything like modern individual freedom, nor did the Protestant Reformation as such lead to it. What led to it were the more-than-religious conflicts between magisterial Protestants and Catholics in the Reformation era, which created a situation that led indirectly, unintentionally, and eventually to the making of a twenty-first-century world that nearly all committed Christians of the Reformation era would have deplored.

It was restrictions on the reach of religion that made religious freedom and religious toleration possible. These constraints facilitated the separation of church and state and led to an emphasis on politically protected individual rights, beginning with the freedom of religion as the right to believe and worship as one chooses. The pursuit of wealth and material possessions that allow people to choose their own pleasures and enjoyments has become an alternative to religion and is nearly universal in its appeal. It demonstrates across the world its power to organize societies otherwise divided over what to believe and how to live. For several centuries now, the large majority of Westerners have given their assent: whatever else they believe and whatever their disagreements, they can agree on this. The hard-won solutions worked out to address the problems·inherited from the Reformation era have been extraordinary achievements in many respects. They've also led to some unintended problems of their own.

Free at Last?

Those individuals who are free to believe what they want as a *result* of secularization are bound to hold differing opinions about the results of this centuries-long *process* of secularization. This is just one corollary of contemporary hyperpluralism. We hold different opinions about where we find ourselves as a whole, whether we think on balance it's a good thing or a bad thing and whether we like particular aspects of it or not. And since we don't know what the future holds or how things will turn out, we might well change our present views, whatever they are, depending on what happens down the road. Narratives depend on knowing how the story ends, but we don't know that yet.

Yet whatever our disagreements about where we are going, it cannot be denied that a massive shift in the place of religion in shared human life has taken place since the Reformation. The Reformation made religion into an unprecedented problem in Western Europe, to which the dominant institutions, ideas, and practices of the modern world have been the response. Because there are so many different, competing views about what is good and bad, right and wrong, desirable or not in the culture we inhabit, it would be impossible to consider them all. I offer here only a few thoughts on which responses to the Reformation seem to have been successful and which have unintentionally emerged as problematic.

First, then, on the plus side: the political protection of individuals to believe and worship (or not) as they please is regarded almost universally in the Western world as a great good. By and large, it has worked as a way of enabling religiously divided Christians, and members of other religious traditions, to coexist in relative peace. In this sense, it did indeed solve the basic problem inherited from the Reformation era that it was intended to address. And insofar as relative social peace is better than recurring violent conflict, this is certainly a good thing. Almost everyone in the Western world thinks that it is morally wrong to try to force someone to believe something against their will and that doing so produces at best resentment and grudging outward conformity to prescriptions, just as it did in early modern Europe. Given the reality of religious pluralism, nearly everybody agrees that protecting individual religious freedom and restricting the scope of religion is far better than any attempt to impose and police some religious views and practices while prohibiting others.

Virtually no one would prefer more wars of more-than-religion to modern individual freedom of religion. What was true in the seventeenth century is even more obvious now, in light of the frighteningly destructive military technology of the twenty-first century. This is one reason why militant Islamism is so disturbing to nearly all Westerners. It is a dramatic, insistent rejection of individual freedom of religion that has been demonstrably combined with a willingness to kill for a particular version of Islam.

Today there are few Westerners who would prefer some form of state-imposed communism, socialism, or fascism to liberal democracy. At a minimum, the political protection of individual rights in modern liberal democracies seems incomparably better than any modern alternatives as a way of addressing the problems inherited from the Reformation era. Only in recent decades have concerted efforts been made to extend the same protections to women, ethnic minorities, children, and disabled persons—and this too is overwhelmingly and rightly regarded as a positive development. (Unborn human beings remain a battleground of contestation.) People overwhelmingly prefer the protection of individual human beings, and commitments to basic values such as equality and freedom, over the appalling brutalization of human beings under tyrannical regimes such as Stalin's Soviet Union or Hitler's Third Reich.

To facilitate secularization, modern liberal democratic states have partnered most heavily with modern industrial capitalism. It has enabled literally billions of people around the world to lead longer, healthier, less onerous, more comfortable, more fulfilling, and more varied lives than were lived by human beings in the preindustrial world. Almost no one who says they yearn for a world before modern technology, modern conveniences, and modern opportunities actually means it. And among those who do, nearly all would need to live for only a few weeks in the conditions of sixteenth- or eighteenth-century Europe to cure them of their nostalgic and escapist fantasies. If nothing else, the need for effective medicine would send them scurrying back to the twenty-first century. At the same time, the lives and working conditions of today's factory laborers in China, Bangladesh, Vietnam, or Mexico bear little resemblance to the lives of the affluent American, British, French, or German consumers who purchase the things they make. Nevertheless, even though the distribution of wealth generated remains shockingly unequal, the impact of industrial capitalism has been stunning in its capacity to satisfy human desires that have contributed to human flourishing. The more sophisticated the means of production and distribution, the greater the capacity, right up to and including the globalizing present.

At the same time, most people would likely agree that however preferable they seem to any realistic alternatives, modern solutions to the problems of the Reformation era have given rise to unintended problems of their own, beyond staggering inequalities of wealth and resources. Arguably the greatest of these, which continues to press on us with ever more urgency, is global climate change. Pretending there's no problem won't make it go away. And what has led to it is the combination of modern liberal democracies and global consumerist capitalism—what in other respects is a great triumph and an impressive solution to the problems of the Reformation era.

Politically protecting individual rights allows you and everyone else to buy as much as you can of whatever you want. Factories and vehicles around the world emit the CO_2 that contributes to global warming when they produce what people want and take people where they want to go. Unless human beings get their collective act together in ways that have never occurred before—within nations, across nations, and among billions of individual consumers—the exercise of individual freedom appears to be leading to a grim future. Earth could become a much warmer planet, in which a radically altered climate makes human flourishing in any ordinary sense impossible. If so, it would be partly an unintended problem made possible by the modern solution to a *different* problem inherited from the Reformation era. The individual freedom that tamed early modern religion as more-than-religion *also* underwrites the modern consumerism sheltered within sovereign nation-states that, through global warming, is threatening the biosphere of our planet. Considering all that is at stake, some current environmentalists understandably sound like secular evangelists, their apocalyptic language and strident tones exhorting a global congregation to become crusaders to save the Earth.

Other downsides to secularization and the ways that freedom is exercised are less global in their implications but perhaps more immediately frustrating. Political culture and public life among the free citizens of the United States have become increasingly polarized, angry, and hysterical in recent years. Many people on all sides engage in hyperbole and demonize their opponents. Well before the election of 2016, a divided American citizenry found a parallel in a gridlocked Congress. Much of what passed for political discourse in the United States remained at the level of bumper-sticker slogans among citizens whose worldviews were often sharply antagonistic.

Yet few observers or analysts imagined that the clash of American voters and their values would result in the election of an ethnonationalist president whose complete lack of political experience was touted by millions of his supporters as one of his strongest attributes. Since Donald Trump was inaugurated on January 20, 2017, we're living in a new and newly uncertain world, with even deeper divisions and angrier adversaries. What happens from here on out, in the United States and around the world, is anybody's guess.

The specific causes of the current antagonisms in the Western world differ from country to country. The particular features of each are rooted in the decisions and actions, politics and processes, of recent decades. But it would be a mistake not to see that more is going on here. These recent developments are also part of much longer historical trajectories that go back to attempts to deal with the problem of religion as more-than-religion that the modern world inherited from the Reformation era. At the heart of recent developments lies their failure to offer anything besides consumerism to take the place of religion as a shared basis for the organization, values, and priorities of human life. If one or another modern philosophy had succeeded in providing such an alternative on the basis of reason between the seventeenth century and the present, as so many modern philosophers tried to provide, then all reasonable people would agree about what is true, what is right and wrong, what we should care about, and how we should live. Then the Enlightenment and modern secularist dream of leaving religion behind would have succeeded.

But nothing like that has come close to happening. Instead, competing secular philosophies find their adherents, just as competing religions do. Despite disagreeing with one another, secular philosophies all lay claim to truth based on reason, which contributes to our hyperpluralism. "Reason alone" has not led people to agree about morality or meaning any more than "scripture alone" did. Dispute about reason has been going on since the seventeenth century, which is why, in the late twentieth century, various critics started calling out the entire endeavor and pronouncing it a failure. They introduced in its place postmodernism, the idea that all values and norms are not discovered by objective reason any more than they're revealed by God; rather, they are constructed by human beings. There is no objective truth in these contentious matters. Such a to-each-his-own claim might sound liberating. But liberals who find this postmodern rejection of objectivity appealing when it serves their own moral and political causes find it appalling when it informs constructions of reality that owe more to Fox News and Breitbart than to the *New York Times* and MSNBC.

So now what? It's hard to see where any persuasive answers about morality and meaning, purpose and priorities can come from that might inform our fragmented societies and support any new consensus. We're too free for that—free even to ignore evidence we don't like or to dispense with logic, if that's our preference, when disputed, divisive questions arise. Persuasive answers won't come from science, no matter how astonishing its technological applications continue to be. Science cannot tell us what we should care about, how we should live, or the sorts of persons we should be. Science describes but it cannot prescribe without ceasing to be science; it is explanatory, not normative. It can't tell right from wrong or good from bad. Those are questions religions have addressed for millennia and, in countless competing ways, still address today, as do rival modern philosophies, even though they are criticized for this by postmodern thinkers.

We find ourselves in our present situation of hyperpluralism because individualism and liberalism have succeeded so well, beginning with an individual freedom *of* religion that has proven simultaneously to be freedom *from* religion. You can believe whatever you want and live however you wish within the laws of the state, and so can everyone else. That's both a great blessing and a big problem. So here we are: so very free and so very far away from Martin Luther and what he started in a small town in Germany five hundred years ago.

ACKNOWLEDGMENTS

It is a pleasure to acknowledge the friends, colleagues, and family members whose input has made this book better than it otherwise would have been. Its shortcomings, needless to say, remain entirely mine.

The book wouldn't have been written at all without the prompting of Rafe Sagalyn, who contacted me and suggested that I might write something about the Reformation that would appeal to a broad audience. I am grateful to Mark Tauber at HarperOne for taking on the project with enthusiasm, to the members of its editorial and marketing staffs, and above all to Miles Doyle, whose editorial suggestions improved the manuscript in many ways. He is a model of editorial professionalism and a pleasure to work with. Craig Harline and Richard Rex, friends as well as colleagues, read the entire manuscript with great care and offered many helpful comments, as did my wife, Kerrie McCaw. Our son, Sean McCaw-Gregory, turned his acute editorial eye on parts of the manuscript and proposed changes that anticipated many of those later made by Miles. Mark Noll read chapter 4 and offered his characteristically generous and excellent advice.

My parents, Mary Lou and Eugene Schaefer, didn't play a direct part in the writing or revision of the manuscript, but they have been a constant support over many decades. It is a pleasure and joy to dedicate the book to them as a small gesture of my gratitude and love.

South Bend, Indiana
March 2017

NOTES

Introduction: Why the Reformation Matters

1 Keith Wrightson, *Earthly Necessities: Economic Lives in Early Modern Britain* (New Haven, CT: Yale Univ. Press, 2000), 55.

2 Andrew Pettegree, *The Invention of News: How the World Came to Know About Itself* (New Haven, CT: Yale Univ. Press, 2014), 54.

3 For Cologne, see Thomas A. Brady Jr., *German Histories in the Age of Reformations, 1400–1650* (Cambridge: Cambridge Univ. Press, 2009), 35. The other two English towns were Norwich and Bristol. E. A. Wrigley, *People, Cities, and Wealth: The Transformation of a Traditional Society* (Oxford: Blackwell, 1987), 160.

Chapter 1: A Reluctant Rebel

1 Martin Luther to John Lang, October 26, 1516, in *Luther's Works*, ed. Helmut T. Lehmann, vol. 48, ed. and trans. Gottfried G. Krodel (Philadelphia: Fortress Press, 1963), 27–28.

2 Luther to Lang, in *Luther's Works*, 48:30.

3 Luther to Lang, in *Luther's Works*, 48:28nn5–6.

4 Franz Posset, *The Front-Runner of the Catholic Reformation: The Life and Works of Johann von Staupitz* (Aldershot, UK: Ashgate, 2003).

5 Luther to Lang, in *Luther's Works*, 48:30.

6 Lyndal Roper, *Martin Luther: Renegade and Prophet* (London: Bodley Head, 2016), 17–34.

7 Martin Brecht, *Martin Luther: His Road to Reformation, 1483–1521,* trans. James L. Schaaf (Minneapolis: Fortress Press, 1985), 129–30.

8 *Erasmus von Rotterdam Novum Instrumentum, Basel 1516: Faksimile-Neudruck mit einer historischen, textkritischen und bibiographischen Einleitung von Heinz Holeczek* (Stuttgart-Bad Cannstatt: Frommann-Holzboog, 1986).

9 Luther to George Spalatin, October 19, 1516, in *Luther's Works,* 48:23–26.

10 George Spalatin to Erasmus, in *The Collected Works of Erasmus,* vol. 4, *Letters 446 to 593, 1516–1517,* trans. R. A. B. Mynors and D. F. S. Thomson, annot. James K. McConica (Toronto: Univ. of Toronto Press, 1977), 166.

11 Brecht, *Martin Luther,* 139–41, 143–44.

12 Andrew Pettegree, *Brand Luther: 1517, Printing, and the Making of the Reformation* (New York: Penguin, 2015), 22, 40, 42–44.

13 James D. Tracy, "Erasmus Becomes a German," *Renaissance Quarterly* 21, no. 3 (1968): 281; *The Collected Works of Erasmus,* vol. 3, *Letters 298 to 445, 1514–1516,* trans. R. A. B. Mynors and D. F. S. Thomson, annot. Wallace K. Ferguson (Toronto: Univ. of Toronto Press, 1976), 63, 89, 301.

14 For Wittenberg's religious institutions and practices, see Helmar Junghans, "Luther's Wittenberg," in *The Cambridge Companion to Martin Luther,* ed. Donald K. McKim (Cambridge: Cambridge Univ. Press, 2003), 20–22.

15 Virginia Reinburg, *French Books of Hours: Making an Archive of Prayer, c. 1400–1600* (Cambridge: Cambridge Univ. Press, 2012), 37–40; Eamon Duffy, *Marking the Hours: English People and Their Prayers, 1240–1570* (New Haven, CT: Yale Univ. Press, 2006), 121–22.

16 *The New Cambridge History of the Bible,* vol. 2, *The Bible from 600 to 1450,* ed. Richard Marsden and E. Ann Matter (Cambridge: Cambridge Univ. Press, 2012).

17 Andrew Colin Gow, "The Bible in Germanic," in *New Cambridge History of the Bible,* 2:213; Bernd Moeller, "Religious Life in Germany on the Eve of the Reformation," in *Pre-Reformation Germany,* ed. Gerald Strauss (New York: Harper and Row, 1972), 23.

18 Thomas à Kempis, *The Imitation of Christ,* ed. and trans. Joseph Tylenda (New York: Vintage, 1998), 34.

19 John C. Olin, ed. and trans., *The Catholic Reformation: Savonarola to Ignatius Loyola* (New York: Harper and Row, 1969), 45 (translation modified).

20 On Maximilian and his relationship to the territories and cities of the Holy Roman Empire, see Brady, *German Histories,* 107–29 (see intro., n. 3).

21 For what follows on the difficulty of carrying out ecclesiastical reforms in the Holy Roman Empire, see Brady, *German Histories,* 131–44, and Euan Cameron, *The European Reformation* (Oxford: Clarendon Press, 1991), 38–48.

22 J. Jeffrey Tyler, *Lord of the Sacred City: The "Episcopus exclusus" in Late Medieval and Early Modern Germany* (Leiden: E. J. Brill, 1999).

23 Martin Luther, *A Disputation against Scholastic Theology,* in *Martin Luther's Basic Theological Writings,* ed. Timothy F. Lull (Minneapolis: Fortress Press, 1989), 16.

24 Luther, *Disputation against Scholastic Theology,* 15, 14.

25 Luther, *Disputation against Scholastic Theology,* 20.

26 For what follows on indulgences, see R. N. Swanson, ed., *Promissory Notes on the Treasury of Merits: Indulgences in Late Medieval Europe* (Leiden: E. J. Brill, 2006).

27 Pettegree, *Brand Luther,* 63–64.

28 David Bagchi, "Luther's *Ninety-Five Theses* and the Contemporary Criticism of Indulgences," in *Promissory Notes,* 332.

29 Martin Luther, "Letter from Martin Luther to Albrecht, Archbishop of Mainz, 31 October 1517," in *The Annotated Luther,* vol. 1, *The Roots of Reform,* ed. Timothy J. Wengert (Minneapolis: Fortress Press, 2015), 52, 53.

30 Luther, "Luther to Albrecht," in *Annotated Luther,* 1:54–55.

31 Pettegree, *Brand Luther,* 75–77. No copies of the German edition survive.

32 Martin Luther, *Disputation for Clarifying the Power of Indulgences [Ninety-Five Theses],* in *Annotated Luther,* 1:39, 40.

33 Luther, *Ninety-Five Theses,* in *Annotated Luther,* 1:35, 37, 39, 40–41, 42, 43, 44–45.

34 Luther, *Ninety-Five Theses,* in *Annotated Luther,* 1:44–45.

35 For reaction to the *Ninety-Five Theses* and early opposition to Luther in general, I am indebted to David V. N. Bagchi, *Luther's Earliest Opponents: Catholic Controversialists, 1518–1525* (Minneapolis: Fortress Press, 1991). On the reactions by Tetzel, Wimpina, and Eck, see also Scott H. Hendrix, *Luther and the Papacy: Stages in a Reformation Conflict* (Philadelphia: Fortress Press, 1981), 32–38; Brecht, *Martin Luther,* 206–7, 211–13.

36 Martin Luther, *A Sermon on Indulgences and Grace,* in *Annotated Luther,* 1:62.

37 Luther, *Sermon on Indulgences,* in *Annotated Luther,* 1:64.

38 Luther, *Sermon on Indulgences,* in *Annotated Luther,* 1:60, 62.

39 Luther, *Sermon on Indulgences,* in *Annotated Luther,* 1:65.

40 Luther, *Sermon on Indulgences,* in *Annotated Luther,* 1:63.

41 Pettegree, *Brand Luther,* 80–81.

42 Erasmus to Thomas More, in *Collected Works of Erasmus,* vol. 5, *Letters 594 to 841, 1517–1518,* trans. R. A. B. Mynors and D. F. S. Thomson, annot. Pieter G. Bietenholz (Toronto: Univ. of Toronto Press, 1979), 327.

43 Martin Greschat, *Martin Bucer: A Reformer and His Times,* trans. Stephen E. Buckwalter (Louisville, KY: Westminster John Knox Press, 2004), 26–29; Brecht, *Martin Luther,* 216.

44 Martin Luther, "Heidelberg Disputation," in *Annotated Luther,* 1:83, 97.

45 Luther, "Heidelberg Disputation," in *Annotated Luther,* 1:90.

46 Posset, *Front-Runner of the Catholic Reformation,* 228; Pettegree, *Brand Luther,* 90–91.

47 On Prierias and his dealings with Luther, on which I have drawn in what follows, see Michael Tavuzzi, *Prierias: The Life and Works of Silvestro Mazzolini da Prierio, 1456–1527* (Durham, NC: Duke Univ. Press, 1997), 104–14.

48 Tavuzzi, *Prierias,* 111.

49 Martin Luther, *Ad dialogum Silvestri Prietatis de potestate papae responsio,* in *D. Martin Luthers Werke: Kritische Gesammtausgabe* (Weimar: Hermann Böhlau, 1883), 1:647.

50 Hendrix, *Luther and the Papacy,* 49–51.

51 Bagchi, "Luther's *Ninety-five Theses*," 346–51.

52 Martin Luther, *The Proceedings at Augsburg*, in *Annotated Luther*, 1:141.

53 Luther, *Proceedings at Augsburg*, in *Annotated Luther*, 1:143.

54 Cardinal Cajetan, "Faith in the Sacrament as Certainty of Forgiveness," in *Cajetan Responds: A Reader in Reformation Controversy*, ed. Jared Wicks, SJ (Washington, DC: Catholic Univ. of America Press, 1978), 55.

55 Luther, *Proceedings at Augsburg*, in *Annotated Luther*, 1:147.

56 Luther, *Proceedings at Augsburg*, in *Annotated Luther*, 1:137.

57 On the meeting at Augsburg and its impact on Luther, see Hendrix, *Luther and the Papacy*, 56–65.

58 Brecht, *Martin Luther*, 260–64.

59 Luther, *Proceedings at Augsburg*, in *Annotated Luther*, 1:150.

60 Luther, *Proceedings at Augsburg*, in *Annotated Luther*, 1:158.

61 Martin Luther to George Spalatin, shortly after December 21, 1518, in *D. Martin Luthers Werke, Briefwechsel* (Weimar: Hermann Böhlaus Nachfolger, 1930), 1:286. See also Hendrix, *Luther and the Papacy*, 75.

62 Martin Luther to Frederick of Saxony, January 13–19, 1519, in *Luther's Works*, 48:105–6.

63 Martin Luther to Leo X, January 5–6, 1519, in *Luther's Works*, 48:100–102.

64 Brecht, *Martin Luther*, 319–21; Hendrix, *Luther and the Papacy*, 87–89.

65 Quoted in Brad S. Gregory, *The Unintended Reformation: How a Religious Revolution Secularized Society* (Cambridge, MA: Belknap Press of Harvard Univ. Press, 2012), 87.

66 Pettegree, *Brand Luther*, 104–5; Mark U. Edwards Jr., *Printing, Propaganda, and Martin Luther* (Berkeley: Univ. of California Press, 1994), 18.

67 On the explicit distinction between the invisible and visible Churches being Luther's original idea rather than taken over from Hus, John Wyclif, or Augustine, I am indebted to Richard Rex, *The Making of Martin Luther* (forthcoming from Princeton Univ. Press), which I am grateful to have read in manuscript.

68 Martin Luther to George Spalatin, ca. February 14, 1520, in *Luther's Works*, 48:153; Hendrix, *Luther and the Papacy*, 97.

69 This paragraph is based mostly on Brecht, *Martin Luther*, 343–48, 366, 390.

70 Martin Luther, *Treatise on Good Works*, in *Annotated Luther*, 1:283, 340, 338, 319.

71 Luther, *Treatise on Good Works*, in *Annotated Luther*, 1:272.

72 Luther, *Treatise on Good Works*, in *Annotated Luther*, 1:268.

73 Hans J. Hillerbrand, ed., *The Reformation: A Narrative History Related by Contemporary Observers and Participants* (New York: Harper and Row, 1964), 80–84 (translation modified).

74 Quoted in Brecht, *Martin Luther*, 347.

75 Martin Luther, *To the Christian Nobility of the German Nation Concerning the Improvement of the Christian Estate*, in *Annotated Luther*, 1:392.

76 Luther, *Christian Nobility*, in *Annotated Luther*, 1:383, 382, 388, 389.

77 Luther, *Christian Nobility*, in *Annotated Luther*, 1:404, 395, 394, 395, 400.

78 Luther, *Christian Nobility*, in *Annotated Luther*, 1:408, 441.

79 Luther, *Christian Nobility*, in *Annotated Luther*, 1:442, 420, 440–41.

80 Luther, *Christian Nobility*, in *Annotated Luther*, 1:434, 428, 451.

81 Brecht, *Martin Luther*, 404–5.

82 Martin Luther, *The Babylonian Captivity of the Church [The Pagan Servitude of the Church]*, in *Martin Luther: Selections from His Writings*, ed. John Dillenberger (Garden City, NY: Doubleday, 1961), 357, 257.

83 Luther, *Babylonian Captivity*, 345, 341.

84 Luther, *Babylonian Captivity*, 283.

85 Luther, *Babylonian Captivity*, 322.

86 Luther, *Babylonian Captivity*, 306, 344.

87 Martin Luther, *The Freedom of a Christian*, in *Annotated Luther*, 1:476, 477.

88 Luther, *Freedom*, in *Annotated Luther*, 1:479, 486.

89 Luther, *Freedom*, in *Annotated Luther*, 1:492, 494, 495.

90 Luther, *Freedom*, in *Annotated Luther*, 1:492, 488.

91 Luther, *Freedom*, in *Annotated Luther*, 1:495–96.

92 Luther, *Freedom*, in *Annotated Luther*, 1:521, 488.

93 Luther, *Freedom*, in *Annotated Luther*, 1:520, 530.

94 Brecht, *Martin Luther*, 416, 420, 423–26.

95 Pettegree, *Brand Luther*, 79.

96 Hillerbrand, ed., *Reformation*, 91 (translation modified).

Chapter 2: A Fractious Movement

1 This account of events in Wittenberg from May 1521 through 1522 is based mostly on James S. Preus, *Carlstadt's "Ordinaciones" and Luther's Liberty: A Study of the Wittenberg Movement, 1521–22* (Cambridge, MA: Harvard Univ. Press, 1974); Ronald J. Sider, *Andreas Bodenstein von Karlstadt: The Development of His Thought, 1517–1525* (Leiden: E. J. Brill, 1974); and Roper, *Martin Luther*, 211–41 (see chap. 1, n. 6).

2 Martin Luther to John Lang, October 26, 1516, in *Luther's Works*, 48:351 (see chap. 1, n. 1).

3 Martin Luther to Philip Melanchthon, January 13, 1522, in *Luther's Works*, 48:365–67.

4 Andreas Bodenstein von Karlstadt, *On the Removal of Images*, in *A Reformation Debate: Karlstadt, Emser, and Eck on Sacred Images*, ed. and trans. Bryan D. Mangrum and Giuseppe Scavizzi, 2nd ed. (Toronto: Centre for Reformation and Renaissance Studies, 1998), 42.

5 This section relies importantly on G. R. Potter, *Zwingli* (Cambridge: Cambridge Univ. Press, 1976); Bruce Gordon, *The Swiss Reformation* (Manchester, Eng.: Manchester Univ. Press, 2002), 46–68; and Philip Benedict, *Christ's Churches Purely Reformed: A Social History of Calvinism* (New Haven, CT: Yale Univ. Press, 2002), 19–32.

6 Huldrych Zwingli, *Divine and Human Righteousness*, in *Huldrych Zwingli: Writings*, vol. 2, trans. H. Wayne Pipkin (Allison Park, PA: Pickwick, 1984), 26.

7 This section draws substantively on R. W. Scribner, *The German Reformation* (Atlantic Highlands, NJ: Humanities Press, 1986); Peter Blickle, *Communal Reformation: The Quest for Salvation in Sixteenth-Century Germany,* trans. Thomas Dunlap (Atlantic Highlands, NJ: Humanities Press, 1992); Andrew Pettegree, *Reformation and the Culture of Persuasion* (Cambridge: Cambridge Univ. Press, 2005); and Brady, *German Histories,* 161–83 (see intro., n. 3).

8 Paul A. Russel, *Lay Theology in the Reformation: Popular Pamphleteers in Southwest Germany,* 1521–1525 (Cambridge: Cambridge Univ. Press, 1986).

9 Argula von Grumbach, *A Christian Writing by an Honourable Noblewoman …* , in *Argula von Grumbach: A Woman's Voice in the Reformation,* ed. and trans. Peter Matheson (Edinburgh: T & T Clark, 1995), 108.

10 Robert W. Scribner, *For the Sake of Simple Folk: Popular Propaganda for the German Reformation* (Cambridge: Cambridge Univ. Press, 1981).

11 Pettegree, *Brand Luther,* 207 (see chap. 1., n. 12).

12 Mark U. Edwards Jr., *Printing, Propaganda, and Martin Luther* (Berkeley: Univ. of California Press, 1994); Pettegree, *Brand Luther.*

13 Robert W. Scribner, "Why Was There No Reformation in Cologne?" *Bulletin of the Institute of Historical Research* 49 (1976): 217–41.

14 Pettegree, *Brand Luther,* 220–24.

15 Bagchi, *Luther's Earliest Opponents* (see chap. 1, n. 35); Edwards, *Printing,* 28–37, 57–82.

16 Martin Luther, *On Secular Authority: How Far Does the Obedience Owed to It Extend?,* in *Luther and Calvin on Secular Authority,* ed. and trans. Harro Höpfl (Cambridge: Cambridge Univ. Press, 1991), 23, 25.

17 My account in this section draws on Peter Blickle, *The Revolution of* 1525: *The German Peasants' War from a New Perspective,* trans. Thomas A. Brady Jr. and H. C. Erik Midelfort (Baltimore: Johns Hopkins Univ. Press, 1981); Tom Scott and Bob Scribner, eds. and trans., *The German Peasants' War: A History in Documents* (Atlantic Highlands, NJ: Humanities Press, 1991); Tom Scott, "The Peasants' War," in *A Companion to the Reformation World,* ed. R. Po-chia Hsia (Oxford: Blackwell, 2004), 56–69; and Brady, *German Histories,* 185–206.

18 Sebastian Lotzer and Christoph Schappeler, *The Twelve Articles of the Upper Swabian Peasants,* in *The Radical Reformation,* ed. and trans. Michael G. Baylor (Cambridge: Cambridge Univ. Press, 1991), 234.

19 Thomas Müntzer, *Sermon to the Princes,* in *Radical Reformation,* 21.

20 Müntzer, *Sermon to the Princes,* 25.

21 Müntzer, *Sermon to the Princes,* 23, and Müntzer, *A Highly Provoked Defense and Answer to the Spiritless, Soft-Living Flesh at Wittenberg,* in *Radical Reformation,* 74, 75.

22 Martin Luther, *Against the Robbing and Murdering Hordes of Peasants,* in *Luther's Works,* ed. Jaroslav Pelikan, vol. 46, ed. and trans. Robert C. Schulz (Philadelphia: Fortress Press, 1967), 50.

23 For this section I have drawn especially on James M. Stayer, *The German Peasants' War and Anabaptist Community of Goods* (Montreal: McGill-Queen's Univ. Press, 1991); C. Arnold Snyder, *Anabaptist History and Theology: An Introduction* (Kitchener: Pandora Press, 1995); and John D. Roth and James M. Stayer, eds., *A Companion to Anabaptism and Spiritualism,* 1521–1700 (Leiden: E. J. Brill, 2007).

24 *The Eleven Mühlhausen Articles,* in *Radical Reformation,* 230.

25 Conrad Grebel, "Letter to Thomas Müntzer," in *Radical Reformation,* 42–43.

26 Michael Sattler, *The Schleitheim Articles,* in *Radical Reformation,* 175.

27 Erasmus, *The Free Will,* in *Erasmus-Luther: Discourse on Free Will,* ed. and trans. Ernst F. Winter (New York: Continuum, 2002), 6.

28 Erasmus, *Free Will,* in *Erasmus-Luther,* 10, 7.

29 Erasmus, *Free Will,* in *Erasmus-Luther,* 15.

30 Erasmus, *Free Will,* in *Erasmus-Luther,* 16, 18–19.

31 Erasmus, *Free Will,* in *Erasmus-Luther,* 35.

32 Erasmus, *Free Will,* in *Erasmus-Luther,* 32.

33 Erasmus, *Free Will,* in *Erasmus-Luther,* 92.

34 Martin Luther, *The Bondage of the Will,* trans. J. I. Packer and O. R. Johnston (Grand Rapids, MI: Fleming H. Revell, 2002), 319.

35 Luther, *Bondage of the Will,* 64, 93.

36 Luther, *Bondage of the Will*, 100, 103–4.

37 Luther, *Bondage of the Will*, 131, 93.

38 Erasmus, *Free Will*, in *Erasmus-Luther*, 94.

39 This section draws significantly on Amy Nelson Burnett, *Karlstadt and the Origins of the Eucharistic Controversy: A Study in the Circulation of Ideas* (Oxford: Oxford Univ. Press, 2011); Heiko A. Oberman, *Luther: Man between God and the Devil*, trans. Eileen Walliser-Schwarzbart (New Haven, CT: Yale Univ. Press, 1989), 232–45; Benedict, *Christ's Churches*, 32–48; and Brady, *German Histories*, 213–24.

40 Martin Luther, *Confession Concerning Christ's Supper*, in *Martin Luther's Basic Theological Writings*, ed. Timothy F. Lull (Minneapolis: Fortress Press, 1989), 400.

41 On Schwenckfeld, see Emmet McLaughlin, "Spiritualism: Schwenckfeld and Franck and their Early Modern Resonances," in *Companion to Anabaptism*, eds. Roth and Stayer, 124–33 (see chap.2, n. 23).

42 In this section I have drawn on Ralf Klötzer, "The Melchiorites and Münster," in *Companion to Anabaptism*, eds. Roth and Stayer, 217–56; Sigrun Haude, *In the Shadow of "Savage Wolves": Anabaptist Münster and the German Reformation during the 1530s* (Boston: Humanities Press, 2000); and Snyder, *Anabaptist History and Theology*, 143–50.

43 Klötzer, "Melchiorites and Münster," 238–39.

44 Ruth Gouldbourne, *The Flesh and the Feminine: Gender and Theology in the Writings of Caspar Schwenckfeld* (Bletchley, UK: Paternoster Press, 2006).

Chapter 3: A Troubled Era

1 James L. Larson, *Reforming the North: The Kingdoms and Churches of Scandinavia, 1520–1545* (Cambridge: Cambridge Univ. Press, 2010).

2 On the Reformation and politics in the Holy Roman Empire, see Brady, *German Histories*, 207–58 (see intro., n. 3).

3 On the character and responsibilities of Lutheran political authorities, see James M. Estes, *Peace, Order, and the Glory of God: Secular Authority and the Church in the Thought of Luther and Melanchthon, 1518–1559*

(Leiden: E. J. Brill, 2005); and Robert von Friedeburg, "Church and State in Lutheran Lands, 1550–1675," in *Lutheran Ecclesiastical Culture, 1550–1675,* ed. Robert Kolb (Leiden: E. J. Brill, 2008), 361–410.

4 Christopher Ocker, *Church Robbers and Reformers in Germany, 1525– 1547: Confiscation and Religious Purpose in the Holy Roman Empire* (Leiden: E. J. Brill, 2006).

5 Joseph Leo Koerner, *The Reformation of the Image* (Chicago: Univ. of Chicago Press, 2004).

6 Geoffrey Parker, "Success and Failure in the First Century of the Reformation," *Past and Present* 136 (1992): 77–79.

7 This and the preceding paragraph are based mostly on Christopher Boyd Brown, *Singing the Gospel: Lutheran Hymns and the Success of the Reformation* (Cambridge, MA: Harvard Univ. Press, 2005), and Brown, "Devotional Life in Hymns: Liturgy, Music, and Prayer," in *Lutheran Ecclesiastical Culture,* ed. Kolb, 205–58.

8 Gerhard Bode, "Instruction of the Christian Faith by Lutherans after Luther," in *Lutheran Ecclesiastical Culture,* ed. Kolb, 168.

9 Gerald Strauss, *Luther's House of Learning: Indoctrination of the Young in the German Reformation* (Baltimore: Johns Hopkins Univ. Press, 1978).

10 For the rift between Philippists and Genuine (or "Gnesio-") Lutherans through the Formula of Concord, see Irene Dingel, "The Culture of Conflict in the Controversies Leading to the Formula of Concord (1548– 1580)," in *Lutheran Ecclesiastical Culture,* ed. Kolb, 15–64.

11 My account of Calvin and Geneva draws on Bruce Gordon, *Calvin* (New Haven, CT: Yale Univ. Press, 2009); William G. Naphy, *Calvin and the Consolidation of the Genevan Reformation* (Louisville, KY: Westminster John Knox Press, 1994); and Benedict, *Christ's Churches,* 77–114 (see chap. 2, n. 5). See also the essays in Donald K. McKim, ed., *The Cambridge Companion to John Calvin* (Cambridge: Cambridge Univ. Press, 2004).

12 Carlos Eire, "Calvinism and the Reform of the Reformation," in *The Oxford Illustrated History of the Reformation,* ed. Peter Marshall (Oxford: Oxford Univ. Press, 2015), 87–88.

13 On both the number of refugees and printing, see Benedict, *Christ's Churches,* 108 (see chap. 2, n. 5).

14 This section draws on Brad S. Gregory, "The Radical Reformation," in
    Oxford Illustrated History of the Reformation, ed. Marshall, 115–51,
    as well as on the articles in Roth and Stayer, eds., *Companion to
    Anabaptism* (see chap. 2, n. 23).

15 Gregory, *Unintended Reformation,* 150 (see chap. 1, n. 65).

16 Brad S. Gregory, *Salvation at Stake: Christian Martyrdom in Early
    Modern Europe* (Cambridge, MA: Harvard University Press, 1999),
    197–249.

17 On radical Protestantism in the English Revolution, see the classic
    work by Christopher Hill, *The World Turned Upside Down: Radical
    Ideas during the English Revolution* (Harmondsworth, UK: Penguin,
    1972); also J. F. McGregor and Barry Reay, eds., *Radical Religion in the
    English Revolution* (London: Oxford Univ. Press, 1984); and Nicholas
    McDowell, *The English Radical Imagination: Culture, Religion, and
    Revolution,* 1630–1660 (Oxford: Clarendon Press, 2003).

18 On Catholicism in the Reformation era, see Robert Bireley, *The
    Refashioning of Catholicism,* 1450–1700 (Washington, DC: Catholic
    Univ. of America Press, 1999); R. Po-chia Hsia, *The World of Catholic
    Renewal,* 1540–1770, 2nd ed. (Cambridge: Cambridge Univ. Press,
    2005); and Simon Ditchfield, "Catholic Reformation and Renewal," in
    Oxford Illustrated History of the Reformation, ed. Marshall, 152–85.

19 H. J. Schroeder, ed. and trans., *Canons and Decrees of the Council of
    Trent* (St. Louis: B. Herder, 1941), 15.

20 On the proceedings and character of the Council of Trent, see John
    O'Malley, *Trent: What Happened at the Council* (Cambridge, MA:
    Belknap Press of Harvard Univ. Press, 2013).

21 For an overview, see Richard L. DeMolen, ed., *Religious Orders of the
    Catholic Reformation* (New York: Fordham Univ. Press, 1994).

22 On Ignatius Loyola and the early Jesuits, see John O'Malley, *The First
    Jesuits* (Cambridge, MA: Harvard Univ. Press, 1993).

23 Jean Delumeau, *Catholicism between Luther and Voltaire: A New View
    of the Counter-Reformation,* with introduction by John Bossy (London:
    Burns & Oates, 1977), 34.

24 William H. McCabe, *An Introduction to the Jesuit Theater: A
    Posthumous Work,* ed. Louis J. Oldani (St. Louis: Institute of Jesuit

Sources, 1983); Jean-Marie Valentin, *Le théâtre des Jésuites dans les pays de langue allemande (1554–1680)*, 2 vols. (Berne: Peter Lang, 1978).

25 Delumeau, *Catholicism between Luther and Voltaire*, 41.

26 Philip M. Soergel, *Wondrous in His Saints: Counter-Reformation Propaganda in Bavaria* (Berkeley: Univ. of California Press, 1993); Craig Harline, *Miracles at the Jesus Oak: Histories of the Supernatural in Reformation Europe* (New York: Doubleday, 2003), 41–48.

27 Louis Châtellier, *The Europe of the Devout: The Catholic Reformation and the Formation of a New Society,* trans. Jean Birrell (Cambridge: Cambridge Univ. Press, 1989).

28 The narrative of this section relies on Brady, *German Histories* (see intro., n. 3).

29 On the Regensburg Colloquy, see Peter Matheson, *Cardinal Contarini at Regensburg* (Oxford: Oxford Univ. Press, 1972).

30 Greschat, *Martin Bucer*, 218–27 (see chap. 1, n. 43).

31 On Reformed Protestantism in the Holy Roman Empire from the 1560s to the Thirty Years' War, see Benedict, *Christ's Churches,* 202–29 (see chap. 2, n. 5), and Henry J. Cohn, "The Territorial Princes in Germany's Second Reformation, 1559–1622," in *International Calvinism, 1541–1715,* ed. Menna Prestwich (Oxford: Clarendon Press, 1985), 135–65.

32 On the rising tensions up to the Thirty Years' War and the war itself, in addition to Brady, *German Histories,* see Peter H. Wilson, *The Thirty Years War: Europe's Tragedy* (Cambridge, MA: Belknap Press of Harvard Univ. Press, 2009), and Ronald G. Asch, *The Thirty Years War: The Holy Roman Empire and Europe, 1618–48* (New York: St. Martin's Press, 1997).

33 Wilson, *Thirty Years War,* 468–70.

34 James K. Farge, *Orthodoxy and Reform in Early Reformation France: The Faculty of Theology of Paris, 1500–1543* (Leiden: E. J. Brill, 1985).

35 On Francis I, his patronage of religious reform and humanism, and his resistance to the Reformation, see R. J. Knecht, *Francis I* (Cambridge: Cambridge Univ. Press, 1982), with reference to Leonardo at 99–100.

36 On the Meaux circle, see Mark Greengrass, *The French Reformation* (Oxford: Blackwell, 1987), 1–20.

37 For the account from the Affair of the Placards to the end of the Wars of
    Religion, I have drawn on Mack P. Holt, *The French Wars of Religion,*
    1562–1629, 2nd ed. (Cambridge: Cambridge Univ. Press, 2005); Robert
    J. Knecht, *The French Civil Wars* (Harlow, UK: Longman, 2000); and
    Benedict, *Christ's Churches,* 127–48.

38 On trials and punishments for heresy in sixteenth-century France, see
    William Monter, *Judging the French Reformation: Heresy Trials by*
    Sixteenth-Century Parlements (Cambridge, MA: Harvard Univ. Press,
    1999).

39 Donald Nugent, *Ecumenism in the Age of the Reformation: The*
    Colloquy of Poissy (Cambridge, MA: Harvard Univ. Press, 1974).

40 On the St. Bartholomew's Day Massacre and the events leading up to it,
    see Barbara Diefendorf, *Beneath the Cross: Catholics and Huguenots in*
    Sixteenth-Century Paris (New York: Oxford Univ. Press, 1991).

41 On seventeenth-century Catholic-Huguenot relations and the erosion of
    Huguenot privileges through the revocation of the Edict of Nantes and its
    aftermath, see Keith P. Luria, *Sacred Boundaries: Religious Coexistence*
    and Conflict in Early-Modern France (Washington, DC: Catholic Univ.
    of America Press, 2005); Geoffrey Treasure, *The Huguenots* (New
    Haven, CT: Yale Univ. Press, 2013); 317–91; and Benedict, *Christ's*
    Churches, 369–78.

42 The narrative in this section through the end of Elizabeth's reign draws
    on Christopher Haigh, *English Reformations: Religion, Politics, and*
    Society under the Tudors (Oxford: Clarendon Press, 1993), and Eamon
    Duffy, *The Stripping of the Altars: Traditional Religion in England, c.*
    1400–c. 1580, 2nd ed. (New Haven, CT: Yale Univ. Press, 2005); and
    through the Restoration, see Robert Bucholz and Newton Key, *Early*
    Modern England, 1485–1714: A Narrative History, 2nd ed. (Malden,
    MA: Wiley-Blackwell, 2009).

43 On Henry VIII's Reformation, see Richard Rex, *Henry VIII and the*
    English Reformation, 2nd ed. (Houndmills, UK: Palgrave Macmillan,
    2006); Ethan Shagan, *Popular Politics and the English Reformation*
    (Cambridge: Cambridge Univ. Press, 2002); and G. R. Elton, *Policy*
    and Police: The Enforcement of the Reformation in the Age of Thomas
    Cromwell (Cambridge: Cambridge Univ. Press, 1972).

44 Diarmaid MacCulloch, *The Boy King: Edward VI and the Protestant*

Reformation (Berkeley: Univ. of California Press, 2002).

45 Eamon Duffy, *Fires of Faith: Catholic England under Mary Tudor* (New Haven: Yale Univ. Press, 2009).

46 For an introductory overview, see the essays in *The Cambridge Companion to Puritanism,* ed. John Coffey and Paul C. H. Lim (Cambridge: Cambridge Univ. Press, 2008).

47 Geoffrey F. Nuttall, "The English Martyrs, 1535–1680: A Statistical Review," *Journal of Ecclesiastical History* 22 (1971): 191–97.

48 David Daniell, *William Tyndale: A Biography* (New Haven, CT: Yale Univ. Press, 1994), 1.

49 On the English Revolution and what led to it, see Austin Woolrych, *Britain in Revolution, 1625–1660* (Oxford: Oxford Univ. Press, 2002).

50 On radical Protestants during the English Revolution, see Hill, *World Turned Upside Down;* McGregor and Reay, *Radical Religion;* and McDowell, *English Radical Imagination.* For Puritans and radical Protestants in the decades immediately prior, see David R. Como, *Blown by the Spirit: Puritanism and the Emergence of an Antinomian Underground in Pre-Civil-War England* (Stanford, CA: Stanford Univ. Press, 2004).

51 On the early Reformation in the Low Countries, I have drawn on Alastair Duke, *Reformation and Revolt in the Low Countries* (London: Hambledon Press, 1990), and Duke, "The Netherlands," in *The Early Reformation in Europe,* ed. Andrew Pettegree (Cambridge: Cambridge Univ. Press, 1992), 142–65.

52 Benedict, *Christ's Churches,* 177.

53 Gregory, *Salvation at Stake,* 91, 216–19.

54 On the emergence and growth of Reformed Protestantism in the Low Countries through the Dutch Revolt and the Eighty Years' War, see Geoffrey Parker, *The Dutch Revolt* (Harmondsworth, UK: Penguin, 1979); Graham Darby, ed., *The Origins and Development of the Dutch Revolt* (London: Routledge, 2001); and Benedict, *Christ's Churches,* 173–201.

55 See the essays in *Reformation, Revolt and Civil War in France and the Netherlands, 1555–1585,* ed. Philip Benedict et al. (Amsterdam: Royal Netherlands Academy of Arts and Sciences, 1999).

56 Guido Marnef, *Antwerp in the Age of Reformation: Underground Protestantism in a Commercial Metropolis, 1550–1577*, trans. J. C. Grayson (Baltimore: Johns Hopkins Univ. Press, 1996).

57 Andrew Pettegree, *Emden and the Dutch Revolt: Exile and the Development of Reformed Protestantism* (Oxford: Clarendon Press, 1992).

58 Gregory, *Salvation at Stake*, 91.

59 Parker, *Dutch Revolt*, 78.

60 Parker, *Dutch Revolt*, 108.

61 Gregory, *Salvation at Stake*, 274.

62 Parker, *Dutch Revolt*, 178.

63 On the Archdukes and Catholicism in the Spanish Netherlands, see Craig Harline and Eddy Put, *A Bishop's Tale: Matthias Hovius Among His Flock in Seventeenth-Century Flanders* (New Haven, CT: Yale Univ. Press, 2000).

Chapter 4: A New World

1 Benjamin J. Kaplan, *Divided by Faith: Religious Conflict and the Practice of Toleration in Early Modern Europe* (Cambridge, MA: Belknap Press of Harvard Univ. Press, 2007).

2 Mark A. Noll and Carolyn Nystrom, *Is the Reformation Over? An Evangelical Assessment of Contemporary Roman Catholicism* (Grand Rapids, MI: Baker Academic, 2005).

3 Stephen Gaukroger, *Descartes: An Intellectual Biography* (Oxford: Clarendon Press, 1995), 65–67; Noel Malcolm, "A Summary Biography of Thomas Hobbes," in *The Cambridge Companion to Hobbes*, ed. Tom Sorrell (Cambridge: Cambridge Univ. Press, 1996), 28–33.

4 My treatment of the Golden-Age Dutch Republic makes use of Maarten Prak, *The Dutch Republic in the Seventeenth Century* (Cambridge: Cambridge Univ. Press, 2005); Simon Schama, *The Embarrassment of Riches: An Interpretation of Dutch Culture in the Golden Age* (New York: Knopf, 1987); and Jonathan Israel, *The Dutch Republic: Its Rise, Greatness, and Fall, 1477–1806* (Oxford: Oxford Univ. Press, 1995).

5 Herbert H. Rowen, ed. and trans., *The Low Countries in Early Modern*

Times: A Documentary History (New York: Harper and Row, 1972), 73–74 (translation modified).

6 Rowan, *Low Countries*, 260–66.

7 Much of the material about the economic success of the Dutch Republic in the following paragraphs is drawn from Jan de Vries and Ad van der Woude, *The First Modern Economy: Success, Failure, and Perseverance of the Dutch Economy, 1500–1815* (Cambridge: Cambridge Univ. Press, 1997).

8 Prak, *Dutch Republic*, 28, 171; de Vries and van der Woude, *First Modern Economy*, 63–65.

9 Prak, *Dutch Republic*, 125.

10 On religious minorities in the Dutch Republic, I have drawn on R. Po-chia Hsia and H. F. K. van Nierop, eds., *Calvinism and Religious Toleration in the Dutch Golden Age* (Cambridge: Cambridge Univ. Press, 2002), as well as Prak, *Dutch Republic*, 211–21.

11 Kaplan, *Divided by Faith*, 172–74. For the museum and the church, in which Catholic masses continue to be celebrated, see the website Museum Ons' Lieve Heer op Solder, https://www.opsolder.nl/en (consulted January 26, 2017).

12 On Catholicism in the seventeenth-century Dutch Republic, see especially Charles H. Parker, *Faith on the Margins: Catholics and Catholicism in the Dutch Golden Age* (Cambridge, MA: Harvard Univ. Press, 2008).

13 Joke Spaans, "Religious Policies in the Seventeenth-Century Dutch Republic," in *Calvinism and Religious Toleration*, ed. Po-chia Hsia and van Nierop, 81.

14 For the character of Dutch Calvinism in the late sixteenth and seventeenth centuries, see Alastair Duke, "The Ambivalent Face of Calvinism in the Netherlands, 1561–1618," in *Reformation and Revolt in the Low Countries*, 269–93 (see chap. 3, n. 51), and Prak, *Dutch Republic*, 208–10.

15 Judith Pollmann, *Religious Choice in the Dutch Republic: The Reformation of Arnoldus Buchelius, 1565–1641* (Manchester, UK: Manchester Univ. Press, 1999).

16 Prak, *Dutch Republic*, 122–25.

17 Prak, *Dutch Republic,* 139.

18 William Temple, *Observations upon the United Provinces of the Netherlands* (London: A. Maxwell, 1673), 183.

19 Temple, *Netherlands,* 178–79.

20 Gregory, *Unintended Reformation,* 266–67 (see chap. 1, n. 65).

21 Harold J. Cook, *Matters of Exchange: Commerce, Medicine, and Science in the Dutch Golden Age* (New Haven, CT: Yale Univ. Press, 2007).

22 De Vries and van der Woude, *First Modern Economy,* 674–80.

23 For the Dutch economic influence on the English, see Steve Pincus, *1688: The First Modern Revolution* (New Haven, CT: Yale Univ. Press, 2009), 50–59, 81–87; and more broadly, Lisa Jardine, *Going Dutch: How England Plundered Holland's Glory* (New York: HarperCollins, 2009).

24 John Locke, *A Letter Concerning Toleration,* ed. James H. Tully (Indianapolis: Hackett, 1983), 26–28.

25 W. M. Spellman, *The Latitudinarians and the Church of England, 1660–1700* (Athens: Univ. of Georgia Press, 1993).

26 Henry D. Rack, *Reasonable Enthusiast: John Wesley and the Rise of Methodism,* 3rd ed. (London: Epworth Press, 2002).

27 Evan Haefeli, *New Netherland and the Dutch Origins of American Religious Liberty* (Philadelphia: Univ. of Pennsylvania Press, 2012).

28 This paragraph is based on Mark Valeri, *Heavenly Merchandize: How Religion Shaped Commerce in Puritan New England* (Princeton, NJ: Princeton Univ. Press, 2009).

29 For an example, see John T. Noonan Jr., *The Lustre of Our Country: The American Experience of Religious Freedom* (Berkeley: Univ. of California Press, 1998).

30 James Madison, "Notes on Debate over Religious Assessment," December 23–24, 1784, in *Jefferson and Madison on Separation of Church and State: Writings on Religion and Secularism,* ed. Lenni Brenner (Fort Lee, NJ: Barricade Books, 2004), 62.

31 James Madison, "Memorial and Remonstrance against Religious Assessments," June 20, 1785, in *Jefferson and Madison,* ed. Brenner, 68.

32 Thomas Jefferson, "Notes on the State of Virginia," 1781–1782, in *Jefferson and Madison,* ed. Brenner, 54.

33 Nathan O. Hatch, *The Democratization of American Christianity* (New Haven, CT: Yale Univ. Press, 1989).

34 Mark A. Noll, *The Work We Have to Do: A History of Protestantism in America* (New York: Oxford Univ. Press, 2002), 57, 53; Hatch, *Democratization,* 220.

35 David Sehat, *The Myth of American Religious Freedom* (New York: Oxford Univ. Press, 2011).

36 Alexis de Tocqueville, *Democracy in America,* ed. J. P. Mayer, trans. George Lawrence (New York: Perennial Classics, 2000), 295.

37 Tocqueville, *Democracy in America,* 290.

38 Tocqueville, *Democracy in America,* 292.

39 Tocqueville, *Democracy in America,* 290–91.

40 Jefferson, "State of Virginia," in *Jefferson and Madison,* ed. Brenner, 24.

41 Thomas Paine, *The Age of Reason,* in Paine, *Political Writings,* ed. Bruce Kuklick (Cambridge: Cambridge Univ. Press, 2000), 268. I am grateful to Mark Noll for discussion about Paine's religious views.

42 Jan de Vries, *The Industrious Revolution: Consumer Behavior and the Household Economy, 1650 to the Present* (Cambridge: Cambridge Univ. Press, 2008).

43 See Albert O. Hirschman, *The Passions and the Interests: Political Arguments for Capitalism before Its Triumph* (Princeton: Princeton Univ. Press, 1977).

44 Adam Smith, *The Wealth of Nations,* ed. Edwin Cannan, with introduction by Robert Reich (New York: Modern Library, 2000), 581.

45 Tocqueville, *Democracy in America,* 291.

46 Tocqueville, *Democracy in America,* 530, 534.

47 Jonathan Mayhew Wainwright, *Inequality of Individual Wealth an Ordinance of Providence, and Essential to Civilization* (Boston: Dutton and Wentworth, 1835), 20.

48 Tocqueville, *Democracy in America,* 532.

49 Mark A. Noll, *The Civil War as a Theological Crisis* (Chapel Hill: Univ. of North Carolina Press, 2006).

50 Tocqueville, *Democracy in America,* 290.

51 Sehat, *Myth of American Religious Freedom;* Philip Hamburger, *Separation of Church and State* (Cambridge, MA: Harvard Univ. Press, 2002).

52 For the next two paragraphs, see Gregory, *Unintended Reformation,* 177–78.

53 J. David Hacker, "Has the Demographic Impact of Civil War Deaths Been Exaggerated?" *Civil War History* 60, no. 4 (2014): 453–58.

54 Grace Davie, *Religion in Britain since 1945: Believing without Belonging* (Oxford: Blackwell, 1994).

55 Victoria de Grazia, *Irresistible Empire: America's Advance through Twentieth-Century Europe* (Cambridge, MA: Belknap Press of Harvard Univ. Press, 2005).